SOS – Secrets of Opening Surprises 13

© 2011 New In Chess
Published by New In Chess, Alkmaar, The Netherlands
www.newinchess.com

Cover design: Steven Boland
Drawing on frontcover: Zander Dekker
Translation: Ken Neat (Chapter 5)
Production: Joop de Groot
Proofreading: René Olthof

Printed in the Netherlands
ISBN: 978-90-5691-341-0

SECRETS OF OPENING SURPRISES

13

Edited by
JEROEN BOSCH

Contributing authors

Arthur Kogan

Simon Williams

Konstantin Landa

Alexander Finkel

Glenn Flear

Dimitri Reinderman

Efstratios Grivas

Adrian Mikhalchishin

John van der Wiel

Ian Rogers

Jeroen Bosch

2011 New In Chess – The Netherlands

Contents

CHAPTER 12 - page 105

Adrian Mikhalchishin

Spanish: Kortchnoi's Idea in the Central Attack

The surprising 5.d4 ♘xd4!?

CHAPTER 13 - page 110

Dimitri Reinderman

Panic in the London

1.d4 ♘f6 2.♘f3 d6 3.♗f4 ♘h5

CHAPTER 14 - page 117

Alexander Finkel

Pirc Defence – Taking off the Gloves

4.f4 ♗g7 5.♘f3 0-0 6.e5 ♘fd7 7.h4!?

CHAPTER 15 - page 124

Jeroen Bosch

New Recipe in Old Indian

The universal antidote g4

CHAPTER 16 - page 130

John van der Wiel

Sicilian Mission: To Boldly Go...

Where No Bishop Has Gone Before

CHAPTER 17 - page 140

Ian Rogers

Surprising Sacrifice in the Giuoco Piano

The cunning 8.♕xd2

CHAPTER 1

Jeroen Bosch

The SOS Files

Light Relief

Let's start this issue of the SOS Files with some light relief. In the next chapter Arthur Kogan explains why he feels that the Najdorf should be met by 6.♕e2!?. In Pamplona earlier this year White opted for the early queen move and it was bull's eye!

□ **Du Plessis**
■ **Sebastian Almagro Mazariegos**
Pamplona 2010

1.e4 c5 2.♘f3 d6 3.d4 cxd4 4.♘xd4 ♘f6 5.♘c3 a6 6.♕e2 e5 The typical Najdorf move isn't all that attractive here.
7.♘f5 d5 White always had a slight edge in Dvirnyy-A.l'Ami, Hoogeveen 2010, after 7...♘c6 8.♗g5 ♗xf5 9.exf5 ♘d4 10.♕d3 ♖c8 11.0-0-0 ♕xf5 12.♕xf5 ♘xf5 13.♗xf6 gxf6 14.♘d5.
8.♗g5! dxe4 9.♖d1 ♕a5 10.♗xf6 gxf6 11.♕xe4

White now has a splendid position after say 11...♗b4 12.♘d6+ or 11...♘c6 12.♗c4 but Black's actual choice was a howler:
11...♕b4?? 12.♘g7+ and Black had to resign as he loses his queen.

Winning Quickly

SOS-1, Chapter 16, p.127

The first-ever winner of the SOS Prize was a young Magnus Carlsen back in 2004. He employed an idea from SOS-1 ('The Improved Lisitsin Gambit') to beat GM Dolmatov in only 19 moves. Surprisingly, there are still players out there who are willing to enter this line as Black. The latest victim is Vladimir Malaniuk, one the greatest experts in the Dutch Defence. Mitigating circumstances are that he was Black against a 2700-player in a rapid game. Nevertheless, his demise was as quick as we could have predicted:

□ **Laurent Fressinet**
■ **Vladimir Malaniuk**
Bastia 2010

1.♘f3 f5
Showing his willingness to enter the Dutch, but this is dangerous in view of our SOS weapon:
2.d3! Rather than the immediate 2.e4 which is the Lisitsin Gambit proper. **2...d6**

3.e4 e5 4.♘c3 ♘c6 5.exf5 ♗xf5 6.d4 ♘xd4 7.♘xd4 exd4 8.♕xd4

This really is a high-risk position for Black: why do they keep ignoring our warnings out there?

8...c6

8...♘f6 9.♗c4! c6 10.♗g5 b5 11.♗b3 ♗e7 12.0-0-0 ♕d7 13.♖he1 ♔d8 14.♖xe7! ♕xe7 15.♕f4 ♗d7 16.♘e4! d5 17.♘xf6 h6 18.♗h4 g5 19.♕d4! 1-0 was the afore-mentioned game Carlsen-Dolmatov, Moscow 2004.

9.♗f4! ♗xc2

9...♕b6 10.♕d2 d5 11.0-0-0 0-0-0 12.♗d3 ♗xd3 13.♕xd3 ♘h6? 14.♕h3+ ♖d7 15.♘xd5! and White won in a few moves, Sandner-Rechel, Germany 2003/04.

9...♕f6 10.♕b4 also favours White.

10.♔d2! ♗g6

Black is also in trouble after 10...♗f5 11.♖e1+ ♔d7 12.g4! ♗g6 (12...♗xg4 is met by 13.♖g1! ♘f6 – 13...♗f5 14.♖xg7+! – 14.♖xg4! ♘xg4 15.♗h3 h5 – 15...♕h4 16.♗xd6! – 16.f3 with an edge for White.) 13.♔c1! ♕b6 14.♕d2 ♕c5 15.g5!? ♘e7? (a blunder in a difficult position. 15...♔c7 16.h4) 16.♗h3+ ♘f5 17.♖e5! 1-0, Mikac-Zelic, Pula 2006.

11.♖e1+ ♔d7 12.g3 ♕b6?! 13.♗h3+

Amazingly all this is known to SOS-readers, Black is already lost.

13...♔c7

In the SOS Files of Volume 2 you will find the following miniature: 13...♔d8 14.♗g5+ ♔c7 15.♘d5+ 1-0, Seel-Horstmann, Bad Wiessee 2003.

14.♗xd6+! ♗xd6 15.♕xg7+ ♔b8 16.♔c1! ♕xf2 17.♘e4! 17.♖e2? ♕f6.

17...♗f4+??

Relatively best is 17...♕f8 18.♕xh8.

18.gxf4 ♕xf4+ 19.♘d2 ♕f6 20.♕d7 20.♖e8+ was a neat mate: 20...♗xe8 21.♕g3+ ♕d6 22.♕xd6+, but the text is of course sufficient.

20...♕f8? 21.♖e8+ 1-0.

Hou about 6...♕e8 in the Nimzo?

SOS-8, Chapter 6, p.50

In the 2010 FIDE Grand Prix in Nalchik Hou Yifan defeated her former compatriot Zhu Chen with an SOS-line in the Classical Nimzo-Indian. Clearly, this idea of Keene has much to recommend itself.

□ **Zhu Chen**
■ **Hou Yifan**
Nalchik 2010

1.d4 e6 2.c4 ♘f6 3.♘c3 ♗b4 4.♕c2 0-0 5.a3 ♗xc3+ 6.♕xc3 ♕e8!?

The queen move was first played by Raymond Keene in 1973. In SOS-8 Sébastien Mazé and Matthieu Cornette explain the main ideas behind this 'mysterious' move:
– Black prevents a possible pin following ♗g5.
– The queen defends the e-pawn, thus preparing ...d6 and ...e5.
– Sometimes the queen aims for square h5; after ...♘e4 and ...f5.
– The queen also makes a queenside strategy involving ...a5-a4 and ...b5 possible.

7.b4
This gains space on the queenside and prepares the fianchetto. However, it also weakens the light squares which is a distinct drawback (White therefore often plays b3 at some point).

● In the opinion of our French authors in SOS-8 White's best move is 7.f3. In 2010 Black has done well so far after 7...d6, and now:
– 8.♗g5?! is inaccurate as Maze/Cornette point out because of 8...♘fd7! and the bishop is badly placed. This position clearly illustrates one of the main points behind 6...♕e8. In the game Kozhuharov-Cornette, Malakoff 2010, there followed: 9.e3 e5 10.d5 a5! 11.b4?! f5 (...h5 is an unpleasant threat) 12.♗h4 axb4 13.axb4 ♖xa1+ 14.♕xa1 ♘a6! 15.♕a3 ♘b6∓ 16.c5? ♘xd5 17.♗c4 ♗e6 18.cxd6 ♘axb4 19.♕b3 cxd6

and White resigned: he is two pawns and hasn't been able to develop his kingside yet.
– 8.e4 e5 (the subtleties of 8...♘fd7 first are explained in SOS-8) 9.♘e2 ♘fd7! 10.g4 (stronger is 10.♗e3 a5 11.b3 ♘a6 12.♘g3 – 12.♕xa5 f5!? – 12...exd4 13.♗xd4 ♘e5 14.♗e2 c5?! – 14...f6 15.0-0 ♘c5 – 15.♗e3 ♘c7 16.0-0 ♘e6 17.♖ad1 ♕e7 18.♖d2± f5 19.exf5 ½-½, Brunner-Cornette, Marseille 2010) 10...a5 11.♗e3 a4! 12.♗g2 ♘c6 13.0-0 b6 14.♖fd1 ♗a6 15.♗f1 ♘a5 (this game demonstrates the strength of Black's queenside strategy) 16.♘g3 ♘b3 17.♖ab1 c5 18.dxe5 dxe5 clearly favoured Black in Kotanjian-Iordachescu, Dubai 2010.
● 7.♘f3 d6 8.g3 a5! 9.b3 a4! 10.b4 b5! 11.c5 ♗b7 12.♗g2 ♗e4! 13.0-0?! (13.♕e3 ♕c6 14.0-0 ♕d5 15.♗b2 ♘c6 and Black was doing well in Hauchard-Bauer, Narbonne 1997. For an analysis of the remainder of the game see SOS-8) 13...♘d5 14.♕d2 f5 15.♘e1! (15.♖e1 f4 16.♘h4 ♗xg2 17.♘xg2 ♕g6 with an attack, Chekhov-Sjoberg, Kecskemet 1991, was mentioned by Mazé/Cornette) 15...♘f6 16.f3 ♗d5 17.♘d3 ♘c6 18.♗b2 ♖d8 with a slight edge in Borzov-Tukhaev, Alushta 2010.
● See SOS-8 for the more restrained 7.g3 and 7.b3.

7...d6 8.♗b2 b6
Sensible play by Hou Yifan. Black played very creatively (and successfully) in Arlandi-Tatai, Chianciano 1989: 8...♘bd7 9.e3 a5 10.♗d3 ♘b6!? 11.♕c2 (11.♘f3 ♘a4 12.♕c2 ♘xb2 13.♕xb2=) 11...♘a4!? 12.♕xa4 (12.♕c3 ♕c6 13.♘f3 ♘a4=) 12...♘xa4 13.♗c1 (13.♖b1) 13...axb4 14.axb4 ♗d7 (14...♘c5) 15.♘e2 b5! 16.0-0 (16.cxb5 ♖fb8∓) 16...bxc4 17.♗xc4 ♘b6 18.♖xa8 ♖xa8 19.♗d3 ♘fd5 20.♗d2 ♖a2∓ and Black won.

9.♕f3
Hoping to punish Black for 6...♕e8? The queen move provokes ...d5 and the closure of

the long diagonal. However, the drawbacks are also clear. White loses time with her queen. Closes her own diagonal a1-h8, as d4-d5 is no longer on the cards. Moreover, ...d5 fits in with Black's light-squared strategy on the queenside. Still, things are not that clear in the game, as Zhu Chen's play can be improved upon.

9...d5 10.♖c1 c6 11.e3 a5?!
Here Black has the equalizing 11...♗a6 at her disposal.

12.bxa5?!
Stronger is 12.b5, for example: 12...cxb5 (12...♗b7) 13.cxb5 ♗d7 14.♕e2! (14.a4 ♕e7 15.♕d1 ♘e4 is a plausible line that favours Black) 14...♘e4 15.f3 ♘d6 16.a4±.

12...bxa5
Not bad is 12...♖xa5!? 13.♗c3 ♖xa3 14.♗b4 ♖a2 and Black is better as 15.♗xf8 ♕xf8 gives Black too much compensation.

13.♕d1
13.♗d3 followed by ♕e2, ♘f3 and 0-0 is a healthier way to develop.

13...♗a6 14.♘f3 ♘bd7 15.♗d3 ♘b6

Black has grasped the initiative by putting pressure on c4. Positionally, White should keep the pawn on c4, which involves a further loss of time.

16.♘d2
– 16.cxd5 ♗xd3 17.♕xd3 cxd5 is clearly better for Black.

– 16.c5 ♘c4 is probably better than 16...♗xd3 17.cxb6 (not 17.♕xd3 ♘c4 18.♗a1 ♕e7 19.0-0 ♖fb8).

16...♖b8   17.♗c3   17.0-0   dxc4.
17...♕e7!   18.♖a1   18.♗xa5   ♕xa3
19.♗xb6 ♕xd3 20.♗c5 ♖fe8∓.

18...♘xc4
18...dxc4 is also unpleasant for White.

19.♘xc4 19.♗xc4 is relatively better to play for opposite-coloured bishops.

19...dxc4 20.♗e2 ♘d5 21.♗xa5 ♖b3
21...♖b2. **22.0-0 ♖xa3**
Hou Yifan is a pawn up, but White's structure is superior, so this does not mean much. More important is Black's piece activity and the tactical chances that this brings. Considering Zhu Chen's 24th and 25th move she must have been in serious time trouble by now.

23.♕c2 ♖a8 24.e4?
This is a serious blunder. It is hard to say what Zhu Chen overlooked. Clearly, allowing the knight to f4 brings nothing but trouble.
24.♕b2 ♖b3 25.♕c1 and White is able to defend.
24...♘f4 25.♗f3?? 25.♗g4 c3 also wins for Black.

25...♖xf3 26.♗d2
And White resigned without waiting for 26...♘e2+.

Beating the French
SOS-3, Chapter 8, p.71

Getting 'Out of the French Book', as Canadian GM Mark Bluvshtein entitled his 2005 article for SOS, is rather difficult, but the unusual 3.♗d3 still seems to do the trick. In a recent game Spanish GM Magem Badals beat his compatriot Oms Pallisse in an attractive little miniature.

☐ **Jordi Magem Badals**
■ **Josep Oms Pallisse**
Barcelona 2010

1.e4 e6 2.d4 d5 3.♗d3!?
A flexible move. Rather than determining the pawn structure (3.e5 and 3.exd5), or obstructing his own development (3.♘d2), or obstructing the possible formation of a pawn chain a la Nimzowitsch (3.♘c3) White leaves it all open. Of course, to obtain such flexibility he has to commit the 'opening sin' of developing his bishop before his knights (Lasker's rule). This is perhaps a small drawback, but there is another one: a possible loss of time. Oms Pallisse responds correctly.
3...dxe4
By far the most natural move. Another typical French idea is 3...c5, when Bluvshtein makes a case for 4.c3, but I have personally preferred 4.exd5, when Black's safest bet is taking back with the pawn à la the Exchange Variation: 4...exd5 (4...♕xd5 5.♘c3 ♕xd4 – 5...♕xg2? 6.♗e4+− – 6.♘f3 – 6.♘b5 – 6...♕d8 gives White enough for the pawn, Bosch-Stellwagen, Dutch tt 2007. See The SOS Files of Volume 8) 5.♘f3 c4 6.♗e2 ♘f6 7.0-0 ♘c6 8.b3 cxb3 9.axb3 ♗e7 10.♘e5 0-0 11.♘xc6 bxc6 12.♘c3 a5 13.♗a3 ♖e8 14.♗xe7 ♕xe7 ½-½, Grafl-Bromberger, Badalona 2010.
4.♗xe4 ♘f6

Winning a tempo for his development, which justifies his previous decision to 'give up the centre' just like in the Rubinstein Variation. Now White places his bishop on the h1-a8 diagonal putting pressure on Black's queenside – fairly unusual for a French Defence!
– 4...c5 5.c3!? (5.♘e2) 5...♘f6 6.♗f3 (6.♗d3 cxd4 7.cxd4 ♘c6 8.♘f3 ♘b4 9.♗e2 ♗e7 10.0-0 0-0 11.a3 ♘c6 12.♘c3 with a typical isolated pawn position, Bontempi-Krivoshey, Porto San Giorgio 2007) 6...♘c6 7.♘e2 e5 8.♗xc6+ bxc6 9.0-0 exd4 10.cxd4 ♗e7 was about equal in (among others) Vedder-Wemmers, Amsterdam 2010. Black has a pair of bishops but also a weaker pawn structure.
– 4...♗e7 5.♘e2 ♘f6 6.♗f3 c5 7.♗e3 ♘bd7 8.♘bc3 cxd4 9.♘xd4 a6 10.0-0 ♘e5 11.♗e2 ♘d5 12.♘xd5 ♕xd5 13.♘f3 ♕xd1 14.♖fxd1 ♘c6 15.c3 was slightly better for White in Collinson-Richter, Hinckley Island 2010. The position resembles a 2.c3 Sicilian gone right for White.
5.♗f3 ♘bd7
Preparing ...c5 in this way is not necessary and therefore this move is, ever so slightly, inaccurate. Good is the straightforward 5...c5 6.♘e2 ♘c6 (6...cxd4 7.♕xd4!? ♘bd7 8.♗e3 ♗c5 9.♕c3 ♕b6 10.♗xc5 – 10.♘d2 ♗xe3 11.fxe3± – 10...♕xc5 11.♕xc5 ♘xc5 12.♘bc3 ♗d7 13.0-0-0±, Jose Queralto-Antonsen, Khanty-Mansiysk ol 2010) 7.♗e3 e5 (7...♕b6 8.0-0?! – 8.♘bc3! see SOS-3 – 8...♕xb2 9.♘bc3 ♗e7?! 10.♘a4 ♕a3 11.c3? c4 12.♗f4 0-0∓, Cihal-Majer Sen, Brno 2010; but stronger was 10.♖b1! ♕a3 11.♘b5 ♕a5 12.♗f4 0-0 13.♘c7 cxd4 – 13...♖b8 14.♗xc6+− – 14.♘xa8±) 8.♗xc6+ bxc6 9.dxe5 ♕xd1+ 10.♔xd1 ♘g4, Sipila-Solomon, Khanty-Mansiysk ol 2010, was already indicated as satisfactory for Black by Bluvshtein, who noted that White had to play 9.c3 instead.

6.♞c3 c5

After all, but now Black can no longer put pressure on d4 with his queen's knight.

7.♞ge2 cxd4 8.♛xd4!?

Because of Black's move order White is not obliged to take back with the knight: 8.♞xd4, which also looks somewhat better for the first player.

8...♝c5 9.♛f4

9...♛e7

9...e5 10.♛g3 favours White who controls the light squares in the centre.

10.0-0 ♝d6 11.♛e3 a6

It is useful to cover square b5 but is does not completely solve Black's problems.

11...♝c5?! is met by 12.♛g5! 0-0 13.♖d1. Perhaps 11...0-0 or 11...♞e5.

12.♞g3

White has a slight edge.

12...♞e5 13.♖d1!?

Magem is not interested in saving his light-squared bishop!

13...0-0 13...♞xf3+ 14.♛xf3 0-0 15.♝g5 is rather unpleasant for Black.

14.b3 ♛c7 14...♞xf3+ 15.♛xf3 ♛c7.

15.♝b2 ♞xf3+ 16.♛xf3 ♖b8?

Black is ambitious and wants to develop à la the Sicilian with ...b5 and ...♝b7, but he has lost his sense of danger for a moment. White has been preparing nasty things along the a1-h8 diagonal and Magem does not miss out on such a chance.

Still playable was 16...♝d7 17.♞ce4 ♞xe4 18.♛xe4 ♝xg3 19.hxg3 ♝c6. And 16...♝e5 17.♖e1± was another possibility.

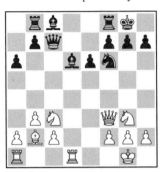

17.♖xd6!

Winning by force in all lines. An important defender is removed and the rook on b8 is badly placed.

17...♛xd6 18.♞ce4 ♞xe4 19.♞xe4

There is no defence now against a devastating check on f6.

19...♛c7

– 19...♛e7 20.♞f6+ ♚h8 21.♝e5! ♖a8 22.♛e4 gxf6 23.♛h4+–.

– 19...♛d8 20.♞f6+ (even simpler is 20.♛g3+–) 20...♚h8 21.♝e5 ♖a8 22.♖d1 ♛e7 23.♛e4+–.

20.♞f6+ ♚h8 21.♛e4 And Black has no defence against checkmate. 1-0

Smyslov's SOS line
SOS-2, Chapter 16, p.121

The Ruy Lopez with 3...g6 is often called the Smyslov Variation, a fitting tribute to the efforts of the 7th World Champion who passed away in March 2010. In the 2010 European Championship 2700-GM Motylev demolished a variation in the 3...g6 Ruy Lopez on which we have repeatedly reported. Check out this attractive game and brush up on your knowledge so this does not happen to you!

☐ **Alexander Motylev**
■ **Michele Godena**
Rijeka 2010

1.e4 e5 2.♘f3 ♘c6 3.♗b5 g6

'Solid but Tricky' is how Glenn Flear dubbed this line in his article for SOS-2. While this sounds like a contradiction in terms it does have the merit of truth. Black often has the option to go either for a solid set-up, or take a more enterprising approach. In short an ideal surprise weapon, that can be played on a regular basis. Apart from Motylev's 4.d4, White has the innocuous 4.♗xc6, 4.♘c3 and especially 4.c3 at his disposal. All these moves are covered by Flear in SOS-2. Please note, if you play 3...g6 it can be useful to also incorporate 3...♘ge7 (the Cozio Variation) in your repertoire – see SOS-8, Chapter 16.

4.d4

The sharpest reaction. White aims to show that in the Open Games Black has no time to fianchetto his bishop.

4...exd4 5.♗g5!

5.♘xd4 ♗g7 6.♗e3 ♘f6 7.♘c3 0-0 8.f3 (8.0-0 ♘g4! 9.♖xg4 ♘xd4 is fine for Black, for example: 10.♗xd4!? ♗xd4 11.♖ad1 ♗xc3 12.bxc3 d6 13.♕g3 ♕e7, S.Polgar-Smyslov, London 1996) 8...♘e7 9.♘de2 (9.♕d2 d5!) 9...d5! 10.exd5 ♘fxd5 11.♗g5 c6 12.♘xd5 cxd5 13.c3 ♕d6 14.♕d2 ♘c6 15.♖d1 ♗e6 and Black was very comfortably placed in Dückstein-Smyslov, Bad Wörishofen 1991 (see SOS-2 for more details).

5...♗e7 6.♗xe7

In his *The Ruy Lopez Revisited* (New In Chess 2009), Ivan Sokolov also mentions the 'illogical' 6.♗f4, citing the game Anand-Smyslov, Groningen 1989, where Black was better after 6...♘f6 7.e5 ♘d5 8.♗h6 a6 9.♗a4 ♘b6 10.♗b3 d5 11.exd6 ♕xd6 12.0-0 ♗e6 13.♗xe6 fxe6 14.♘bd2 0-0-0.

6...♕xe7

6...♘gxe7 7.♘xd4 d5 8.♘c3 is somewhat unattractive for Black, and to avoid the dangers in the present game I would recommend the alternative on the next move.

7.♗xc6!

7.0-0 is either answered by 7...♘f6 8.e5 ♘h5!, with a decent game for Black (see the SOS Files of Volume 3), or by 7...♕c5 8.♗xc6 dxc6 9.♕xd4 ♕xd4 10.♘xd4 ♗d7 11.♘c3 0-0-0, which is Sokolov's preference.

7...♕b4+?!

Very tricky, but also very risky as Motylev brilliantly demonstrates. The queen check is a speciality of GM Julian Radulski. Much more solid is 7...dxc6, when play might continue 8.♕xd4 ♘f6 9.♘c3 ♗g4 10.♘d2 (10.0-0 ♗xf3 11.gxf3 0-0) 10...♗e6 (10...c5 11.♕e3 0-0-0; 10...0-0) 11.f3 c5 12.♕e3 0-0-0 13.0-0-0 ♖d4 14.♖he1 ♖hd8 with equality in Organdziev-Radulski, Vrnjacka Banja 2004 – see the SOS Files of SOS-3.

8.c3 ♕xb2

9.♗a4!

This is the new Star Move! Motylev preserves his bishop for the attack, not worrying about the rook he will lose on a1. The result is a very romantic game in the spirit of Anderssen and Morphy. Until now White took on d4: 9.♕xd4 bxc6 (9...♕xa1? 10.0-0 f6 11.e5! dxc6 12.exf6, with a killing attack, was given by Flear) 10.0-0 ♕xa1 (10...♗a6 and now Flear's 11.♘bd2! is strong) 11.♕xh8 ♔f8 12.♘g5 (12.♘e5 ♕xa2 13.♕xh7? d6! 14.♘xc6 a5! 15.f4 ♗a6 16.♖e1 ♗d3 17.e5 ♗e4! 0-1, Bjarnason-Radulski, Le Touquet 2007) 12...♗a6! 13.♘xh7+ ♔e7 14.♕e5+ ♔d8 15.♖d1 ♗e2! 16.♕g7 ♔e7 and the game Spasov-Radulski, Borovets 2008, soon ended in a draw by perpetual check (see the SOS-Files of SOS-10).

9...♕xa1 10.0-0 b5?

Hoping to gain time or to shut out the bishop. Yet this can be shown to be a losing mistake. 10...c5 11.♕d2 is also too risky (the queen on a1 is completely out of play), which leaves 10...♕xa2. If you want to insist on 7...♕b4+ then this should be the start of your (computer-assisted) analysis.

11.♗b3 c5

The idea is nice (shutting out the bishop), and while your engine will quickly reveal 12.♘xd4! this is not so easy to find over the board. Don't forget that in this game Black is a grandmaster too.

12.♘xd4! 12.cxd4 c4!. **12...cxd4**
13.♕xd4 f6 Forced – if Black loses the rook on h8 his position is wrecked anyway.
14.e5! Opening the position with the black king stuck in the middle. **14...♗b7**

15.♘a3 ♕b2 16.exf6 The immediate 16.♘xb5 also wins.

16...♘h6

White wins after 16...0-0-0 17.♘xb5 ♗c6 18.♘xa7+ ♔c7 19.♘xc6 dxc6 20.♕a7+.

17.♕e5+ ♔d8 18.♘xb5

All units barring the rook are in on the attack. Black's forces are scattered over the board.

18...♕d2 19.♕c7+ ♔e8 20.♘d6+ and Godena resigned.

Motylev's 9.♗a4 led to a very nice victory. You may want to investigate 10...♕xa2, but there is a very safe line available in the form of 7...dxc6, rendering Smyslov's Variation absolutely payable.

Reading SOS Successfully

SOS-12, Chapter 4, p.34
SOS-6, Chapter 3, p.24

In the previous SOS volume Alexander Finkel wrote on an Alekhine favourite (6.g4) versus the French that in modern times has mainly been played by Swedish GM Jonny Hector. Not so long after the publication of SOS-12 one of our readers, Boris Grimberg, was able to employ Hector's weapon versus GM Ivan Farago in Germany's biggest open tournament. Farago had a tough time against such a 'booked-up' opponent. When playing through the game we were struck by how effortlessly it all seems.

☐ **Boris Grimberg**
■ **Ivan Farago**
Deizisau 2010

1.e4 e6 2.d4 d5 3.♘c3 ♗b4 4.♘e2 dxe4 5.a3 ♗e7

For 5...♗xc3+ 6.♘xc3 see Chapter 7 of the present volume.

6.g4 e5

The most natural response, although Finkel feels that 6...♗d7 and 6...h5 are no worse.

7.h3 exd4?! 8.♕xd4 ♘c6

After 8...♕xd4 9.♘xd4 the ending is not so easy for Black, according to Finkel on the basis of several of Hector's games.

9.♕xe4 ♘f6 10.♕g2!

Interestingly White gains an edge here by fianchettoing his queen! In the game we will see that Black has trouble finding a safe haven for his queen. The queen on g2 is safe from any attacks by enemy pieces, and supports the pushing of the kingside pawns.

10...0-0 11.g5!?

Somewhat impatient, but difficult to find fault with. After 11.♗d2 ♗e6 12.0-0-0 ♕c8 13.♘f4 ♖d8 14.g5 ♘e8 15.♘cd5! White was much better in Hector-Heika, Hamburg 2005. (See SOS-12).

11...♘d7

Nor does Black achieve equality after either 11...♘h5 12.♗d2 ♕d6 13.0-0-0 ♗f5 14.♘d5, or 11...♘e8 12.♗d2 followed by queenside castling.

12.♗d2 ♘b6 13.0-0-0 ♘c4?! 14.♗f4

So far White has only made 'natural' moves – that is if you are in for 6.g4 and that sort of thing. It's a pleasant edge that White is enjoying. First of all because Black's queen is awkwardly placed, and, secondly, since

White's plan of attacking on the kingside is so simple to execute.

14...♗d6 15.♗xd6

Keeping the tension with 15.♔b1 or 15.♘d5 also deserves consideration.

15...♘xd6 16.h4 ♗f5 17.♘g3 ♕d7

17...♗e6 18.♘ge4±. **18.♘xf5** To be able to develop the bishop to d3 with tempo. The crude 18.h5 was also strong.

18...♕xf5 19.♘d5 ♔h8?!

This is understandable in view of a sometimes painful check on f6. Consider for instance: 19...♖ac8? 20.♗d3 ♕d7? 21.♘f6+, and wins.

The pawn sacrifice 19...♖ae8 brings no compensation after 20.♘xc7 ♖e5 21.♘d5.

19...♘e4 offered most resistance.

20.♗d3 ♕d7 21.h5

Chess is often a very difficult game, but here it all seems so simple!

21...♘e7

White also wins after 21...♘e5 22.h6 g6 23.♕g3, and 21...♖ad8 22.h6 g6 23.♖he1.

22.♘f4 22.h6 was even stronger. **22...♕c6 23.♕g4 f5? 24.♕e2 ♘e4** 24...♖ae8 25.h6. **25.♗b5!**

This wins by force, but the game would also not have lasted much longer after 25.h6.

25...♘b6 25...♕c5 26.♘g6++−. **26.♖d7 a6 27.♗c4**

27...♕c6

It smacks of despair, but this is actually the strongest move in the position! 27...♖ae8 loses after 28.♖xe7 ♖xe7 29.♘g6+.
28.♖xe7 ♘g3 29.fxg3 ♕xh1+ 30.♔d2 ♖ad8+ 31.♗d3 ♕g1 32.♕e5 Or 32.h6.
32...♕f2+ 33.♔c3 ♖g8 34.h6 1-0.

In SOS-6 I wrote about the so-called Aussie Attack. This is a particularly risky line, but you know how it is: high risk – high benefit. In the game below avid SOS-reader Daniel Bisby beats *Dangerous Weapons* editor GM John Emms with a novelty that was mentioned in SOS-6. A deserved win and the winner of the SOS Prize.

☐ **Daniel Bisby**
■ **John Emms**
London Chess League 2009

1.e4 c5 2.♘f3 e6 3.d4 cxd4 4.♗g5!?
This is the Aussie Attack!
4...♘f6 5.e5 h6 6.♗h4 6.♗c1 is the safer option, as indicated in SOS-6.
6...g5 7.exf6 Black is OK after 7.♗g3 ♘h5 8.♘bd2 ♘c6 9.♗b5 g4!, as I mentioned in the earlier article.
7...gxh4 8.♕xd4 ♘c6 9.♕xh4 ♕b6 10.♘bd2
Played like a man. 10.b3 is too insipid.
10...♕xb2 11.♖b1 ♕xc2 12.♗b5

12...a6
12...♖g8!? 13.0-0 (13.♔e2 is mentioned by Bisby, with the idea of 13...♖xg2? 14.♘e1!, although he mentions that it 'must be rubbish'!) 13...♕g6 to exchange queens with 14...♕g4 was indicated in SOS-6.
13.♗xc6 ♕xc6 14.0-0 b5 15.♘e5 ♕d5 16.♕h5 ♖h7
Interestingly, I gave this position in SOS-6 with the following comments: 'and Black had everything defended for the moment in Liu Pei-Qi Jingxuan, Suzhou 2006. White should now perhaps have played 17.♖fd1 (rather than 17.♘df3) and if you love to attack then here's your chance. White may well be better!'. Clearly, Bisby loves to attack and his strong opponent lasted for only a few more moves!

17.♖fd1! d6

This loses by force, but Black's position is very hard to play in practice.

18.♘dc4! ♕e4

Black also loses after 18...♕c5 19.♘xd6+! ♗xd6 20.♖xd6 ♕xd6 (20...♖a7 21.♖bd1 ♗d7 22.♕g4+−) 21.♖d1

21...♕c7 (21...♕c5 22.♕g4 ♖h8 23.♘xf7!+−) 22.♕g4 ♖h8 23.♕g7 ♖f8 24.♘g6! ♕c5 25.♘xf8 ♕xf8 26.♕xf8+ ♔xf8 27.♖d8 checkmate!

19.f3 ♕f4

Black is lost in all lines:

– 19...♕f5 20.♕xf5 exf5 21.♘xd6+ ♗xd6 22.♖xd6+−.

– 19...♕c2 20.♖bc1 ♕e2 21.♖d2+−.

– 19...♕xb1 20.♖xb1 bxc4 21.♕g4 dxe5

22.♕xc4 ♗d7 23.♕e4 ♖c8 24.♕xh7+−.

20.♘xd6+ ♗xd6 21.♖xd6 ♕xf6

22.♖bd1?

Letting Black off the hook for a moment. Correct was 22.♕g4!, when White wins after 22...♔f8 (22...♖g7 23.♕e4) 23.♖e1! and now there are all sorts of nice geometrical motifs, for example: 23...♖g7 24.♕d4 ♗g8 25.♖d8+ ♔h7 26.♕e4+ ♕f5 27.♕xa8 ♕g5! 28.♖h8+! ♔xh8 29.♕xc8++−.

22...♖a7?

22...♕g5, to stay in the game.

23.♖d8+

And Black resigned, as he loses his rook to a knight fork after taking twice on d8.

CHAPTER 2

Arthur Kogan

Sicilian Najdorf: the Czebe Attack

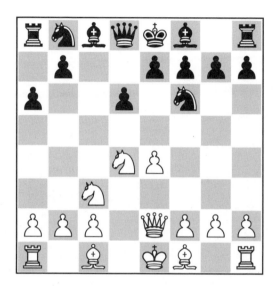

Let's play 6.♕e2!?

1.e4 c5 2.♘f3 d6 3.d4 cxd4 4.♘xd4 ♘f6 5.♘c3 a6

The Najdorf is usually played by those who take their openings very seriously and prepare and memorize long lines for hours. So, it makes sense to surprise them at an early stage, and test their creativity instead of their memory. Personally, I have played 6.♕f3 quite successfully (see SOS-5, Chapter 13, p.107), but perhaps this line is less surprising than it used to be. Therefore without further ado I present you

6.♕e2!?

This is slightly similar to 6.♕f3. White prepares to castle queenside as quickly as possible, and anticipates the Najdorf move 6...e5.

Other attacking ideas include e5, f4, g4 or even ♘d5, depending on Black's set-up. Actually, these days the queen move has become quite common in several lines of the 6.♗g5 Najdorf. The point is that having the queen on e2 will not disturb the rook on d1 on the half open file. Moreover, with the queen on e2 there are often threats against the black king on e8 in combination with moves like e5, ♘d5 or even ♘f5. All this seems to compensate for the bishop on f1, that will feel sad for a while but can join the game from g2 after the customary push of g4 in many lines. At such an early stage in the game Black also has a wide choice. I will mainly show the basic ideas by combining the limited practical experience with my own analysis. There is still a lot of space for improvements and creativity for all the SOS fans out there!

While it is hard to divide the limited available material into main lines and side variations, I first present the following game excerpts with a few notes:

– 6...♘c6!? was tried by Murey, but I believe that White is better after 7.♘xc6 bxc6 8.e5! ♘d5

and now 9.♗d2! would be my recommendation. White is planning to take on d5, followed by ♗c3, when Black will have trouble developing his kingside.

Instead, the game went 9.♕c4!? ♗b7 (not bad is 9...e6 10.♕xc6+ ♗d7 11.♕c4 ♖c8, with very decent compensation to say the least) 10.exd6 ♕xd6 11.♗d2 g6 12.♕d4 e5 13.♕a4 ♕b4 14.♕b3 ♕xb3 15.axb3, and White still holds a modicum of an advantage, but the players soon agreed to a draw in Balinov-Murey, Seefeld 2002.

– 6...♕c7 is another logical move, that was played by the Najdorf expert Karjakin: 7.♗e3 (7.♗g5 can transpose to lines of the 6.♗g5 attack) 7...e5 8.♘b3 ♗e7 9.0-0-0 ♗e6 10.♘d5 ♗xd5 11.exd5 h5 12.♔b1 ♘bd7 13.h4 (here I would recommend 13.f4!± and if 13...h4 then 14.♖g1 followed by g4) 13...♖c8 14.c4 a5, and Black had serious counterplay in Rodriguez Guerrero-Karjakin, San Sebastian 2006.

– 6...♕b6!? is also logical, as in many Sicilians, to chase the knight from its active post. Here Black is clearly aiming to take advantage of 6.♕e2. However, White will soon gain a tempo on the queen with ♗e3. Play is similar to certain lines of the Scheveningen, where ♕e2 is also played sometimes. Here are some ideas for your 'brain bag': 7.♘b3 (not 7.♕c4?! ♘c6) 7...e6 8.g4! ♗e7 (8...♘c6 9.g5 ♘d7 10.f4 ♕c7 11.a3 b6 12.♗e3 ♗b7 13.♗h3 0-0-0 14.f5 ♖e8 15.0-0-0±, Perez Candelario-Röder, Campillos 2006) 9.g5 ♘fd7 10.f4 ♘c6 11.♗e3 ♕c7 12.0-0-0 b5 13.♗g2 ♗b7 14.♔b1 b4 15.♘d5!?

(making optimal use of the queen on e2, now that Black hasn't castled yet; actually, 15.♘a4 0-0 16.h4 also doesn't look so bad for White) 15...exd5 16.exd5 ♘a5 17.♘xa5 ♕xa5 18.♗d4 ♔d8 19.♖he1 ♖e8 20.♕h5 (20.♗xg7) 20...f6 21.♕f7±, Pikula-Misailovic, Budva 2009.

In all the above lines White clearly had decent chances to emerge with an opening advantage. Now, let's delve more deeply by means of the following division:

I   6...g6
II   6...b5
III   6...e6
IV   6...e5

Variation I – 6...g6

6...g6
Trying to transpose to a Dragon is fairly logical.

7.♗g5
7.f3!? is not so bad either, because ...a6 is not always useful in the Dragon, and Black will have to take care of a possible e4-e5, for example: 7...♗g7 8.♗e3 0-0 9.0-0-0

7...♗g7 8.0-0-0

8...0-0!
This looks very risky because of 9.e5, but I still consider it the best move for Black.
● Attila Czebe is the main practioneer of 6.♕e2. Our expert preferred 8...♘bd7 when confronted with 6.♕e2 himself. The game went 9.f4 ♕c7, and now White misplayed with 10.♗xf6?! ♘xf6 11.e5 dxe5 12.fxe5, and Black was more than OK after 12...♗g4! 13.♘f3 ♘d7 14.♘d5 ♕c5 15.♕e4 ♖c8 16.♘c3 ♗f5, Sommerbauer-Czebe, Oberwart 2005.
I would recommend the improvement 10.♔b1 (10.g4!? is interesting. 10.♘f3 is also logical, but I consider 10.♔b1 to be more useful: when the game opens up the king should be on b1 – 10...♘b6 11.e5 dxe5 12.fxe5 ♘g4 13.♗f4 f6 14.♖e1)
– 10...b5 11.♗xf6!. Now it works better. After 11...♘xf6 12.e5 dxe5 13.fxe5 ♗g4 (13...♘g4 14.e6) 14.♘f3 ♘d7 15.♕e4!

♗xf3 16.gxf3 ♖d8 17.f4± White looks better with his nice centre and that poor bishop on g7!.
– 10...0-0 11.♘f3! (11.g4!? with ♗g2 and ♘d5 is a more positional plan but also an option)

and White seems to have the better chances, for example: 11...♘b6 (11...b5? 12.e5 dxe5 13.fxe5 ♘g4 14.♘d5±) 12.e5 dxe5 13.fxe5 ♘g4 14.♗f4±.
● 8...♕a5 also make sense and was played once: 9.h4! ♘c6 10.♘b3! (so the queen is not so safe on a5 after all!) 10...♕d8, and here I would recommend 11.♘d5! (11.♔b1 0-0 12.♘d5±; 11.h5!? ♘xh5 12.♘d5 ♗e6 13.g4, with compensation in Sipos-Stavrianakis, Szombathely 2009) 11...♘xd5 12.exd5 ♘e5 13.h5!, with a nice initiative for White.

9.e5
9.f4?! was played by the always creative Swedish GM Hector. He got into trouble after 9...♗g4! 10.♘f3 ♕a5 11.h3 (or 11.e5 dxe5 12.♕xe5 – 12.fxe5 ♘c6!∓ – 12...♕b4!) 11...♗xf3 12.♕xf3 ♖c8. Black already has fine counterplay. The following move doesn't help: 13.♗xf6? ♗xf6 14.♘d5 ♕xa2, and Black was much better in Hector-Cheparinov, Malmö 2007.
An alternative for the forcing sequence after 9.e5 is 9.h3!?.

21

9...dxe5!

This is what I would recommend Black to play. It leads to a very complicated game.

9...♕a5 didn't stop our expert to score a nice win after 10.♗xf6! exf6 11.exd6 ♖d8 12.♕e7 ♗f8 13.♕c7 (13.♕xf6 ♖xd6 14.♕f4±) 13...♕g5+ 14.♔b1 ♖e8 15.♘f3 ♕f5 16.♗d3 ♕d7 17.♘d5 ♕xd6 18.♕xd6 ♗xd6 19.♘xf6+ ♔f8 20.♘xe8 ♔xe8 21.♗xg6 1-0, Czebe-Galyas, Balatonlelle 2007.

10.♕xe5

10.♘e6 is not that clear. After 10...♗xe6! 11.♖xd8 ♖xd8 Black will have very active piece play for the queen.

10...♘g4

The start of an impressive tactical display.

11.♕e1 ♗xd4 12.♗xe7

12...♗e3+! 13.♕xe3 ♕xd1+ 14.♘xd1

♘xe3 15.♗xf8 ♘xd1

15...♘xc2 16.♗h6±.

16.♗c5 ♘xb2 17.♔xb2 ♗e6 18.♗d3±

And White's bishops seem to give him the better chances in this endgame. He can play on both sides of the board.

Variation II – 6...b5

6...b5 7.♗g5

Also interesting is 7.♘d5!?.

7...e6

Play may be compared to 6.♗g5 e6 7.♕e2 and now 7...b5. Black's normal antidote to 7.♕e2 is 7...h6 8.♗h4 ♗e7!.

8.0-0-0

8...♘bd7

Against the logical 8...b4 I would recommend to go for an attack with 9.e5!? bxc3 (9...dxe5 10.♘xe6) 10.exf6 gxf6 11.♕f3! fxg5 12.♕xa8 cxb2+ 13.♔b1 ♕b6 14.♖d3!, with unclear play.

Or the characteristic sacrificial idea 9.♘d5!? exd5 10.exd5+ ♗e7 (or 10...♕e7 11.♕c4! ♕b7 12.♖e1+ ♗e7 13.♗xf6 gxf6 14.♗d3 with a dangerous attack) 11.♗xf6 gxf6 12.♖e1 intending ♕f3.

9.♘d5!

Such aggressive ideas should always be considered when one has a development advantage with the opponent's king still in the centre.

9...♗b7

Also critical is 9...exd5 10.exd5+ (10.♘c6 ♕c7 11.exd5+ ♘e5 12.f4 ♗g4!) 10...♕e7 (10...♘e5 11.f4 ♗g4 12.♘f3 illustrates the difference with 10.♘c6; 10...♗e7? 11.♘c6+−) 11.♕d2!, with multiple threats, for example: 11...♘e4 12.♗xe7 ♘xd2 13.♗xf8±, or 11...♕e5 12.♖e1 ♘e4 13.f4! ♘xd2 14.fxe5 dxe5 (14...♘xe5 15.♗xd2) 15.♗xd2 ♗b7 16.♘c6 f6 17.♗d3 which looks better for White.

10.♘xf6+ gxf6

Or 10...♘xf6 11.e5±.

11.♗h4 h5 12.♔b1 ♖c8 13.f4 ♖c5 14.♕e3

And White was clearly better in Czebe-Szabo, Budapest 2005. I would recommend playing g3 followed by either ♗g2 or ♗h3, with a decent positional edge.

Variation III – 6...e6
6...e6 7.g4!

7.f4!? also makes sense and led to interesting play in Spasov-Vazquez, Tunja 1989: 7...♗e7 (7...b5 8.a3) 8.♗e3 ♕c7 9.g4 ♘fd7 10.g5 b5 11.a3 ♘c6 12.♕d2 ♖b8 13.h4 ♘b6 14.♘xc6 ♕xc6 15.h5 ♘c4 16.♗xc4 ♕xc4 17.♗d4, and White is better and won after 17...♖g8 18.b3 ♕c6 19.h6 e5 20.♗e3 exf4 21.♗xf4 gxh6 22.♖xh6 ♕c5 23.0-0-0 ♗e6 24.♗xd6 ♗xd6 25.♕xd6 ♕xd6 26.♖xd6 a5 27.♖xh7.

7...♘c6 8.♘b3 b5 9.♗g2 ♗b7 10.0-0

Motylev is playing for a typical Scheveningen, with a few additional tempi.

10...♗e7 11.a3 That's why Vallejo tried the creative: **11...g5?!** However, he got into trouble after: **12.e5! dxe5 13.♖d1 ♕c7 14.♗xg5 ♘h5 15.gxh5 ♗xg5 16.♕g4 ♗e7 17.♕g7±**

Motylev-Vallejo Pons, Wijk aan Zee II 2009.

Variation IV – 6...e5
6...e5

The most critical answer, following the basic idea of the Najdorf to obtain central control and fight for the d5-square. So here Black intends to push ...d6-d5 one day!

7.♘f5!

Following the creative spirit! After other moves the queen is misplaced on e2.

See, for example what happened in Perez Candelario-Rabadan, Madrid 2008: 7.♘f3 ♗e7 8.♗g5 ♗e6 9.0-0-0 ♘bd7 10.♗xf6 ♘xf6 11.♘xe5 ♖c8 12.♘d3 ♕a5!, and with ideas to sac on c3, and ...b5-b4 Black had more than enough compensation.

7...d5

The direct approach!

● Also logical is 7...♗xf5 8.exf5, and now:
– 8...♘c6 9.♗g5 ♗e7 10.0-0-0 (or 10.♗xf6) 10...0-0 11.♗xf6! (my improvement over 11.h3? ♘d4 12.♕d3 ♖c8, as in Rudolf-Majdan, Dresden 2008) 11...♗xf6 12.♘d5, and White has the better chances, owing to his good control of d5. The plan is to play ♕e4 and push the g- and h-pawns to start a kingside attack.
– After 8...♗e7 I would recommend 9.g4 ♘c6 10.♗g2 ♘d4 11.♕d1, with nice pressure along the h1-a8 diagonal, but also good is 9.♗g5 ♘bd7 10.g4 (10.0-0-0 ♖c8).

● 7...g6 is weakening but was also tried a few times: 8.♘e3 (8.♘h6!? ♘c6 9.♗g5

♗xh6 10.♗xh6 ♘g4 11.♗d2 ♘d4 12.♕d1 ♕h4 13.g3 ♕f6 14.f4 is another interesting line, since Black's activity might be just an illusion, as White intends ♘d5, c3 and ♗e2) 8...♗e6 9.g3 (more solid and less weakening than 9.g4!? ♘c6 10.♗g2 ♗h6 11.♘cd5 ♖c8 12.c3 ♗xd5 13.exd5 ♘e7 14.h4, with unclear play, although White has some initiative and later won in Czebe-Wang, Zalakaros 2008; or 9.♘ed5 ♘bd7 10.g3) was played by the Hungarian GM Czebe, one of the biggest fans of 6.♕e2.

– 9...h5!? 10.♗g2 h4 11.0-0 (here 11.♘ed5± followed by ♗g5 and castling queenside is a possible improvement) 11...♗h6 12.♖d1 hxg3 13.hxg3 ♘c6 14.♕d3 ♘d4, with good play for Black in Romero Holmes-Harikrishna, San Sebastian 2006.
– 9...♘c6 10.♗g2 ♗g7 11.0-0 0-0 12.f4 (or 12.♘cd5) 12...exf4 13.gxf4 ♘h5 14.f5 ♗d7 15.♘ed5 ♕h4 16.♕f2 ♕xf2+ 17.♖xf2 ♘f6 18.♗g5 ♘xd5 19.exd5 ♘d4 20.f6 ♗h8 21.♘e4±, Czebe-Meszaros, Hungary 2009.

8.♗g5 d4

This is a logical improvement on 8...♗xf5?! 9.exf5 ♘bd7 10.0-0-0, and Black's centre is in trouble: 10...♗e7 (10...d4 11.♖xd4) 11.♗xf6! ♘xf6 12.♕xe5 0-0 13.♘xd5 ♘xd5 14.♖xd5 ♗g5+ 15.♔b1 ♕b6 16.♕d4!±, Balinov-Dudas, Austria 2001/02.

Now I propose
9.0-0-0!
playing for f4 is the main idea now.
Less clear but also interesting is 9.♗xf6 gxf6
10.0-0-0 ♗d7! (10...♗e6) 11.♕h5 (11.♘b1
is less attractive, because of 11...♗e6)
11...dxc3 12.♗c4 ♕b6 13.♕xf7+ ♔d8
14.b3 – White intends to double on the
d-file.
9...♕a5
– 9...♘c6 is maybe better, but White has
good attacking chances after 10.f4.
– 9...♗e6 10.♘d5! is an important detail,
based on some intricate tactics: 10...♗xf5
(10...♗xd5 11.exd5 ♕xd5 12.♘xd4)
11.♘xf6+ gxf6 12.exf5±, and taking on g5
will lose the rook on h8! So White keeps the
better position by playing ♗h4, g4 and ♗g2:
12...♘c6 13.♗h4 ♕d5 14.♔b1 (14.♕c4±)
with ♖g1 and g4 and ♗g2 coming up.
– 9...♗d7 leads to similar play as in the previous note, after 10.♘d5 ♗xf5 11.♘xf6+
gxf6 12.exf5.
10.♗xf6 gxf6
And here comes an important move:

11.♕h5!!
And with ♗c4 coming up White has a very
strong attack! For example:
11...dxc3
Or 11...b5 12.♘d5 ♕xa2 13.♘xf6+ ♔d8
14.♘d5 ♗e6 15.♕g5+ ♔c8 16.♕f6±.
**12.♗c4   ♕c7   13.♗xf7+   ♕xf7
14.♖d8+!±**

I tried to show you the key ideas behind
6.♕e2. I hope that you got enough inspiration to try it out for yourself!

CHAPTER 3
Jeroen Bosch
The North Sea Defence

Viking provocation or just testing the waters?

Magnus Carlsen had a tough time at the 2010 Olympiad in Khanty-Mansiysk, losing three of his games and some 15 elo-points in the process. Some pointed to the experimental mode in which he was playing some of his games as the reason for this failure. Especially his 6th round game against Michael Adams made him vulnerable to such criticism. Employing 1.e4 g6 2.d4 ♞f6 3.e5 ♞h5 will inevitably raise a few eyebrows, but online observers went much further, as did his former coach Garry Kasparov in an interview published on ChessVibes.com: 'I don't approve of this. In fact I think it's almost an insult to play such an opening against someone like Adams, a well-known top player. In

my opinion Magnus deserved to loose (sic) this game.'

Arguably, the opinion of one of the greatest players in the history of our game is informative on such matters. Kasparov raised the level of chess and the level of opening preparation to a very high degree. His professionalism goes hand in glove with a seriousness, and a feeling of responsibility at how chess ought to be played by top players. Clearly, opening frivolities such as his former pupil is allowing himself here are to be frowned upon. Yet, is it really ethically unsound to direct your knight to the edge of the board at such an early stage against a player who deserves your respect? I find it hard to believe that Carlsen intended to insult Adams. And, observing the players during the game, I did not have the feeling that Adams was motivated by a desire to punish his opponent for his lack of respect. Although, with Adams's low-key exterior this is admittedly hard to gauge.

From another point of view one might also argue that Carlsen had so much respect for his opponent that he saw no chance to outplay him in a 'respectable' opening, and therefore went for something out-of-the box to obtain some chances of playing for a win as Black. Perhaps we could even invoke the spirit of the famous Dutch historian Johan Huizinga and call Magnus Carlsen a true 'Homo Ludens', whose great results in chess are inspired by 'playfulness'. Whenever, I see Carlsen's games I am not only impressed by his incredible strength, but also by the fact that, at this awesome height, he still seems capable of improving. If you look at it from this light, then it becomes very sensible to push to the outer limits of what is possible in chess.

Personally, I must confess that this opening idea has been hidden in my file of SOS ideas for many years but so far I had been reluctant to write on it, feeling that it is just a tad too dubious. However, I gave up all resistance after this game: if a 2800+ player can play it and achieve a very decent position against such a strong player as Adams then surely us lesser mortals can have a go at it sometimes? Meanwhile, Carlsen was certainly not the first strong GM to play in this way. Miles played it a few times, while others gave it an occasional outing, among them: Morozevich, Aronian (in a blindfold game in Amber), Hodgson, Hillarp Persson and Campora.

Interestingly, the idea of 2...♘f6 and 3...♘h5 was devised at approximately the same time (around 1983-1985) by two creative thinkers independently of each other. In the Netherlands Gerard Welling was inspired by Nimzowitsch-Alekhine, New York 1927: 1.♘f3 ♘f6 2.b3 d6 3.g3 e5 4.c4 e4 5.♘h4!? to come up with what he called the Horseshoe Variation. While in Sweden independent thinker Rolf Martens called it the Norwegian Defence. When both of them came to learn of this, Martens re-dubbed the line the North Sea Defence (Gerard Welling, personal communication). Readers who are interested in the ideas of the Swedish opening researcher may consult New In Chess Magazine 1999/8, 'The unorthodox explorations of Rolf Martens' by Jesper Hall. Those who want to read more on the history of this variation are advised to visit the ChessCafe.com website. In the May 2008 issue of his online column 'Over the Horizons', Stefan Bücker presents a well-balanced and highly informative view of the Norwegian Defence, and for those who want to dig even further his bibliography will come in useful. Now without further ado, let's look at the moves!

☐ **Michael Adams**
■ **Magnus Carlsen**
Khanty-Mansiysk Olympiad 2010

1.e4 g6
Not nearly as provocative as Tony Miles' 1...a6 versus reigning World Champion Anatoly Karpov at the 1980 European Team Championship in Skara!
2.d4 ♘f6
This provokes the advance of the e-pawn, in the spirit of Alekhine's Defence.
3.e5
The only way to 'refute' the North Sea Defence.
3.♘c3 is not very principled, as it allows Black to transpose into the Pirc (3...d6). However, true Vikings will play 3...d5, when

after 4.e5 Black has a choice between 4...♘h5 and 4...♘e4.

● 4...♘h5, and now:

– 5.h3 ♘g7 6.♗f4 c5 7.dxc5 d4 8.♘e4 ♘e6 9.♗d2?! ♕d5! and Black was doing fine in Spaan-Geselschap, Dutch tt 1995/96.

– 5.♘ge2 ♗g4 (subtle opening play, or a sign of disrespect for his weaker opponent? Possibly just Homo Ludens at his best!) 6.h3 ♗e6 7.g3 c6 8.♗g2 ♕d7 9.♗e3 ♘a6 10.♕d2 ♘c7 11.♗h6 f6 12.g4 ♘g7 13.♗f4 h5, and Miles later obtained an excellent position, but uncharacteristically lost track and the game, Jose Queralto-Miles, Andorra 1996.

– After 5.g4 ♘g7 6.♗g2 c6 7.♗h6 ♘e6 8.♗e3 (8.♗xf8 ♔xf8 9.♕d2 ♘g7 10.h3 h5 was Eriksson-G.Hjorth, Sweden 1992) 8...h5 9.gxh5 ♖xh5

Black has positional compensation for his

lack of development. I give you the remaining moves of this high-level game because they illustrate the general strategy that both sides may follow: 10.♕d2 ♘a6 11.♘ge2 ♘ac7 12.h4 ♘g7 13.♘g3 ♖h8 14.♗f3 ♗e6 15.h5 ♕d7 16.0-0-0 gxh5 17.♘xh5 ♘xh5 18.♗xh5 0-0-0 19.♘e2 ♗g7 20.♘f4 ♗h6 21.♘d3 ♗xe3 22.♕xe3 ♗g4 23.♘c5 ♕f5 24.♗xg4 ♕xg4 25.♖hg1 ♕f5 26.♖g5 ♕h7 27.♖dg1 b6 28.♘d3 draw, Hernandez-Campora, Ayamonte 2004. Both players are rated above 2500.

– 5.♗e2 ♘g7 (5...♘c6!? only works when White falls for 6.♗xh5 – 6.♘f3 a6 is how Rolf Martens wanted to play this position, but it looks too exotic. Bücker recommends 7.0-0 ♘g7 8.♘a4! – threatening c4 – , with an edge for White – 6...gxh5 7.♗e3 ♗f5 and Black's control of the light squares compensate for his damaged pawn structure, while 8.♕xh5 ♗xc2 9.e6 is exciting but better for Black after 9...♗g6 10.♕xd5 ♕xd5 11.♘xd5 0-0-0 12.♘f4 ♘xd4 13.♗xd4 ♖xd4, Katz-Kuraszkiewicz, Germany 1993)

6.♗h6 (logical play by White – 6.♘f3 should be met by 6...♗g4, although White must be at least somewhat better; 6.f4 is met by 6...h5 to control the light squares on the kingside) 6...c5?! (Welling later tried to improve his own play with 6...♘f5 7.♗xf8 ♔xf8 8.♘f3 c6 9.♕d2 h5 10.0-0, Tolhuizen-Welling,

Eindhoven 1988. Now 10...a5 has been suggested by Gunnar Hjorth in an extensive theoretical article in the *Correspondence Chess Informator* (Vol 7, 1995). The engines agree that this is best, but I would still prefer White!) 7.dxc5 d4 8.♘b5 ♘c6 9.♘f3 ♘e6 10.♗xf8 ♔xf8 11.♕d2 (11.c3! dxc3 12.♕xd8+ ♘exd8 13.♘xc3, as in Daamen-G.Welling, Eindhoven 1988, is better for White) 11...a6 12.♘a3 ♘xc5 13.0-0-0 ♗e6 14.♔b1 (as Welling has pointed out, it is important that after 14.♘xd4 ♘xd4 15.♕xd4 ♕xd4 16.♖xd4 ♗xa2 the bishop cannot be trapped with 17.b3?, because of 17...♗xb3) 14...♔g7 15.♘xd4 ♘xd4 16.♕xd4 ♕c7 17.♕e3 b5

Black has obvious compensation for the pawn. After 18.♖d4 ♖ab8 19.♖hd1 ♖hc8 20.g4 ♘a4 21.f4 ♕a5 22.f5, the stem game Bosboom-Welling, Dutch tt 1987, continued with 22...b4. Instead, 22...♘c3+! would have won on the spot: 23.bxc3 ♕xa3 24.fxe6 b4!, Welling.

● Personally, I would be less keen on these blocked positions, which is why I would prefer 4...♘e4 5.♗d3 (5.♘ce2 f6 6.f3 ♘g5; 5.♘xe4 dxe4 6.f3 – 6.♗c4 ♗g7 7.♗e3 c5 8.c3 cxd4 9.cxd4 ♘c6 10.♕d2 0-0 11.♘e2 ♘a5∓ Amberger-Andersen, Esbjerg 2008 – 6...c5 7.d5 ♗g7 is fine for Black, Gunlycke-Crouch, Oxford 2003) 5...♘xc3

6.bxc3 c5 7.f4 ♘c6 8.♗e3 ♕a5 9.♕d2 c4 10.♗e2 ♗f5,

and although the e-pawn hasn't moved, I bet that many players of the French wouldn't mind being Black here, Rabiega-Paulsen, Berlin 2000.

When Aronian confronted Grischuk with the North Sea Defence the Russian copped out with 3.f3, and after 3...c6!? (3...d5 4.e5 ♘h5; 3...d6) 4.c4 d5 5.e5 ♘fd7 6.♘c3 dxc4 7.♗xc4 ♘b6 8.♗b3 ♘a6 9.♘ge2 ♘c7 10.0-0 ♗e6 11.♗xe6 ♘xe6 12.f4 ♕d7 13.f5 ♘g7 14.e6 fxe6 15.fxg6 0-0-0 it was clear that both players were in a very 'playful' mood that day, Grischuk-Aronian, blindfold Monte Carlo 2006.
After 3.♗d3 Black again has the option to go for a Pirc, but principled is 3...d5 4.e5 ♘h5.
3...♘h5

4.♗e2

Most players will opt for this developing move that also attacks the trusty steed.

– In fact 4.♘f3 may well be stronger (as after 4.♗e2 d6 it turns out that taking the knight gives Black a lot of counterplay). Black has to attack the centre with 4...d6, when I would like to show you the game Hillarp Persson-Andersen, Copenhagen 2010. Remember that Hillarp Persson has also defended the black cause(!): 5.♗c4 (5.♘c3 dxe5 6.♘xe5 – the pawn sacrifice 6.♗e3!? has been suggested by Michiel Wind – see Bücker's ChessCafe.com article for more details – 6...♗g7 looks quite decent for Black) 5...dxe5 (very risky, 5...♘c6 6.♕e2 has been analysed by Hjorth – 6...♗g4 – and Martens – 6...a6. Personally, I would prefer 6...d5, or Bücker's 6...♗g7) 6.♘xe5 e6 7.♕f3 (sacrificing a pawn) 7...f6! 8.♘d3 ♕xd4 9.♗b3 e5 10.♘c3 ♕g4 (Black should keep this resource in reserve with 10...♘c6!? 11.♘b5 ♕d7) White was now better after 11.♕d5! ♕d7 12.g4! ♘g7 13.♘e4 ♕e7 14.g5 ♘d7?

15.♕xd7+ (how to annotate this move? Only a true artist plays in this way! The mundane 15.gxf6 ♘xf6 16.♗a4+! c6 17.♗xc6+! bxc6 18.♕xc6+ ♔f7 19.♕xa8 wins for White. Possibly Hillarp Persson overlooked that at the end of this line 19...♗b7 fails to

20.♘d6+ ?) 15...♔xd7 16.gxf6 ♕e8 17.fxg7? (17.♗g5 followed by a timely f7 favours White) 17...♗xg7 18.♗g5 ♕f8 19.0-0 ♔c6 20.♘c3 ♗g4 21.♗a4+ b5! 22.♗xb5+ ♔b7, and Black was completely winning but the game ended in a draw in 106 moves!

– 4.g4?! ♘g7 5.♗h6?! d6 6.♕e2? ♘c6 was clearly better for Black in Hallebeek-Welling, Eindhoven 1988.

– 4.f4 d5! and this is certainly no worse than 1.e4 g6 2.d4 d6 3.♘c3 c6 4.f4 d5 5.e5 h5, which goes back to Gurgenidze's 1.e4 c6 2.d4 d5 3.♘c3 g6 4.e5 ♗g7 5.f4 h5.

– After 4.♗c4 d5 5.♗d3 ♘g7 is logical once you have absorbed Black's way of thinking in this line.

4...d6

Rolf Martens deserves considerable praise for inventing this whole concept. Black immediately puts pressure on White's centre, just like in the Alekhine. Of course, taking on h5 is now crucial for his whole idea. Gerard Welling's philosophical concept behind 2...♘f6 was to fianchetto the knight here – going for a kind of Gurgenidze System.

It must be said that his followers make for an impressive line-up as well: 4...♘g7 5.♘f3 d5 6.h3 (6.c4 c6 7.♘c3 dxc4 8.♗xc4 ♘e6 9.♗e3 ♗g7 10.♕d2 with a very pleasant edge for White in Burmakin-Morozevich, Sochi 2005

– the game ended in a draw) 6...h5 (6...♘e6 7.0-0 ♗g7 8.♗e3 0-0 9.c4 c6 10.♘c3 dxc4 11.♗xc4 was Ferguson-Hodgson, Kilkenny 1999. To my mind, White's play with an early c4 – just as in Burmakin-Morozevich – more or less refutes the set-up with 4...♗g7) 7.0-0 c6 8.b3 a5 9.c4 ♘a6 10.♘c3 ♘c7 11.cxd5!? ♘xd5 12.♘xd5 cxd5 13.♘g5 ♗d7 14.♗d3 ♘e6 15.♕f3! and White was superior in Lautier-Miles, Biel 1996.

5.♘f3
Adams decides that he will not be provoked, undoubtedly after assessing that Black will have considerable compensation after 5.♗xh5 gxh5 6.♕xh5. Indeed, after 6...dxe5 7.♕xe5 (7.dxe5 ♕d5 and Black soon retrieves his pawn: 8.♘f3 – 8.♘e2 ♕xg2 9.♖g1 ♕h3; 8.f3 ♘c6 – 8...♕e4+ 9.♗e3 ♕xc2) 7...♖g8

you will find several games in your database from this position. White has a pawn, Black has some pressure and an important light-squared bishop. Hjorth's, very plausible, main line continues 8.♕e2 ♘d7 9.♕d5 (9.♕e4 ♘f6 10.♕f3 and now 10...c6 – 10...♕d5!? – transposes) 9...c6 10.♕f3 ♘f6 11.h3 (perhaps White may also hope for something after returning the pawn with 11.0-0!? ♗g4 12.♕d3 ♗xe2 13.♕xe2 ♕xd4 14.♘c3) 11...♕a5+ (11...♗e6!?; 11...♕d5!?) and now Bücker is right in claiming an edge for White after

12.♘bc3 ♕f5 13.♘f4! ♕xc2 14.0-0.
Not so popular in practice is 5.f4, an ambitious approach recommended by Stefan Bücker. This certainly looks dangerous for Black.

Hjorth points out that after 5.exd6 cxd6 White can still not profitably take on h5 with 6.♗xh5 because of 6...♕a5+.

5...♘c6 6.exd6
6.0-0 ♗g7 (6...dxe5 7.d5!) 7.exd6 ♕xd6 (7...exd6 would transpose back into the main game after 8.d5 ♘e7 9.c4 0-0 10.♘c3) 8.♘a3 0-0 (8...♕xd4 9.♘xd4 ♕xd4 10.♘b5) 9.c3 ♘f6 10.♘c4 ♕d8 11.♘fe5 ♘xe5 12.♘xe5 ♗e6 13.♗f3 c6 with near-equality in Taylor-Hillarp Persson, Cobo Bay 2005. Play is similar to the Kengis Variation in the Alekhine (4.♘f3 dxe5 5.♘xe5 g6). Releasing the tension, with something like

6.h3 dxe5 7.dxe5 ♕xd1+ 8.♗xd1, Hagesaether-Andersen, Aarhus 2009, is obviously fine for Black.

6...exd6 Also playable is 6...♕xd6. **7.d5** Gaining space, White could also continue his development with 7.0-0 ♗g7 8.c4 0-0 9.♘c3. **7...♘e7 8.c4 ♗g7 9.♘c3 0-0 10.0-0**

Adams certainly hasn't tried to refute Carlsen's audacious opening choice. Instead, he has settled for a healthy position with perhaps a slight plus for White. On the upside for our Viking: he has a playable position in which there is sufficient play left. I suspect that both players were satisfied here!

10...♗g4

White has a space advantage, so trading pieces is a good idea for Black. What is more, the light-squared bishop has no future anyway (where else to put it but on g4?), and exchanging it for the knight increases Black's central control over the dark squares d4 and e5.

11.♖e1 ♖e8 12.h3 ♗xf3 13.♗xf3 ♘f6

Black has lost some time with ♘g8-f6-h5-f6, but if you just look at the position you will see that this has not resulted in a disadvantage in development. Indeed, after White's next both sides have more or less fully developed and are ready for the middlegame. Black is certainly OK here despite his opening experiment (or is it because of it?).

14.♗f4 ♘d7 15.♖c1 Or 15.♕d2 ♘e5 16.♗e2 ♘f5, with a decent game.

15...♘e5 16.b3 a6

Here 16...♘xf3+ 17.♕xf3 ♘f5 18.♘e4 h6 (covering square g5; not 18...♕d7 19.♗g5±) would limit White's advantage to a minor edge.

17.g3 17.♗e4 was a decent alternative.

17...♘f5?!

Again avoiding the simplifying 17...♘xf3+ 18.♕xf3 ♘f5 when Black has equal chances. It seems that Carlsen's ambition is to blame for the final result, rather than his choice of opening.

Indeed, as Magnus Carlsen wrote on his weblog: 'Despite the unusual opening choice I was happy with my position entering the middle game. Becoming a bit too optimistic I played for a win but underestimated his attack and lost deservedly.'

18.♗g2 Now Adams preserves the bishop, but Carlsen hunts for the other one with the slightly weakening

18...g5?! This very concrete move must have been Carlsen's idea. 18...h6.

19.♗xe5!

A wise and very practical choice. In the resulting position with bishops of opposite colours the looseness of the pawn on g5 is felt most clearly. Still, play is nearly equal. Giving the bishop for the other knight equalizes on the spot: 19.♗e3 ♘xe3 20.♖xe3 f5. Trying to preserve the bishop pair leads to complications: 19.♗d2 ♘d3 20.♖xe8+ ♕xe8 21.♖b1 (not 21.♗xg5 ♘xc1 22.♕xc1 and there is no compensation after 22...♕e5) 21...♗d4, and now:

● White can play for a slight edge with 22.♔h2!? when the lines fork:

– 22...♘xf2 23.♕f3 ♕e5 24.♖e1 g4 25.♖xe5 (25.hxg4 ♘h6! 26.♖xe5 ♘hxg4+ 27.♔g1 ♘h3+ 28.♔h1 ♘hf2+ 29.♔g1 ♘h3+ is either a perpetual, or more or less equal after 30.♔f1!? ♘h2+ 31.♔e2 ♘xf3 32.♖e4 ♘hg1+ 33.♔d3 ♗e5) 25...gxf3 26.♖xf5 fxg2 27.♔xg2 ♘d3±;

– Not 22...♗xf2? 23.♘e4 ♗xg3+ 24.♘xg3 ♘xg3 25.♕f3 and wins.

– 22...♕e5 23.♕g4 ♗xc3 24.♗xc3 ♕xc3 25.♕xf5 ♕d2 26.♖f1 ♘e5 27.♗e4± or 27.c5±.

● 22.♘e4 ♘xg3!

– 23.♗e3! ♘xe4 24.♗xd3 (24.♗xd4 ♘f4∓) 24...♗xe3 25.♕xe3 f5! 26.♗xe4 ♕xe4 27.♕xg5+ ends in a perpetual.

– 23.♘xg3 ♗xf2+ 24.♔h1 (24.♔h2 ♗xg3+ 25.♔xg3 ♕e5+ 26.♔f3 ♖e8∓) 24...♗xg3 25.♕f3 ♘f2+ 26.♔g1 ♗h4 is very unclear.

– 23.♘f6+ ♗xf6 24.fxg3 ♕e5∓.

19...♗xe5 20.♘e4

Threatening 21.♕g4 and therefore forcing

20...♘g7 White is now more comfortable because of the pawn on g5.

21.♕d2 h6 22.f4 gxf4 23.gxf4 ♗f6 24.♔h2

24.♘xf6+ ♕xf6 25.♗f3 ♘f5 is certainly not better for White.

24.♗f3 ♗h4 25.♖e2 f5 and Black is nearly equal.

24...♘h5?!

Carlsen misses the stronger 24...♗h4! 25.♖g1 f5 when 26.♘g3 (26.♘f2 ♕e7 27.♖ce1 ♕f7; 26.♘c3 ♕e7 followed by 27...♕e3 is even slightly unpleasant for White) 26...♗xg3+ 27.♔xg3 ♘h5+ 28.♔h2 ♔f7 (28...♔h7) 29.♗f3 ♕h4 30.♗xh5+ ♕xh5 should end in draw.

25.♖g1 ♔h7?! 25...♔h8. **26.♖cf1 ♖g8 27.♕e2 ♘g7**

28.♕d3

Even stronger was 28.♘xf6+! ♕xf6 29.♗e4+ ♔h8 30.♗b1! (to set up a well-known battery along the b1-h7 diagonal) 30...♕d4 31.♕g4 (threatening 32.♕h4) 31...♕f6 32.♕d1. Now ♕d3 or ♕c2 is back on the cards, after 32...♘e8 33.♕c2 White should win following 33...♖g7 34.♖g4!.

28...♔h8 29.♗f3

This is a terrible position for Black.

29...b5

29...♘f5 30.♘g5 hxg5 31.♕xf5 ♗d4 32.♖xg5 ♕f6 33.♕g4 and White wins.

29...♗h4 30.♕d4 ♕e7 (30...♔h7 31.♘g5+ hxg5 32.fxg5 ♗xg5 33.♗e4+ f5 34.♗xf5+

♘xf5 35.♖xf5 ♖g6 36.♕g4+−) 31.♖g4! f5 32.♖g6! ♔h7 33.♖fg1 and the knight cannot be taken, which is why White's strategical dominance cannot be contested. If 33...fxe4? then 34.♗xe4+−.

30.♗d1!

Again we see the battery along the diagonal b1-h7 deciding the issue.

30...bxc4 31.bxc4 ♗h4 32.♗c2 f5 33.♖g6! ♔h7 34.♖fg1 ♕e7

34...fxe4?? 35.♕xe4 and mates.

35.♘g3

35.c5! is how the engines would have finished Black off. Adams's move is more than sufficient though: 35...fxe4 36.♕xe4 ♕xe4 37.♗xe4 and Black has to return the piece with 37...♘f5 38.♗xf5 ♖xg6 39.♖xg6, winning at least another pawn.

35...♗xg3+ 35...♖af8 36.♕d4!.

36.♕xg3 ♕f7 36...♘h5 loses after 37.♕f3 ♖xg6 38.♗xf5.

37.♗d1! ♖ae8 38.♖xh6+

And Carlsen resigned because of 38...♔xh6 39.♕g5+ ♔h7 40.♕h4+ ♘h5 41.♗xh5.

CHAPTER 4

Simon Williams

The Williams Anti-Grünfeld Variation

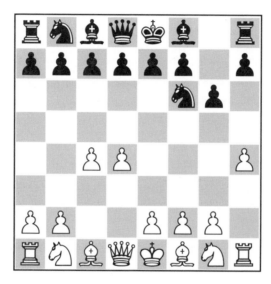

1.d4 ♘f6 2.c4 g6 3.h4!?

Struggling to keep up with the latest opening novelties can be a tough struggle, even for the most dedicated of chess players. It is especially tricky to get a good position from the opening if you do not have enough time. Enough time to search the internet for the latest improvements that top GMs seem to come up with on a regular basis.

One of the first strong players that I knew, Mike Basman, was a maverick. A maverick who had a rather different outlook on chess. His philosophy was that he would just play some strange opening moves. He did this in order to avoid any theory. This was certainly an intriguing, attractive and fresh outlook on the game. This way of approaching the game

often gave him interesting and exciting games, the only problem was that his openings were not based on sound principles. For a start 1.g4 (his little baby!) did create a big hole on f4 and, as the famous saying goes, pawns cannot move backwards!

From my perspective I was getting annoyed playing against the Grünfeld opening. The theory was too much for my little brain to take in. I was always looking at ways to take my opponent out of familiar ground from as early a stage as possible. I started experimenting with 1.d4 ♘f6 2.c4 g6 3.♘c3 d5 4.h4!? (see SOS-3, Chapter 3, p.28). This brought me some good results but then a couple of my opponents started to play

4...c5! In my opinion this move destroys any hopes that White has of getting an opening advantage (see The SOS Files of volume 12). So back to the drawing board...

I then had a crazy thought: what would happen if I played h4!? one move earlier? Could my opponent still play 3...d5? Well, the answer to this is, no, I do not believe he can! 3...d5? looks like an error! An error that should give White a good position! If you are not convinced, look at the first two games of this chapter.

Basically from that moment onwards I would always play 3.h4!? if I expected my opponent to reply with the Grünfeld. I believe that this is a very dangerous weapon against the Grünfeld. It loses some of its strength against the King's Indian Defence and especially the Benko set-up, but if used at the right moment it can bring devastating results!

The other interesting point was that when I searched 3.h4!? on ChessBase I stumbled across the first player to ever venture this move, and guess who it was? Well, Mike Basman of course!

Anyway, I hope that the games below give you an interesting insight into the ideas behind the strange push 3.h4!?. A word of warning though, I would only play this move if you know your opponent prefers the Grünfeld opening!

□ **Simon Williams**
■ **Alexandre Platel**
Dieppe 2009

1.d4 ♘f6 2.c4 g6 3.h4

I am going to be bold and call this the 'Williams Anti-Grünfeld Variation'. This forces Black to think from an early stage, which is always an attractive idea. Let's just take a quick look at what can happen if White tries to play h4 on move 4.

3.♘c3 d5 4.h4!? c5! Black immediately hits out against White's centre. This is the best way to take advantage of 4.h4. This is out of the scope of this article, but it does give Black a very satisfactory position. (4...♗g7? is an error due to 5.h5!, when play could very easily transpose to the next game in this chapter after 5...♘xh5 6.cxd5 c6 7.e4! cxd5 8.e5 and White has a nice position. This is one of the attractions of this variation!)

3...d5?!

In my opinion this move is already a mistake! Black's other options are 3...♗g7 and 3...c5. These moves will be looked at in more detail in the last game of this chapter. I will give you a little taster now...

– 3...♗g7 4.♘c3 0-0 (4...d5?! is an error, as White can now play 5.h5!, transposing to the next game: 5...♘xh5 6.cxd5 c6 7.e4! cxd5 8.e5 ♗f8 9.g4 ♘g7 10.♗g2) 5.e4 d6 6.h5 ♘xh5 7.♗e2 ♘f6 8.♗g5.

– 3...c5!? tries to enter an improved version of the Benko Gambit: 4.d5 b5 5.cxb5 a6.

4.cxd5

4...♕xd5

It looks a bit odd to capture this way, but the alternative 4...♘xd5 falls straight into White's hands. There are two good moves here:

– 5.e4 – unlike the main line Grünfeld Black no longer has the option of capturing

White's knight on c3, so he has to waste a tempo: 5...♘b6 (5...♘f6 6.e5 ♘d5 7.h5 – I prefer White's position here; the h-pawn march has been a success!) 6.h5 and White has good attacking chances.

– 5.h5 immediately also looks better for White, for example 5...♗g7?! 6.h6 ♗f8 7.e4 and Black will find it hard to develop his kingside, whilst White has taken over control of the centre.

5.♘c3

Why not develop and attack?

5...♕a5

In similar spirit to the Scandinavian. Black could have also tried 5...♕d8, but then White can continue in standard fashion with 6.e4, when again I believe that White's chances are to be preferred. Just compare this to the normal Grünfeld and we can see that White is doing well.

6.♗d2

A sensible move that creates some future threats against the black queen. We have basically reached a position where there is no theory, so both sides can just enjoy playing chess!

6...♕b6

Black tries to punish me for my strange opening play, but this is a very risky plan. Black's other options were:

– 6...♗g7, when White should just continue

with 7.e4, with an advantage due to his strong centre.

– 6...c6 gives the black queen an escape route back to d8. This would have been the most sensible choice: 7.e4 with ♗c4 and ♘ge2 to follow (♘f3 would allow ...♗g4, which is an annoying pin and one which White should avoid).

7.h5!?

Using the h-pawn! If you are willing to play 3.h4!? then you must also be willing to sacrifice the pawn at a moment's notice! My general plan was to open up the h-file and to gain some time.

7...gxh5

Black elects to keep his knight on f6, but the problem with this is that he opens up his kingside. For a start the black king will now never feel entirely safe on g8.

After 7...♘xh5 I was planning to play 8.e4!? ♕xd4 9.♘f3, with quick development: 9...♕d8 10.♗c4 – I am ready to play ♕b3 and 0-0-0, when my initiative must be worth the invested material.

8.e4

Offering a pawn...

8...♕xd4

Black accepts the offer. This is greedy, but the most critical approach.

8...♗g7 allows me to continue with 9.e5, when Black's knight is forced away to a passive square. White is better.

9.♘f3

Developing with tempo.

9...♛b6

Black could have played 9...♛d8, when I was planning 10.♗c4 with ideas of ♛b3 and e5. The position certainly looks dangerous for Black, he is lagging behind in development.

10.♗e3!

Forcing Black to take another pawn! I had a crafty idea in mind...

10...♛xb2

This is the only move that makes any sense.

11.♗d4!

After this move Black's position falls apart, the queen has been rushing around the board like pacman on drugs, but Black has forgotten to castle or to develop his pieces!

11...c5

The position is not easy for Black – it is too late to try and develop some pieces. For example, 11...♗g7? allows 12.♘d5 and White is going to win the rook on a8.

12.♖b1

Another White piece enters the game.

12...♛a3 13.♘b5! ♛a5+ 14.♗c3 ♛d8

So the queen arrives back at its starting square. In the meantime I have managed to activate most of my pieces. The end comes very quickly.

15.e5!

When you have the initiative you must use it, otherwise it will drift away.

15...♘g4

Black is basically lost, for example: 15...♘e4 16.♛a4, threatening the knight, ♘c7 mate and ♘d6 mate! Or 15...♛xd1+ 16.♖xd1 ♘e4 17.♘c7 mate. Or 15...♘d5 16.♛xd5 ♛xd5 17.♘c7+.

16.e6 f6

The following finish was extremely pleasing to play...

17.♛a4! Threatening a nasty discovered attack on the king!

17...♘c6

There is no defence, for example 17...♗g7 18.♖d1 (18.♘c7+ is also strong!) 18...♛b6 19.♘c7+ ♚f8 20.♖d8 mate.

18.♖d1 ♛b6

Can anyone spot the finish?

19.♗a5! ♘xa5 19...♕xa5+ 20.♕xa5 ♘xa5 21.♘c7 mate. **20.♘c7** Mate.

We can see from this game that Black has to treat 3.h4!? with a certain amount of respect, otherwise things can go horribly wrong!

We will now look at another game where Black insists on playing an early ...d5. This time one move later than the last game, again it seems that White gets a good position after this push.

☐ **Simon Williams**
■ **Patrik Hugentobler**
Samnaun 2008

1.d4 ♘f6 2.c4 g6 3.h4!?

This game transposes to a line that can be reached after 3.♘c3 d5 4.h4 ♗g7?! (4...c5!) 5.h5 ♘xh5 6.cxd5 (see SOS-3, Chapter 3, p.28).

3...♗g7 A sensible reply, the problem is the way that Black follows the move up.

4.♘c3 d5?!

Again I believe that this move is an error, but if Black insists on playing the Grünfeld it is very likely that he will play in this way. A better approach is 4...0-0, which will be looked at in the next game: 5.e4 d6 6.h5!?.

5.h5!

Correct! White uses the h-pawn to divert Black's knight away from f6. This is a standard plan in this opening. This is superior compared to 5.cxd5 ♘xd5 6.h5, because Black can strike out with 6...c5!.

5...♘xh5

The most common reply.

● Black has also played 5...c6 6.h6 ♗f8 7.♗g5. This also looks better for White. The game Dambrauskas-Ivoskaite, Panevezys 2007, continued 7...♘e4 8.♘xe4 dxe4 9.♕d2 ♗e6 10.e3 f6 11.♗f4, and White is clearly better, as Black has problems developing his kingside pieces and on top of this he has a weak pawn on e4.

● But 5...gxh5?! is an ugly move and White got a good position in Kanep-Lelumees, Tallinn 2005, after 6.cxd5 ♘xd5 7.♖xh5 (7.e4!?) 7...♘f6 8.♖g5!? (a strange plan!) 8...♔f8 9.e4 h6 10.♖g3 and now Black's kingside was already under strong pressure.

● 5...0-0 looks like suicide to me, but it has been tried out by the odd, brave/foolish player. Kadas-Kis, Hajduboszormeny 1995, continued 6.hxg6 hxg6 7.cxd5 (I would have wipped out 7.♗g5!? – the plan is to play ♕d2, ♗h6, ♗xg7 etc. checkmate...) 7...♘xd5 8.e4 ♘xc3 9.bxc3 c5:

– Now I am not convinced about 10.e5?!, which seems to give Black too much counterplay: 10...♘c6 11.♘e2 cxd4 12.cxd4 ♗f5 13.♗b2 ♘b4.

Two interesting options are:

– 10.♗h6, which probably leads to a slightly better endgame after 10...♗xh6 11.♖xh6 cxd4 12.cxd4 ♕a5+ 13.♕d2,

– and 10.d5!?, which looks like the most fun, for example 10...♗xc3+ 11.♗d2 ♗xa1!? (very risky!) 12.♕xa1 f6 13.♗c4 and White has a strong attack.

6.cxd5 c6

Black is aiming to strike out against White's centre, but this allows a cute idea. Black has also tried 6...c5 7.dxc5 ♕a5, in

Sulyok-A.Nemeth (Hungary tt 1994), which continued 8.e4 ♕xc5, and here White should have just played 9.♘f3, with a promising position: 9...♗xc3+ 10.bxc3 ♕xc3+ 11.♗d2.

7.e4!

Sacrificing a pawn for a strong initiative.

7...cxd5

Or 7...♘f6!? 8.dxc6 and

– after 8...bxc6 Seres-Dembo, Budapest 2001, continued 9.♗e2 ♗a6 10.♘f3 ♕a5 11.0-0 (11.♗d2!?), with a better position due to Black's pawn formation.

– after 8...♘xc6 9.d5 ♘e5 10.f4 ♘eg4 11.e5 ♕b6 12.♕e2 ♘h5 13.♕b5+ White has a big advantage.

– 8...0-0!? was played in Seres-Balinov (Budapest 1999): 9.cxb7 ♗xb7 10.f3 ♘c6 11.♗e3 ♕c7 and now White should have either played 12.♕d2 ♖fd8 13.♘ge2 or 12.♖c1!?, with an advantage in both cases.

8.e5

This is White's idea. Black's knight on h5 is in danger of being trapped, and his kingside in general is cramped.

8...♗f8

This is pretty much forced in order to stop White from playing g4.

8...f5 is bad due to the simple 9.♗e2, with a big advantage.

9.g4 ♘g7 10.♗g2

Black now has a choice of two ways to defend d5. I believe that my opponent picked the correct one.

10...♗e6!

At least by avoiding ...e6 Black gives his bishop potential for the future.

10...e6 was played in Shliperman-Ady, New York 1999. White got a very good position after 11.♗h6!, a common idea which stops Black from moving his bishop, so Black's whole kingside is trapped in: 11...♘c6 12.♘ge2 ♗d7 13.♕d2 f6 14.exf6 ♕xf6 15.♖h3 ♗b4 16.♖f3 ♕e7 17.♗g5 ♕d6 18.a3.

11.♕b3

Another, possibly, stronger idea was 11.♘h3!?, which I would recommend you to play if you ever reach this position. For example 11...♘c6 12.♘f4 h5 13.♘xe6 ♘xe6 14.♗e3, after which White can continue with f4-f5.

11...♕d7

This is a mistake. A stronger plan would have been 11...♘c6!, with a roughly equal position, for example 12.♘ge2 (12.♗e3!? is another possibility) 12...♕d7 13.f3, and Black's position is still cramped but he has no major weaknesses. I expect the position is roughly equal.

12.♗xd5

Simple and good.

12...♗xd5 13.♕xd5

13...♘c6?

This is the biggest mistake that Black plays – after this his position is pretty hopeless. Black should have played 13...♕xd5, which is still good for White but not terminal, for example 14.♘xd5 ♘e6 15.♘e2 ♘c6 16.♗e3 0-0-0 17.♘df4 ♘cxd4 18.♘xe6 ♘xe6 19.♗xa7.

14.♕xd7+ ♔xd7 15.♘f3 e6

Black's kingside is not taking part in the game and he will suffer for this.

16.♗h6!

This standard plan again. White stops Black from developing his dark-squared bishop and therefore his rook on h8.

16...♘b4 17.♔e2

17...♘e8

A desperate attempt at co-ordinating the kingside pieces, but the h-pawn is too high a price to pay.

18.♗xf8 ♖xf8 19.♖xh7 White is win-

ning. The rest is easy. **19...♖c8 20.♘g5 ♔e7 21.a3 ♘c6 22.♖d1 ♖d8 23.♔e3 ♘c7 24.f4 ♘d5+ 25.♘xd5+ ♖xd5 26.♘e4 ♖b5 27.b4 ♖d5 28.♘f6 ♖dd8 29.d5 exd5 30.♘xd5+ ♔e6 31.♔e4** Black resigned. The position is hopeless, for example 31...♔d7 (31...a6 32.f5+ gxf5+ 33.gxf5+ ♔d7 34.e6+) 32.f5 gxf5+ 33.gxf5 ♔c8 34.b5 ♘a5 35.e6.

We will now look at what happens if Black avoids playing the slightly dubious ...d5 advance. This is the best way to play and I am going to suggest some interesting ideas that will keep the position lively! In this game we will concentrate on the King's Indian set up, which is one of Black's most common ways of meeting 1.d4.

☐ **Simon Williams**
■ **Michal Meszaros**
Reykjavik 2009

1.d4 ♘f6 2.c4 g6 3.h4!? ♗g7 4.♘c3 d6 5.e4

5...0-0

5...c5 makes a lot of sense and has been given an outing at the highest level. Black is acting against a wing assault with a central attack. This is quite possibly Black's best reply to 3.h4!?.

6.d5 e6! (this is a good way to play against an early h4. Black is basically trying to punish White for his 'arrogant pawn lunge'! By opening up the centre Black is starting play against White's king. I expect that the position should be roughly equal here. 6...b5 is also very playable, as after 7.cxb5 a6 Black reaches a favourable Benko Gambit, as White's pawn on h4 seems a bit out of place in this structure) 7.dxe6 (another option which is in the spirit of the opening was 7.h5!? – you should not feel afraid about sacrificing this pawn, that is the idea of the variation! In this case White gains some tempo, an open h-file and a favourable exchange of pieces by playing this push. Play could continue 7...♘xh5 8.♗e2 ♘f6 9.♗h6 ♗xh6 10.♖xh6 – White has managed to swap off Black's best minor piece, which will mean that Black will always have a slightly weakened kingside if he castles. The position is interesting and requires practical examples) 7...♗xe6 8.♗e2 ♘c6 9.♘f3 (9.h5!? was more consistent: 9...♘xh5 10.♗xh5 gxh5 11.♘d5, but White cannot claim an advantage here, as Black has very good control of the dark squares) 9...0-0 (now White's pawn on h4 looks rather stupid!) 10.♗f4 ♖e8!? 11.♕xd6 ♕a5 and Black had very good play for the sacrificed pawn and he went on to win quite convincingly in Kazhgaleyev-Radjabov, Khanty-Mansiysk 2005.

6.♗e2

I had good memories of this move, but a very interesting alternative was 6.h5!? with the brutal idea of opening up the h-file. This can lead to some interesting possibilities! For example 6...♘xh5 7.♗e2 ♘f6 8.♗g5. I have only found one game in this variation, Shirazi-Delorme, Pierrefitte rapid 2003, which continued 8...c5, which must be best (8...e5? is a typical mistake with the bishop on g5: 9.dxe5 dxe5 10.♕xd8 ♖xd8 11.♘d5 and White is winning material; 8...♘bd7 looks too slow: 9.♕d2 with ♗h6 and checkmate to follow). Black hits out in order to create counterplay. Yet if we compare this to 5...c5 we can see that in this position Black has really wasted a tempo castling. That is why I would consider 5...c5 to be one of Black's strongest replies.

After 8...c5 9.d5 Black now has a number of ways to continue. Again all these possibilities require practical examples. Anyway, let's have a look:

– 9...e6! is the most logical and I expect best way for Black to play the position. The open e-file will become a useful asset to Black: 10.♕d2 exd5 11.♘xd5!? ♖e8 12.f3 with a roughly equal game.

– 9...b5 looks a bit slow to me. White's attack on the kingside is going to land first, for example 10.cxb5 (10.f3!?) 10...a6 11.♕d2! (there is no point messing about on the queenside: 11.bxa6? ♗xa6 12.♕d2 ♘bd7 13.♗h6 ♗xh6 14.♕xh6 ♕b6 15.♖b1 ♘e5 looks better for Black) 11...axb5 12.♗h6! (White has a simple plan: ♗xg7, ♕h6, e5!, ♘e4) 12...b4 13.♗xg7 ♔xg7 (13...bxc3? 14.♕h6 ♖e8 15.♗xf6 exf6 16.♕xh7+ ♔f8 17.♕h6+ ♔e7 18.bxc3 White is clearly better) 14.♕h6+ ♔g8 15.e5! (White is close to winning!) 15...dxe5 16.♘e4 ♘bd7 17.♘g5. Powerful play!

– 9...♘a6? is too slow, as after 10.♕d2 ♘c7 11.♗h6 e6 12.♗xg7 ♔xg7 13.♕h6+ ♔g8

14.g4 White is winning: 14...♖e8 15.e5 (15.g5!) 15...dxe5 16.d6 ♕xd6 17.g5 ♘d7 18.♘e4 and Black resigned in Shirazi-Delorme, rapid 2003.

6...c5!
Black should always aim to play this and then ...e6 in this variation.

7.d5 e6
Black will gain good play after ...exd5 and then ...♖e8. In the past I faced 7...a6?!, but I won a nice game after 8.a4 e6 9.h5 exd5 10.hxg6 d4 11.gxh7+ ♔h8 12.♘d5 ♘xe4 13.♘f3 ♗g4 14.♘h4 ♖e8 15.♘f4 ♕f6 16.f3 ♘g3 17.fxg4 ♘xh1 18.g5 ♕d8 19.♕d3 ♗e5 20.♘hg6+ fxg6 21.♘xg6+ ♔g7 22.♕h3 ♗g3+ 23.♔f1 ♔xg6 24.♕h6+ ♔f5 25.♗g4+ ♔e5 26.♕g7+ ♔e4 27.♕g6+ ♔e5 28.♕f5 mate, Williams-Palliser, London 2000.

8.h5 At least this move is consistent!
8...exd5 9.hxg6 hxg6
9...d4 10.gxh7+ ♔h8 11.♘d5 ♘xe4 12.♘f3 – White's attractive idea is to play ♘h4, ♘f4 and then ♘g6+! with mate to follow.

9...fxg6!? looks like the best approach, as Black might be able to start an attack down the f-file.

10.exd5 The position is roughly equal.
Black will attack down the e-file and queenside whilst White will try to create some attacking chances on he kingside.

10...♖e8 11.♗g5?!
Premature. 11.f3 was better.

11...♕b6! Black is planning to play ...♘e4!, which frees up his bishop on g7.
12.♘a4?
A mistake, I had to try 12.♕d2, but Black must be better after 12...♘e4 13.♘xe4 ♖xe4.
12...♕c7?
Black misses 12...♕b4+, which would have given him a large advantage after 13.♗d2 (13.♔f1 ♗d7) 13...♕xc4.
13.f3 Planning ♔f2 and then g4, which gains space on the kingside.
13...a6 14.♘c3 b5 15.♕d2
Trying to keep the queenside closed!
15.cxb5 axb5 16.♘xb5 ♕b6 is very risky, as Black's pieces are ready to spring to life.
15...♘bd7 16.g4 It may have been worth playing 16.♗h6 ♗h8 first, who knows!

16...b4!? This closes the queenside.
17.♘d1 ♘e5 18.♔f1 18.♘e3 was equal.
18...♘h7 19.♗h6 ♗h8 20.♘e3 ♕e7!

This is a very good plan. Black brings his queen around to the kingside where I may have overextended myself.

21.♘h3 21.♘g2 was slightly better.

21...♕f6! Black is now clearly better.

22.f4 g5! Taking advantage of the placement of my king. **23.♔g2 ♘g6** Suddenly Black's pieces flood into my position. I was feeling rather uncomfortable here! **24.♗d3**

24...♕xb2?! A stronger plan was 24...gxf4 25.♗xg6 f3+ 26.♔f2 ♕xg6 27.♘f4 ♕e4, when Black is on the verge of winning.

25.♕xb2 ♗xb2 26.♖ae1 ♗g7?

Throwing away the advantage. Black should have played 26...♗c3 27.♖e2 ♘f6, which leaves me tied up.

27.♗xg7 ♔xg7 28.fxg5 A silly error. I should have played 28.♔g3!, which is equal, for example 28...gxf4+ 29.♘xf4 ♘f6 30.g5.

28...♘xg5!

29.♘xg5??

The final mistake. It was time to bail out with 29.♗xg6!=, when the game should end in a rather fortunate draw for me. 29...♔xg6 30.♘f4+ ♔g7 31.♘h5+ ♔g6 32.♘f4+ ♔g7 33.♘h5+ ♔f8? would have been a misguided winning attempt, as after 34.♘f6 ♖e7 35.♖h8+ ♔g7 36.♖e8! White is better.

29...♘f4+ 30.♔f3 ♘xd3

Black's queenside pawn mass is going to win the game.

31.♖h7+? The final error!

31...♔g6 32.♖eh1 ♔xg5 33.♖7h6 ♘e5+! 34.♔g3 ♘g6 35.♘f5 ♗xf5 36.♖1h5+ ♔f6 37.gxf5 ♖e3+ 38.♔f2 ♖ae8 39.fxg6 fxg6 40.♖h1 ♖e2+ 41.♔g3 ♔g5

White resigned.

I decided to include the next game as it demonstrates what can go wrong if someone is not in his comfort zone. When I was preparing for this game I noticed that my opponent always played the Grünfeld, hence why I played 3.h4. My opponent smelled a rat and went for a King's Indian set-up but it was clear that he was not at home in this system. That is one of the great advantages of 3.h4!?. Your opponent will often get confused and this will make him play inferior moves. Anyway onto the game.

□ **Simon Williams**
■ **Peter Poobalasingam**
Hastings 2008/09

1.d4 ♘f6 2.c4 g6 3.h4!? d6

3...c5!? is a very important alternative! This advance makes a lot of sense. White has apparently wasted a move playing h4 so Black aims to punish White by steering the game into Benko territory. Personally I would only play 3.h4!? if I expected my opponent to play the Grünfeld. If I had any inkling that they might hit me with 3...c5, the Benko approach, then I would avoid playing 3.h4!?. I expect that after this move White cannot really hope of gaining an advantage. I had one game in a local league match that continued 4.d5 b5 5.h5!? (an interesting way to try and take the game in uncharted waters) 5...♘xh5 and now in Williams-Wells I tried 6.d6?!, which is a bit over the top! I should have just continued 6.cxb5 a6 7.e4 d6, with an interesting Benko position! Black has sacrificed a pawn on the queenside whilst White has done the same on the kingside. I expect the position is roughly equal, White can aim to play ♗e2 and ♗h6 at the correct moment, with hopes of starting a kingside attack. An interesting battle lies ahead.

4.♘c3 ♘bd7?!

This is not as flexible as 4...♗g7, as the black knight can no longer move to c6. This is the first indication that my opponent was not totally at home.

4...♗g7 was looked at in the previous game.

5.e4

5...e5

5...♗g7 transposes to Azmaiparashvili-Radjabov, Benidorm, 2003. It seems to me that Black may have committed his knight to d7 rather prematurely: 6.♗e2 (White prepares to play h5, which is the standard plan in this variation!) 6...e5 (6...c5 is also play-

able if Black wants to lead the game into a Benko Gambit, play could continue for example with 7.d5 b5 8.cxb5 a6, when one interesting idea would be 9.h5!?, which aims to take advantage of the early charge of the h-pawn: 9...♘xh5 – with this move Black figures that he will rely on getting enough counterplay from his light-squared bishop – 10.♗xh5 gxh5 11.bxa6 ♗xa6 12.♘ge2 and Black has good counterplay in the spirit of the Benko but he also has some weaknesses on the kingside. Practical examples are needed!) 7.d5 (and not 7.h5? exd4 8.h6 dxc3 9.hxg7 ♖g8, when Black is better) 7...♘c5 8.♕c2 h5 (this is often the best way for Black to stop White from causing any problems with h5) 9.b4 ♘cd7 10.♖b1 a5 11.a3 axb4 12.axb4 c6 13.♘f3 0-0 14.♗g5 ♕c7 15.♘d2 and White's position was to be slightly preferred due to the space that he had gained on the queenside.

6.d5 ♘c5 7.♕c2 a5

Black decides that he should stop me from expanding on the queenside with b4. A sensible plan.

8.♗e2

This is the normal approach. By playing ♗e2 I prepare the 'threat' of h5. How should Black deal with this threat?

8...h6?!

This is another indication that my opponent

is not comfortable with the subtleties of the position. This is a mistake which will leave Black with some serious positional weaknesses after 9.h5 g5. As a rule Black should always meet h4 with h5.

8...h5! stops the h-pawn in its tracks. This does leave the g5-square weak but this is not a serious problem. At least by playing in this manner Black can target my pawn on h4 and maybe play for the break ...f5 at a later moment. The position is roughly equal here: 9.♗g5 ♗e7! 10.♘f3 ♘g4.

9.h5! g5

The pawn structure has changed and Black has three main problems: 1) Black has saddled himself with a major weakness on f5. This is his main problem for the rest of the game. 2) Black's dark-squared bishop is also very bad and it does not have much potential to break out. 3) Black's standard way to break out in the King's Indian – ...f5 – is going to be very hard to achieve now. Basically Black is left with a very passive position. I would say that White has a nice advantage here.

10.♗e3 b6

11.♗d1!

The idea behind this move is to target Black's f5-square. My plan is to play ♘e2, ♘g3 and then at a later moment ♘f5. The knight is on a better route to f5 here compared to f3.

11.♘f3 was also possible. I could continue with ♘d2, ♘f1, ♘g3 and then ♘f5. 11...♗g4?! would be a mistake, as after 12.♘d2 ♗xe2 13.♔xe2 Black's f5-square is even more weak due to the exchange of light-squared bishops.

11...♗d7 12.♘ge2 c6

13.♗xc5!?

This move simplifies matters. I also want to play against Black's bad dark-squared bishop.

13...bxc5 14.♘g3

A fair bit of manoeuvring goes on now, but my basic plan is to swap off the light-squared bishops and then land a knight on f5.

14...cxd5 15.cxd5 ♗e7 16.♗e2 ♔f8 17.♗b5

Trying to execute the first stage of my plan, the exchange of light-squared bishops.

17...♗c8

18.♘d1

Preparing ♘e3 and then ♘f5. It is all about the f5-square that Black has made permanently weak after ...h6?! and ...g5.

18...♘e8 19.♘e3 ♘g7

Bringing another piece to the defence of f5. Passive defence is rarely a good plan though.

20.♗e2

Preparing ♗g4.

20...♖b8 21.0-0 ♔g8 22.b3

A useful waiting move. In order to win I will probably have to make a break on the queenside as well, and this move prepares a3 and b4 at a later stage.

22...♔h7 23.♗g4 ♗a6 24.♖fb1!

Now that the kingside is under control, my aim is to open up the queenside.

24...♖f8 25.♕c3

There is no need to rush. From c3 the queen supports an eventual b4 push.

25...♗b5 26.a3 ♗e8 27.b4!

Black is horribly passive and it is no surprise that his position collapses quickly.

27...axb4 28.axb4 ♖b5 29.♖a7 cxb4 30.♖xb4 ♕b8 31.♖xb5 ♕xa7 32.♖b1

32...f5? Desperation which quickens the end, but the position was pretty miserable anyway, for example 32...♗d8 33.♕b4 and I am threatening ♕xd6 as well as an exchange of queens with ♕b7.

33.♘exf5 ♗d7 33...♘xf5 34.♗xf5+ ♔h8 35.♕b4. **34.♕e3** An exchange of queens simplifies matters and avoids any complications. **34...♕c7 35.♕b6! ♕xb6 36.♖xb6 ♗xf5 37.♗xf5+**

I had a pleasant choice, but I wanted to avoid a simplified opposite-coloured bishop endgame, which may arise after 37.♘xf5 ♘xf5 38.♗xf5+.

37...♔g8 37...♘xf5 38.♘xf5 is hopeless for Black. **38.♖b7 ♗f6** 38...♘xf5 39.♘xf5 is a classic example of a strong knight versus bad bishop position! **39.♗e6+ ♔h8 40.♖d7 ♘e8 41.♘f5 ♗g7 42.♘e7** 43.♘g6 is next, so Black threw in the towel.

Well, I hope this chapter has given you the inspiration to be adventurous and to give 3.h4!? a try. In chess it is sometimes more fun to think outside of the box, if in doubt just take a look at Mike Basman's games!

CHAPTER 5

Konstantin Landa

The Scotch Game: Carlsen Leads the Way

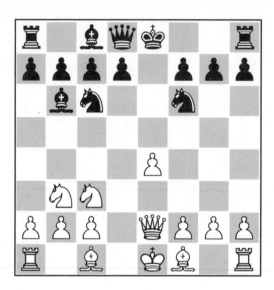

Preparing to castle queenside

☐ **Magnus Carlsen**
■ **Etienne Bacrot**
Nanjing 2010

1.e4 e5

At the present time this is the soundest move. Players who are ready to make this move at the board usually possess a more developed positional understanding. For players with a tactical, attacking style, 1...c5 is more appropriate, of course.

2.♘f3 ♘c6

We will leave to one side the searches for an advantage after 2...♘f6. This is a tedious matter, but nevertheless not hopeless. According to the present world champion

Viswanathan Anand 'The Petroff Defence is not yet completely a draw'.

3.d4!?

Why do I attach any marks as early as the third move? I think that the Scotch Game is made for those who want to embark on 'their' play from the very first moves! The opening is absolutely correct, and White obtains exactly the same disappearing advantage as after other continuations, but... the variation has not been so seriously studied as other continuations. The resulting positions are complicated and very concrete! Black has to keep a very careful eye on his opponent's threats. Lengthy manoeuvring in this opening hardly ever occurs, which is usually very unpleasant for the player with the black pieces. Just think what can happen after the classical 3.♗b5. In the complicated Ruy Lopez one has to 'rack one's brains' over the Chigorin, Breyer and Zaitsev Variations and much other information which is of absolutely no use in a specific game for the commander of the white pieces. Your opponent may be excellently prepared in one, individual variation, but you have to remember them all! What is the point, with a head aching from preparation, of going into a complicated middlegame?

In my view, this is a direct way to obtain a zero in the tournament table, unless you are a player in the world's top hundred! Nowadays White counters this problem by playing the Spanish Exchange Variation...

3...exd4 4.♘xd4 ♗c5
The main line of modern theory. After 4...♘f6 5.♘xc6 bxc6 6.e5 ♕e7 7.♕e2 ♘d5 8.c4, despite the favourable assessment for Black of the resulting positions, not everyone likes the obscure structure and the complexity of the positions arising.

For example, after 8...♗a6 9.b3, if I did not know the theoretical lines I would feel the desire to resign at the sight of the 'dead' bishop on a6...

Of course, it is not all so simple and Black holds on thanks to dynamic factors, but the feeling that White must be better does not leave me for a second.

5.♘b3
But this is interesting! Earlier Magnus looked for an advantage in two directions:
– In the endgame after 5.♘xc6 ♕f6 6.♕f3 (6.♕d2 practically went out of use at the start of this century; after 6...dxc6 7.♘c3 ♗d4 8.♗d3 ♘e7 9.0-0 ♘g6 Black began achieving very respectable results) 6...dxc6!? (in return for White's slightly better pawn structure, Black obtains free development. The 'classical' position of the variation arises after 6...bxc6 7.♘d2. 6...♕xf3 7.gxf3 bxc6 8.♗e3 ♗xe3 9.fxe3 is also possible) 7.♗c4 ♕xf3 8.gxf3 ♘f6 9.♗e3 ♗xe3 10.fxe3 ♔e7. In my view, in the given version of the endgame White has no advantage.

– The second way of fighting for an advantage came to the fore quite a long time ago – White tries to reinforce his knight at d4 in all possible ways, even to the detriment of the normal development of his knight at c3: 5.♗e3 ♕f6 6.c3!?. The resulting position has its own, very extensive theory, but in recent times here too Black has adapted and White has been unable to obtain not just an advantage, but even a hint of a playable position.
The aggressive 6.♘b5 (the Blumenfeld Attack)

was examined in SOS-3 (Chapter 7, page 62).

5...♗b6

The retreat 5...♗e7 looks rather passive. White can continue calmly developing his pieces by 6.♘c3 ♘f6 7.♗e2 0-0 8.0-0 d6 9.♗f4 with a spatial advantage.

5...♗b4+, somewhat disrupting the coordination of the white pieces, is far more cunning: 6.c3 (6.♗d2!? a5 7.a3 ♗xd2+ 8.♕xd2 ♘f6 9.♘c3 0-0 10.0-0-0 is also interesting) 6...♗e7, and now two continuations can be recommended for White:

– The classical occupation of the centre by 7.c4 ♘f6 (a game of my own from the 2004 world championship continued 7...♗f6 8.♗d3 d6 9.0-0 ♘ge7 10.♘c3 ♗xc3 11.bxc3 0-0 12.♘d4 f5 13.f4! ♘xd4 14.cxd4 fxe4 15.♗xe4 d5 16.cxd5 ♘xd5 17.♗a3 ♖f7 18.♕b3 ♘f6, Movsesian-Landa, Tripoli 2004, and here White would have gained a promising position after 19.♗c2! b6 20.♕d3 ♗b7 21.♖ae1±) 8.♘c3 0-0 9.♗e2 ♖e8 10.0-0 a5 11.f3 a4 12.♘d4 a3 13.b3 ♗b4 14.♕d3 d6 15.♗e3 ♘xd4 16.♗xd4, and White is slightly better, Petrosian-Smorodsky, Tbilisi 1944.

– 7.g3 (evoking memories of Richard Réti) 7...♘f6 8.♗g2 d6 9.0-0 ♗g4 10.f3 ♗e6 11.♘d4, and in both cases White has the easier game thanks to his advantage in space.

6.♘c3

The 'classical' way to play this line was 6.a4, but Carlsen has in mind to castle on the queenside.

6...♘f6

The move recommended by the computer. The other plan with the development of the knight at the more stable position e7 will be examined in the next game.

7.♕e2

White deploys his pieces as in the Sicilian Defence, where the plans for attacking the black king have already been worked out in detail.

7...0-0 8.♗g5 h6

9.♗h4

9.h4?! must be deemed too drastic in view of 9...d6! (of course, the immediate 9...hxg5? is bad, as after 10.hxg5 White gains a strong attack) 10.f3 (the principled continuation, but it effectively loses the game; chances of a fight are retained by 10.♗e3 ♖e8 11.♗xb6 axb6 12.f3 – 12.0-0-0 b5! – 12...d5 13.0-0-0 ♗d7!) 10...hxg5 11.hxg5 ♘g4! 12.fxg4 ♕xg5 13.♕f3 ♗xg4 14.♕g3 ♘e5 and White has not achieved anything, Rublevsky-Anand, Bastia 2004 (however, 14...♘b4 15.♗d3 ♖ae8 was even stronger).

9...a5! 10.a4

White is contemplating castling long, and therefore the inclusion of the moves by the rooks' pawns of both sides is clearly advantageous to Black. The very sharp variations where the advance of the black a-pawn is ignored have not yet occurred in practice. 10.0-0-0!? (with 'eyes wide shut') 10...a4 11.♘d2, and now:

– 11...a3 12.e5 axb2+ 13.♔b1 ♘d4
(13...♖e8 14.♗xf6 gxf6 15.♕g4+ ♔h8
16.♕h4 ♔g7 17.exf6+ ♕xf6 18.♕xf6+
♔xf6 19.♘d5+ ♔g7 20.♘xb6 cxb6 21.♘c4
d5 22.♘xb6 ♖a5 23.♘xd5±) 14.♕d3 d5!
15.exf6 ♗f5 16.♕g3 ♗xc2+ 17.♔xb2 g6
18.♖c1. The position is a mind-boggling one,
but I would prefer to be Black – the white king
is too exposed (18...♗f5 19.♘b3 c6).

– 11...♗d4 (this seems safer for Black)
12.♘b5! a3 13.♘xd4 ♘xd4 14.♕e3 axb2+
15.♔xb2 ♘e6 16.♗c4 d5 17.♘f3 c6 unclear.

10...♘d4

Etienne decides to simplify the position immediately.

Before the present game this position had
only been considered by non-human minds.
An internet rapid game between two engines
continued as follows: 10...d6!? 11.0-0-0
♗e6 12.♕e1!? (for a human, such a move is
impossible to make at the board! 12.f3 looks
more 'human', with the idea after
12...♕e7?! of sticking the knight on the central
square: 13.♘d5 ♗xd5 14.exd5 ♖ae8
15.♕xe7 ♘xe7 16.♗b5 and White has the
advantage) 12...♕e7 13.f4 ♖ae8 14.♘d2
♗d4 15.♘b5 ♗g4 16.♘f3 ♕xe4 17.♕xe4
♖xe4 18.♖xd4 ♘xd4 19.♘fxd4 c6 20.♗d3
cxb5 21.♗xe4 ♘xe4 22.♖e1 d5 23.♘xb5
♖c8, and the result of a tense struggle was a
roughly equal endgame, 'Fredis'-'Hoshad',
playchess.com 2006.

11.♕d3

If White goes along with Black by playing
11.♘xd4, then after 11...♗xd4 12.0-0-0
♗xc3 13.bxc3 ♕e7 14.e5 ♕a3+ 15.♔b1?
(15.♔d2 ♕xa4 16.♗xf6 gxf6 17.♕e3 ♕h4
18.g3 ♕g5 19.f4 ♕g7∓) 15...♗a6 the inclusion
of the moves a5 – a4 is clearly felt.

11...♘xb3 12.cxb3 Now the white king
has acquired a 'home' at a2.

12...♖e8 13.0-0-0 d6 14.♕c2

14...♗d7?

A loss of a tempo, which effectively already
ruins Black's game! Although in the given
position the computer gives assessments in
favour of Black, for some reason all the time
one wants to give an advantage to White – he
has easy play in the centre and on the
kingside. Apparently there are still positions
in which silicon is powerless. It was essential
to cover the d5-point, even at the cost of
weakening the d6 pawn: 14...c6 15.♗c4
(Black can meet 15.♗g3 with 15...d5! 16.e5
♘h5) 15...♕e7 16.♖he1 ♗e6 17.f4 ♗xc4
18.bxc4 ♕e6 19.♕d3, with a slightly inferior
but defensible position. Of course,
Black cannot play 14...♗e6? 15.e5 g5
16.♗g3 ♘h5, when 17.♗b5! ♗d7 18.♗c4! is
very strong for White.

It is not possible to escape from the unpleasant
pin by 14...g5?! 15.♗g3 ♘h5 16.e5
♘xg3 17.hxg3 ♖xe5 18.♖xh6 ♗f5 19.♗d3

g4 20.♔b1, when Black comes under a strong attack.

15.♗c4 ♗e6 Again 15...g5 16.♗g3 (16.e5!?) 16...♘h5 17.e5! was bad for Black.

16.♖he1

White has a decent advantage. Even 'visually' it is evident that he has a pleasant and easy game, with all his pieces standing in the centre, and that Black's game is very difficult.

16...♕e7 17.e5

Magnus decides to 'fracture' Black's position immediately, exploiting the advantage of having his rooks on the central files. White's other possibility was 17.f4 ♗xc4 18.bxc4 ♕e6 19.♗xf6 ♕xf6 20.♘d5 ♕d8 21.♘xb6 cxb6 22.g3±.

17...dxe5 18.♖xe5 ♕f8

18...♖ad8? would have lost to 19.♘d5, with a pin on the diagonal and on the file!

19.♗xf6 gxf6 20.♖e2 ♕g7

No better is 20...♗xc4 21.bxc4 ♖xe2 22.♕xe2 ♖e8 23.♘e4 ♖e6 24.♕f3±, when White gradually steals up on the weakened black king.

21.♗xe6 ♖xe6 22.♖xe6 fxe6

23.♖d3!

Strongly played! White's aim is the black king. While the black bishop is 'chilling out' at b6, White begins a very strong attack.

23...♔h8 24.♖g3 ♕h7 25.♕d2 ♗c5

25...♖g8 26.♖xg8+ ♔xg8 27.♕d8+ ♔g7 28.♕e7+ ♔g6 29.♕xe6±.

26.♘e4 ♗e7 27.♖h3 ♔g7

The knight is taboo: 27...♕xe4 28.♕xh6+ ♔g8 29.♖g3+ ♔f7 30.♕h5+ ♔f8 31.♕h8+ ♔f7 32.♖g7 mate.

28.♕d7 ♔f7

29.♘g5+! Very pretty. 29.♘xf6 ♔xf6 30.♖f3+ ♔g5 31.♕xe6 would also have concluded the game.

29...fxg5 30.♖f3+ ♔g8

30...♔g6 31.♕xe6+ ♔h5 32.♖h3 mate.

31.♕xe6+ ♔h8 32.♖f7 ♗d6

32...♕d3 33.♕xh6+ ♔g8 34.♕g7 mate.

33.♖xh7+ ♔xh7 34.♕f7+ ♔h8 35.g3 ♖a6 36.♔b1 ♗b4 37.f4 gxf4 38.gxf4

Black resigned. A quite timely decision – he is not able to create any fortress, and White wins easily.

□ **Teimour Radjabov**
■ **Evgeny Tomashevsky**
Plovdiv 2010

1.e4 e5 2.♘f3 ♘c6 3.d4 exd4 4.♘xd4 ♗c5 5.♘b3 ♗b6 6.♘c3

Very recently, in the latest European Club Championship, this position occurred again. Evgeny Tomashevsky, a solid positional player, chose a different plan.

6...d6!?

A flexible move: for the moment Black has

not decided where to develop his king's knight. In addition, the immediate development of the bishop at g5 is not possible.

7.♕e2
All the same!
7...♘ge7
Black, having evidently observed the horror of the Carlsen-Bacrot game, chooses a solid arrangement of his forces. It is no longer possible to pin the knight on e7, but in this branch too, in my view, Black has problems! Naturally, if 7...♘f6 there immediately follows 8.♗g5!.
8.♗e3 0-0 9.0-0-0 ♗e6 10.f4

10...♔h8
Black responded badly in the source game: 10...f5? 11.g4!? (the simple 11.e5 d5 12.♕f2± would also have given an advantage) 11...♖e8 12.♖g1 fxg4 (Black should

have taken the other pawn 12...fxe4, although in this case too White's chances of a direct attack after 13.♔b1! are considerable) 13.♗xb6! axb6 14.f5 ♗f7 15.♕xg4 with a deadly attack on the kingside, Shmirina-T.Mamedyarova, Budva 2003.
11.♔b1 ♕e8 12.♗xb6 axb6 13.g4 f6
With a good knowledge and a little imagination, in the contours of this position one can see a mirror reflection of the Caro-Kann Defence, only it is not the light-squared, but the dark-squared bishops which have been exchanged. A drawback to Black's position is the insecure position of his monarch on the kingside.
14.h4 ♕f7

15.f5!
Setting up a bind and preparing a direct attack on the king. White gives up the e5-square, but the black knight there only looks nicely placed.
15...♗xb3 16.cxb3 White recaptures with this pawn, keeping the a-file closed!
16...♘e5 17.g5 ♖ad8 18.♗g2 ♖d7 19.♖hf1 ♖fd8 20.♕e3 ♖e8 21.♕g3 ♖ed8 22.♕e3
Indecision No.1...
22...♖e8 23.♕g3 ♖ed8 24.♖d2
Black is very passively placed, whereas White has a mass of possibilities, one of which consists in playing his knight to e6. I

also took part in this tournament and I witnessed this game. At this point, to be honest, I had no doubts about what the result would be.

24...c6 In any case Black must undertake something, to avoid being suffocated.

25.♕f4?!

Indecision No.2. The direct switching of the knight to e6 should have been calculated. In all variations White has a significant advantage: 25.♘e2 d5 26.♘f4 dxe4 27.♖xd7 ♖xd7 28.♗xe4 ♘d5 29.♗xd5 cxd5 30.gxf6 gxf6 (30...♕xf6 31.♘h5 ♕d6 32.f6 g6 33.♖e1 gxh5 34.♖xe5 and Black has no defence) 31.♖c1 ♘c6 32.h5! (intensifying the threats to the black king) 32...d4 33.h6 ♕g8 34.♕xg8+ ♔xg8 35.♖g1+ ♔f7 36.♔c2±.

25...b5 26.♖fd1 ♕g8 27.♖d4 ♕f7 28.♖4d2 ♕g8

29.♗h1?!

Indecision No.3. Why not 29.♘e2 ? – after 29...d5 30.♘d4 dxe4 31.♗xe4 ♘d5 32.♗xd5 ♖xd5 33.♘e6 ♘g6! (33...♖xd2 34.♖xd2 ♖xd2 35.♕xd2+−) 34.♖xd5 ♖xd5 35.♕c1 ♖xd1 (35...♘xh4 36.♖xd5 cxd5 37.♕f4 ♘g6 38.♕c7 ♘e5 39.♕xb7 fxg5 40.♘xg5±) 36.♕xd1 ♘xh4 37.♕g4 fxg5 38.♕xg5 ♘g6 39.a3 White retains a great advantage (39...♕e8 40.♕g4!). I cannot explain Teimour's rejection of the knight manoeuvre to e6. Possibly he underestimated how strong the steed would be there.

29...♕f7 30.♖d4 ♕h5 31.b4 ♕g4 32.♕xg4 ♘xg4

Without the queens it is easier for Black to defend, of course, but even so the advantage is still with White.

33.♖g1 ♘e5 34.♖f1 ♘f7 35.♖g1 ♘e5 36.♖f1 ♘f7 37.♖g1 ♘e5

Draw by repetition.

What conclusion can be drawn from the material we have studied? To me it is obvious that the Scotch Game is quite a dangerous weapon against players who begin with 1...e5.

In addition, the line with the bishop retreat to h4, discovered by Magnus Carlsen, is highly venomous for Black. Although in many lines the computer gives Black the advantage, this opinion is unjustified in this position. Experience and a more detailed analysis show that it is much more difficult for Black to defend, than for White to attack! In the last two games which we have analysed, Black was unable to equalise. We now await revelations at the Anand-Kramnik level in this opening. But until they have been expressed, one can play this line and win at any level!

CHAPTER 6

Jeroen Bosch

Budapest Gambit Delayed

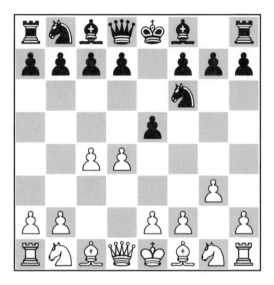

Catalan with 3...e5

1.d4 ♞f6 2.c4 e6 3.g3 e5

A real surprise! Pawns can't move backwards so a certain amount of caution is always required. However, that does not explain Black's slow-motion e-pawn which goes from e6 to e5. In fact, Black argues that in the Budapest Gambit an additional tempo (3.g3) is detrimental to White's position. There are two arguments in favour of this line of reasoning. Firstly, White's main line against the Budapest proper (1.d4 ♞f6 2.c4 e5 3.dxe5 ♞g4) is 4.♗f4; with a pawn on g3 the bishop feels less comfortable on f4, though. Secondly, White often plays e3 in the Budapest Gambit, which does not combine very well with 3.g3. Naturally, Black has to watch out for those

positions where g3 comes in handy, and these do occur in the Budapest.

The witty 3...e5 was first played by the multiple Hungarian Champion Gedeon Barcza (against Pal Benko in 1948). A young Lajos Portisch has also played it (unsuccessfully), but 3...e5 has mainly been tried by the Brazilian IM Herman van Riemsdijk. On the whole, you won't find many games with this Delayed Budapest Gambit. Disregarding the objective merits of the tempo loss for a moment, this may also be explained by the fact that Budapest players will embark on their favourite gambit on the second move, and those who don't play the gambit will certainly not consider it a tempo down. Yet, I feel that this gambit against the Catalan has been underestimated, and I intend to show you why.

4.dxe5

As they say, the only way to refute a gambit is by accepting it. Of course White could argue that with the additional 3.g3 it makes sense to investigate positions that could also result from the English Opening:

● 4.♗g2 exd4 5.♕xd4 ♘c6

This attack on the queen proves White wrong. It is impossible to believe in a white opening advantage after Black regains tthe time lost in the opening (2...e6 and 3...e5) with this natural developing move. 6.♕d1 (6.♕d2 ♗c5 7.♘c3 d6 8.♘f3 0-0 9.0-0 ♖e8 10.e3 ♗e6 11.b3 ♕d7 was fine for Black in Cobo-Van Riemsdijk, Tucuman 1971) 6...♗b4+ (6...♘e5!? 7.♘d2 ♗b4 8.♕b3 ♕e7 9.a3 ♗c5 10.♘h3 a5 11.♘f4 a4 12.♕c3 d6, Neelotpal-Sharbaf, Mashhad 2010, and having cramped White's queenside, Black is doing very OK) 7.♘d2 d5!? (7...0-0) 8.cxd5 ♘xd5 9.♘f3 0-0 10.0-0 ♖e8 11.♘b3 ♘f6 12.a3 ♕xd1 13.♖xd1 ♗f8 14.♔f1 ♗f5 15.♘fd4 ♘xd4 16.♘xd4 ♗e4 17.♗xe4 ♘xe4 18.♗f4 c6 with equal chances in the stem game Benko-Barcza, Budapest 1948.

● 4.♘f3 e4 (4...exd4 5.♘xd4 – if Black now continues quietly, he might well end up in an English Opening a (useful) tempo down. So

he went: 5...d5 6.♗g2! ♗b4+ – 6...dxc4 is a better attempt, but I would prefer White – 7.♘c3 0-0 8.cxd5 ♘xd5 9.♕b3!, and White had an edge after 9...♗xc3+ 10.bxc3 ♘b6 11.♗a3 ♖e8 12.0-0, Pachman-Brat, Prague 1954. As an afterthought, 4...♗b4+!? is interesting) 5.♘fd2.

Now 5...c6 6.♗g2 d5 7.0-0 ♗d6?! (7...♗e7 8.cxd5 cxd5 9.f3 ♘c6 is about equal) 8.cxd5 cxd5 9.f3 0-0? 10.fxe4 ♘g4 11.♕b3 ♘c6 12.e3 ♘xh2? 13.♔xh2 ♕h4+ 14.♔g1 ♕xg3 was easily refuted by 15.e5+–, Molnar-L.Portisch, Budapest 1956. Black can just improve with 7...♗e7, but he can also play 5...d5 6.cxd5 (or 6.♗g2 ♘c6!?, while 6...c6 transposes to Molnar-Portisch) 6...♕xd5 7.e3 ♗b4 8.♘c3 ♗xc3 9.bxc3 0-0, with interesting play.

4...♘g4

Here we are in the realm of the Budapest Gambit with the addition of g2-g3.

It makes sense to make 5.♘f3 the main line of our investigation. Together with 4.♗f4, 4.♘f3 is, after all, the main line against the 'regular' Budapest Gambit.

5.♘f3

● Nobody has ever dared **5.♗f4**, convinced as they are that the combination of a bishop on f4 and a pawn on g3 is unhealthy. Yet, things are not that clear.

Now, I don't like 5...♗b4+ because of 6.♘c3 (not 6.♘d2 g5), when the additional g3 favours White.

– After 5...♘c6 6.♘f3 Black may consider 6...♗c5!? (in the main line of the Budapest Gambit Black gives a check with the bishop, but here after 6...♗b4+ 7.♘c3! – 7.♘bd2 ♕e7 8.♗g2 ♘gxe5 9.0-0± – 7...♗xc3+ 8.bxc3 ♕e7 9.♕d5 the extra tempo is very useful and renders this line almost unplayable for Black) 7.e3 f6!? 8.exf6 ♕xf6 9.♘c3 ♗b4 and the bishop on f4 is slightly awkward, but there is nothing concrete for Black.

– 5...g5!?. This is less odd than it looks. In the Budapest Gambit after 1.d4 ♘f6 2.c4 e5 3.dxe5 ♘g4 4.♗f4 they also play 4...g5 (Mamedyarov and a young Topalov have done so). Then White's best answer is 5.♗g3, when he can obtain an edge with a fairly quick h4. Now he is forced to be more modest.

6.♗d2 ♘xe5 (6...♗g7) 7.♘f3 (7.♘c3 ♘bc6 8.♘f3 ♗g7 9.♗g2 0-0 is a normal continuation. White has a slight edge) 7...♗g7 (7...♘xf3+ 8.exf3 ♕e7+ 9.♗e2±) 8.♘xe5 (8.♘xg5?! ♘xc4) 8...♗xe5 9.♗c3 ♘c6 (not 9...♕f6 10.♗xe5 ♕xe5 11.♘c3 d6, with a positional edge for White) 10.♗g2, with a slight advantage but nothing special.

● Dubious is **5.f4?!** ♗c5 6.♘h3 d6, and Black has ample compensation.

● **5.e6** cannot unduly worry Black, although it is more tricky here than in the Budapest proper.

5...♗b4+ (the exciting way to play it; 5...fxe6 6.e4 ♘e5 is also playable; worse is 5...dxe6 6.♕xd8+ ♔xd8, which equalizes in the regular Budapest Gambit, as with the pawn on g3 White can put some pressure on Black's queenside with ♗g2) 6.♗d2 ♕f6 7.exf7+ ♔xf7 8.♘f3 ♕xb2 9.♗xb4 ♕xb4+ 10.♘bd2 ♖e8 or 10...♖f8.

● The book refutation of our SOS line is **5.♘c3**, which is based on a game Tukmakov-Van Riemsdijk, Groningen 1990, where White gained an edge after 5...♘c6?! 6.♗g2 ♗c5?! (6...♘gxe5)

7.♘h3! (this is the point – White can harmoniously develop all his pieces without having to play e3) 7...♘cxe5 8.0-0 0-0 9.♘e4 ♗e7 10.b3 d6 11.♘f4 ♘f6 12.♘c3 c6 13.♕c2.

However, Black's fifth move is the culprit, and after 5...♘xe5! Black is doing well.

The pawn sacrifice 6.♘f3 ♘xc4 7.♕d5 is not very convincing, when Black the returns

material with 7...♘b6 (7...♘d6) 8.♕e5+ ♕e7 9.♕xc7 ♘a6 10.♕f4 ♘b4, with active piece play. And 6.b3 can be favourably met by 6...♗b4! 7.♗b2 (7.♗d2 0-0 8.♗g2 ♖e8) 7...0-0 or even 7...♕f6!?.

● Somewhat similar to Tukmakov-Van Riemsdijk is **5.♗g2** ♗c5?! 6.♘h3 ♘xe5 7.0-0 d6 8.♘c3 0-0 9.b3 a6 10.♘f4±, J.Horvath-G.Horvath, Zalaegerszeg 1991. However, here too, Black has 5...♘xe5!.

● **5.♕d4** was given an exclam by Eric Schiller, but Black has 5...d6, which is a promising gambit (incidentally **5.♕d5** can also be met by 5...d6). 6.exd6 ♗xd6! (6...♘c6? 7.♕e4+ ♗e6 8.dxc7 ♕d1+ – 8...♕xc7 – 9.♔xd1 ♘xf2+ 10.♔e1 ♘xe4 11.♗g2 f5 was not entirely clear in Malo-Arpa, Aragon 1998, but White should have a slight edge).

And now:
– 7.♘f3 0-0 8.♗g2 ♘c6 9.♕d2 (9.♕d1? ♗c5!∓) 9...♗e6, and Black has more than enough for the pawn.
– Not 7.♕xg7? ♗e5, and wins.
– 7.c5? was given an ! by Schiller, but 7...♘c6 favours Black.
– 7.♕e4+ ♗e6 (7...♗e7) 8.♘c3 (8.♕xb7 ♘d7; 8.♗h3 ♘d7 9.♗xg4 ♘f6 10.♕xb7 ♘xg4) 8...♘c6, with compensation.

● **5.e4** is a serious move – in the Budapest Gambit 4.e4 is often associated with

Alekhine. After 5...♘xe5 6.f4 Black should play 6...♘ec6 7.♗e3 (7.♗g2 ♗c5 8.♘e2 d6 9.♘bc3 0-0 10.♘a4 ♗b4+ 11.♗d2 a5 is about equal, Hanks-Perez, Tel Aviv ol 1964. On move 7 Black can also play 7...♗b4+) 7...♗b4+ and now:

– 8.♔f2 ♕e7 9.♗g2 ♗c5 10.♕d2 ♗xe3+ 11.♕xe3 ♘b4 was Quinteros-Van Riemsdijk, Sao Paulo 1978. Black is doing fine in this complicated position.

– In Laznicka-Timman, Paks 2010, there followed 8.♘d2 ♕e7 9.♗g2 ♘a6 10.♘e2 ♘c5 11.♕c2 f5 (this looks strong, but Laznicka counters with a temporary pawn sacrifice) 12.♘c3 ♗xc3 13.♕xc3 ♘xe4 14.♘xe4 fxe4 15.0-0-0. White is a pawn down, but he has two bishops, an edge in development, and open files for his rooks. Black's position is more difficult to play. On move 10 I would prefer 10...0-0 intending ...♗c5, but please note that the immediate 10...♗c5 favours White after 11.♗xc5 ♘xc5 12.0-0 d6 13.♘c3.

– 8.♘c3 ♗xc3+ 9.bxc3 ♕e7

Play has transposed directly into the Budapest Gambit, a line which is known to favour Black. You will find several games in your database (two by Keres as White) following 1.d4 ♘f6 2.c4 e5 3.dxe5 ♘g4 4.e4 ♘xe5 5.f4 ♘ec6 6.♗e3 ♗b4+ 7.♘c3 ♕h4+! (so Black actually provokes g3!) 8.g3 ♗xc3+! 9.bxc3

♕e7. Viktor Moskalenko explains the ins and outs in his *The Fabulous Budapest Gambit* (New In Chess, 2008).

5...♗c5

Black develops just like he does in the Budapest Gambit and provokes e3. Here the combination of e3 and g3 will lead to Budapest positions in which White can develop his bishop to the long diagonal (not bad), but Black may profit from the weakened light squares. The subsequent moves are pretty much forced.

6.e3 ♘c6 7.♗g2 ♘gxe5 8.♘xe5 ♘xe5

Black has retrieved his gambit pawn with a perfectly normal position. Just imagine: you could also have been defending some slightly worse Catalan around this stage!

9.0-0

9.♘c3 0-0 10.0-0 d6 11.b3 a5 (11...♗g4! is OK for Black) 12.h3 ♕f6?! 13.♘d5! ♕d8 (Black had probably overlooked 13...♘f3+ 14.♕xf3 ♕xa1 15.♕e2!, and White more or less wins) 14.♗b2 c6 15.♘c3 ♕e7 16.♘e4, with a slight edge for White in Quinteros-Tempone, Mar del Plata 1995.

9...d6

Or the immediate 9...0-0.

10.b3

10.b4 looks frightening, and is an argument in favour of 9...0-0. Yet, after 10...♗b6 11.c5 dxc5 12.♕xd8+ ♔xd8 13.♗b2 (13.♖d1+ ♔e7 14.♖d5 f6 15.bxc5 ♗a5) 13...f6 14.bxc5 ♗xc5 White has a certain amount of compensation for the pawn, but nothing special.

10.♕c2 0-0 11.b3 ♕f6 (11...c6) 12.♗b2 ♕h6!? (12...♗f5) 13.♗xe5 (or 13.♘c3 ♗h3 14.♘d5 ♗xg2 15.♔xg2 c6) 13...dxe5 14.♘c3 f5 15.♖ad1 c6, with a favourable Dutch in Terasti-Laihonen, Tampere 1997.

10...♗g4

Gaining time and taking advantage of the weakened light squares. Alternatively, there is 10...0-0.

11.♕c2

11...♘f3+!?

Black is also doing well after 11...♗f3.

12.♔h1 0-0 13.♘d2

Admitting that Black is fully equal. White suffers slightly after 13.♗b2 ♕g5! 14.♘d2 ♕h5. Note that 13.h3?! is well-met by 13...♕f6!.

13...♘xd2

Draw. Küttner-Frenzel, Ruhla 1957.

CHAPTER 7

Alexander Finkel

French Defence: Obtaining Two Bishops

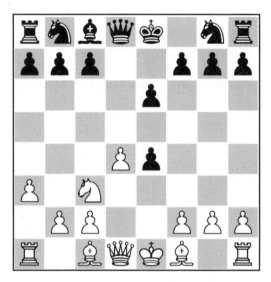

Winawer: 4.♘e2 dxe4 5.a3 ♗xc3+ 6.♘xc3

After covering 5...♗e7 in the previous issue of SOS, the following article is dedicated to Black's other popular reply on 5.a3: 5...♗xc3+, which is considered by modern theory as the most solid way to treat 4.♘e2.

The big question is whether White has sufficient resources to fight for an opening advantage if Black doesn't have aggressive intentions and is satisfied with equality, even if this means giving up serious attempts to play for a win?! Objectively speaking Black should be able to keep the balance if he is well prepared for this line, however even in that case White may pose him some tough problems to solve.

Black's play in this line may be classified into three main categories: he either tries to hold a slightly inferior endgame in which White enjoys a minimal but rather annoying advantage due to his bishop pair (even though in some of the lines Black neutralizes White's pressure in the endgame almost by force); or he tries to keep his extra pawn on e4, which usually allows White to gain a dangerous initiative, as Black has to play ...f5, weakening the dark squares on the kingside and in the centre (which is obviously welcomed by White, since his dark-squared bishop may just turn into a monster!); or he tries to give back the pawn on e4 at the right moment, initiating some trades along the way (bingo!).

It should be emphasized that by choosing the 4.♘e2 line White deliberately gives up the fight for a serious opening advantage (although he may get a really nice edge in case Black gets greedy or incautious). However, in most cases White emerges out of the opening with a very solid position and good prospects to turn his symbolic plus into something more tangible.

In the illustrative games I tried my best to cover every important alternative by Black, so after reading this article you should have a rather clear idea what to do regardless of Black's opening choice.

□ **Daniel Campora**
■ **Paulo Dias**
Santo Antonio 2001

1.e4 e6 2.d4 d5 3.♘c3 ♗b4 4.♘e2 dxe4 5.a3 ♗xc3+ 6.♘xc3 e5?!

It seems that this straightforward attempt to simplify the position is not sufficient for equality. Moreover, White has more than one way to secure a small, but long-lasting opening advantage.

Instead, 6...♘f6 7.♗g5 favours White who will win back the pawn with some edge. While 6...f5?! was played in the famous game Alekhine-Nimzowitsch, Bled 1931.

After 7.f3! exf3 8.♕xf3 ♕xd4 (Larsen has indicated 8...♕h4+ 9.g3 ♕xd4 10.♗f4! c6 11.♕h5+ g6 12.♕e2 ♕g7 13.0-0-0 as favouring White; 8...♘f6 9.♗f4 0-0 10.0-0-0) 9.♕g3 ♘f6 10.♕xg7 ♕e5+ (White is also better after the stronger 10...♖g8 11.♕xc7 ♘c6 12.♗f4!, as originally indicated by Alekhine) 11.♗e2 ♖g8 12.♕h6 ♖g6 13.♕h4 ♗d7 (13...♖g4!?, Kasparov) 14.♗g5! ♗c6? (14...♘c6 15.0-0-0 0-0-0) 15.0-0-0 White won quickly.

7.dxe5

This seemingly unpretentious move appears to be less logical than 7.♗e3 (White's plan is just to complete development of the pieces leaving the black pawn on e4 for dessert!) 7...♘c6 (7...exd4 8.♕xd4 ♘f6 9.♕xd8+ ♔xd8 10.0-0-0+ ♘bd7 11.♗c4 ♔e7 12.♖he1 c6 13.♘xe4 ♘xe4 14.♗g5+±, Thomas-Hollis, Bristol 1968) 8.♗b5 ♗d7 9.dxe5 ♘ge7 10.♕h5 ♘g6 11.0-0-0 ♕c8 12.e6 ♗xe6 13.♗xc6+ bxc6 14.♕c5±, Hector-Lyrberg, Sweden 2005/06.

7...♕xd1+

8.♘xd1!?

Just as on the previous move White has another decent alternative: 8.♔xd1 ♗f5 9.♘d5 ♔d7 (9...♘a6 10.♗g5 ♗e6 11.♗b5+ c6 12.♗xa6 ♗xd5 13.♗xb7 ♖b8 14.♗a6 ♖b6 15.♗e2 ♖xb2 16.♔d2±, Letzelter-Huss, Buenos Aires ol 1978) 10.♗f4 ♘c6 11.♗b5 a6 12.♗xc6+ ♚xc6 13.♘c3 ♘e7 14.♔e2 ♘g6 15.♔e3 ½-½, Fegebank-Barkowski, Bargteheide 1989.

8...♘c6 9.♗f4 ♘ge7 10.♘c3 ♗f5 11.0-0-0 ♘g6 12.♗g3 ♘gxe5

Perhaps Black should've preferred a capture with the other knight in order to prevent White's next move.

12...♘cxe5!? 13.♖e1 (13.h4 h5 14.♗b5+ c6 15.♗a4 ♘d7 16.♖he1 ♘c5=) 13...0-0-0 14.♘xe4 ♖he8 15.♘c3 ♘c6 16.♖xe8 ♖xe8 17.♗b5 a6 18.♗xc6 bxc6 19.♖d1 is only slightly better for White.

13.♗b5! 0-0?!

This natural move is obviously an inaccuracy allowing White to trade his pair of bishops for Black's pair of knights causing an irrepairable damage to Black's pawn structure. After the correct 13...a6! 14.♗xe5 axb5 15.♗xg7 ♖g8 16.♗f6 ♖xg2 17.♘xb5 ♖c8 18.♖hg1 ♖g6± Black has excellent chances to hold.

14.♖d5! f6 15.♗xc6 bxc6 16.♖c5 ♗g6 17.♖e1 Black just has too many weaknesses to protect!

17...♖fe8

Removing a rook from the f-file is tough decision to make, but he hardly had anything better. 17...♖ae8!? 18.♖a5 ♖f7 19.♖xa7 f5 20.♗f4 ♘g4 21.♖e2±.

18.♗xe5 ♖xe5 19.♖xe5 fxe5 20.♘xe4 ♖d8

The rook endgame after 20...♗xe4 21.♖xe4 ♖e8 22.♔d2 ♔f7 23.♖a4 ♖a8 24.♖a6 is hopeless for Black.

21.f3 ♔f7 22.♘f2 ♖e8 22...♖d5?! 23.♘g4 ♔e6 24.c4 ♖a5 25.♔d2 ♔f5 26.♔c3+−. **23.♘g4!? e4 24.f4 ♔e6 25.♘e3 ♖f8** 25...c5 26.♔d2 h5 27.♔c3 ♗f5 28.g3 g6 29.♖d1±. **26.g3 ♗e8 27.♖d1 g5?!**

28.f5+!?
28.fxg5!? ♖f3 29.♖e1±.
28...♔f6 29.♖d8!
This move practically decides the game as trading the rooks would lead to an easily winning endgame.
29...h5 30.♔d2 h4
Also losing is 30...♔e7 31.♖d4.
31.♖a8 hxg3 32.hxg3 ♖h8 33.♔c3 ♔e5 34.b4 a6 34...c5 35.b5. **35.a4 ♔d6 36.♔d4 ♔e7 37.g4 ♖h1 38.♖xa6 ♖b1 39.c3 ♖b3 40.♖a8 ♖a3 41.♘c4**
Black resigned. A great example of endgame technique by Campora!

□ **Igor-Alexandre Nataf**
■ **Manuel Apicella**
Marseille ch-FRA 2001

1.e4 e6 2.d4 d5 3.♘c3 ♗b4 4.♘e2 dxe4 5.a3 ♗xc3+ 6.♘xc3 ♘c6

The main reply. Black's basic idea in this line is to return the pawn under more favourable conditions.

7.♗b5 ♘e7 8.♗g5

White's only attempt to fight for an opening advantage. Other moves do not pose Black any problems:

– 8.♗e3 0-0 9.♕d2 e5! 10.dxe5 ♕xd2+ 11.♗xd2 a6 (11...♘xe5 12.♘xe4 ♗f5 13.f3 ♗xe4=) 12.♗xc6 ♘xc6 13.0-0-0 ♘xe5 14.♘xe4 ♘g4! with even chances, Mokry-Casper, Olomouc 1983.

– 8.♘xe4 a6 9.♗xc6+ ♘xc6 10.♗e3 0-0 11.♕d2 b6 12.0-0-0 ♗b7 13.f3 ♕d5 14.♘c3 ♕a5 equal, Kassimov-Tarlev, Anapa 2009.

8...f6 9.♗e3

9...f5?!

As I previously mentioned, Black shouldn't be too greedy. The pawn on e4 is not worth weakening the dark squares on the kingside, especially since White's dark-squared bishop doesn't face any opposition.

9...a6?! 10.♗xc6+ ♘xc6 11.♕h5+ ♔f8 12.0-0-0 ♕e8 13.♕h4 ♘e7 14.♕xe4 ♘f5 15.♗f4±, Skaric-Govedarica, Belgrade 2007.

10.♕h5+!?

Another promising option was 10.f3: 10...exf3 11.♕xf3 0-0 12.0-0-0 ♘d5 13.♘xd5 ♕xd5 14.♕xd5 exd5 15.♗f4 with compensation, Westerinen-Djurhuus, Oslo 1988.

10...g6 11.♕h6 ♔f7 12.0-0-0

12...♘d5

After the text Black is doomed to a passive defence, therefore the ugly 12...♘g8 deserved attention, intending to play ...h6 later on: 13.♕f4 ♘f6 (13...♘ce7 14.♘xe4 ♘d5 15.♘g5+ ♔g7 16.♕e5+ ♘gf6 17.♗d2±, Cordovil-Vega Holm, Loures 1998) 14.♕h4?! (14.f3!?) 14...h6 15.♗xh6 ♘g4 16.♕xd8 ♘xd8 17.♗e3 ♔g7 unclear, Gankin-Paveliev, Moscow 2008.

13.♘xd5 exd5

Or 13...♕xd5 14.c4 ♕d6 15.♗f4 ♕f8 16.♕xf8+ ♖xf8 17.♗xc7 with a slight plus.

14.♗f4

The weakness of the dark squares in Black's camp fully compensates White for the lack of pawn.

In a later game White immediately traded his light-squared bishop for Black's knight, securing the penetration of the other one to e5: 14.♗xc6!? bxc6 15.♗f4 ♕f8 16.♕h3 h6 17.♗xc7 ♕e7 18.♗e5 ♕g5+ 19.♔b1 ♖e8 20.♕c3 ♗d7 21.h4 ♕xg2 22.♕e3±, Moreda-Daneri, Mar del Plata 2009.

14...♕f8 The only move, for if 14...♗d7? then 15.♗xc6 ♗xc6 16.♗e5 ♕f8 17.♕h3±. **15.♕h4** 15.♕h3!?, Pilnik-Czerniak, Buenos Aires 1941. **15...♕e7 16.♕g3 ♗e6 17.h4** 17.♗xc6!?. **17...h5** 17...♖ac8 18.h5 is annoying.

18.♗xc7

Restoring the material balance and keeping the pressure.

18...♖hc8 19.♗d6 ♕d8 20.♔b1 a6?!

Black should have kept the knight on the board in order to cover the dark squares on the kingside: he is slightly worse after 20...♘e7! 21.♗e2 ♖c6 22.♗e5 ♖ac8 23.♖d2 ♘g8.

21.♗xc6 ♖xc6 22.♗e5 ♖ac8 23.♖d2 b5 24.♕f4 a5 25.♖h3 b4 26.♖g3

Everything is set up for ♕h6.

26...♗d7

White keeps the initiative after 26...bxa3!? 27.♕h6 a2+ 28.♔xa2 ♕g8 29.♔b1.

27.a4

27...♖c3!?

Finding a very interesting defensive resource! 27...♖e6.

28.♕h6!

Of course not 28.bxc3? bxc3 29.♖e2 ♕b6+ 30.♔c1 ♕b2+ 31.♔d1 ♖c4! 32.♕g5 ♕a1+ 33.♕c1 ♖xa4 34.♗f4 ♕b2! and Black is better.

28...♖xg3 28...♕g8? 29.bxc3 bxc3 30.♖e2+−. **29.♕g7+ ♔e6 30.fxg3 ♗e8** 30...♕g8? 31.♕f6 mate.

31.g4! ♕xh4?

The decisive mistake! After the correct 31...hxg4 32.h5! ♕e7! (32...gxh5 33.♕h6+ ♔f7 34.♖f2) 33.♕xe7+ ♔xe7 34.h6 ♗xa4 35.g3 (35.h7 e3 36.♖e2 f4 37.h8♕ ♖xh8

38.♗xh8 ♔e6 and the ending is not clear: 39.g3?! g5 40.♗e5? f3−+) 35...g5 36.h7 f4 37.gxf4 gxf4 38.♗xf4 ♖h8 39.♖h2 ♔f7 40.♗e5 g3! Black holds the draw.

32.gxf5+ gxf5 33.♕h6+ ♔f7 34.♕g7+ ♔e6 35.♕h6+ ♔f7 36.♖f2!

Now it's all over.

36...♗d7 36...♕xf2 37.♕f6+ ♔g8 38.♕g7 mate. **37.♕g7+ ♔e6** 37...♔e8 38.♗f6+−. **38.♕g6+ ♔e7 39.♕d6+ ♔e8 40.♗f6**

Black resigned.

☐ **Francesco Bentivegna**
■ **Milan Drasko**
Cutro 2005

1.e4 e6 2.d4 d5 3.♘c3 ♗b4 4.♘e2 dxe4 5.a3 ♗xc3+ 6.♘xc3 ♘c6 7.♗b5

Black equalizes after 7.d5 exd5 (7...♘ce7?! 8.♕g4!) 8.♕xd5 ♘ge7 9.♕xd8+ ♘xd8 10.♘xe4 ♗f5 11.♗d3 (11.♗b5+ ♘dc6 12.f3 0-0-0 13.0-0 ♘d4) 11...♘e6 12.♗d2 0-0-0 13.0-0-0 ♘d4!? (13...♗g6) 14.♔b1 ♘ec6, Zelcic-Psakhis, Batumi 1999.

7...♘e7 8.♗g5 f6 9.♗e3 0-0

Indisputably Black's best reply.

10.♕d2

Not good is 10.♘xe4? f5 11.♘g5 f4 12.♗d2 ♕d5! 13.♗xc6 ♘xc6 14.♘f3 ♘xd4

15.♘xd4 ♕xd4∓, Dragicevic-Höggström, Sweden 2007/08.

10...a6!?

This logical move, forcing White to define the future of the light-squared bishop, appears to be an excellent alternative to the mainstream 10...e5, which is considered Black's safest choice by modern theory.

11.♗xc6

Objectively speaking Black doesn't face any problems once White gives up the light-squared bishop, however 11.♗c4!? is also hardly sufficient for an advantage: 11...♔h8 12.0-0-0 e5 13.d5 ♘a5 14.♗a2 ♗g4 15.b4 ♗xd1 16.♖xd1 f5 17.g3 b6 18.bxa5 ♕d6 19.♔b2, Rogulj-Pfeifer, Venice 2005.

11...♘xc6 12.0-0-0

12.♘xe4 e5 with an equal position, Gipslis-Casper, Jurmala 1987.

12...b6 13.♘xe4 ♗b7 14.f3

14...♕d7

Both sides have just one weakness: White's pawn on d4 versus the black one on e6. Neither White or Black have an active plan to improve their position, so it's mostly about manoeuvring and... more manoeuvring!

– 14...♖f7 15.♕f2 ♖d7 16.h4 ♕f8 17.h5 ♖ad8?! (17...h6) 18.h6 g6 19.♕h4 ♖f7 20.g4±, Moussard-L.Roos, Pau 2008.

– 14...♕e7 15.♕c3 ♖ad8 16.h4 ♕f7 17.h5 h6 18.b3 f5 19.♘d2 f4 20.♗f2 ♖d5 unclear, Vujadinovic-Holzke, Budapest 1991.

15.♖he1 ♖ad8 16.♕e2

16.♗f2 ♕f7 17.♕e2 ♖d7 18.♘c3 ♖fd8 19.♕xe6 ♘xd4 20.♗xd4 ♖xd4 21.♖xd4 ♖xd4 22.♕e8+ ♕xe8 23.♖xe8+ ♔f7 was equal in the game Hector-Casper, Germany Bundesliga 2001/02.

16...♖fe8 17.♔b1 ♕f7 18.♖d2

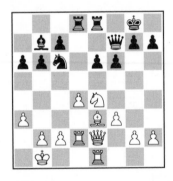

18...♖e7!?

Black is not satisfied with a draw, which would be most likely result after the thematic 18...e5, so he keeps on regrouping his pieces, hoping to outplay White later on (in which he eventually will succeed!).

19.♖ed1 ♖ed7 20.♗f2 ♘e7!? 21.♘c3

21.h4, gaining some aggression on the kingside in order to force Black to push the liberating ...e5, deserved attention: 21...♘g6 22.g4 e5 23.dxe5 ♘xe5 24.♗g3 equal.

21...♘g6 22.♗g3 h5 23.h3?!

A minor concession, which eventually costs White the game! There was no need to allow Black to push ...h4.

23.h4 ♘e7 24.♗f2 intending 24...♘f5 25.g4 with a slightly better position.

23...h4 24.♗h2 ♘e7 25.♕e1 ♘f5∓ 26.♗g1 ♖e7 27.♗f2 ♕h5 28.♖e2 ♖de8 29.♘e4 a5 29...♗d5!?. **30.c4**

Not a bad idea, but it was also possible just to sit and wait...

30...♗a6 31.♕c3 31.♖c2. **31...♕g6 32.♔a1 ♖d8 33.♖ed2 ♖ed7**

34.♗e1?!

It was about time for White to force a change in the pawn structure and get some fresh air for his pieces: 34.d5!? exd5 35.cxd5 ♔h7 36.♕c2 ♗b7 37.♘c3 and chances are even.

34...♗b7 35.b3?

Cracking under the pressure. White obviously underestimated the transfer of the black queen to f4.

35.♗f2 ♕h6 36.♕b3 ♕f4 37.d5 ♔h7∓.

35...♕h6!∓ 36.♗f2 36.♔b2 ♘e3 37.♖c1 f5∓. **36...♕f4!**

The knight has no place to retreat to...

37.♕c2 c5 38.dxc5?

The last chance to put up some resistance was 38.d5 exd5 39.cxd5 ♗xd5 40.♘c3 ♗c6 41.♖xd7 ♖xd7 42.♖xd7 ♗xd7 43.♔b2.

38...♗xe4−+ 39.♖xd7 ♗xc2 40.♖xd8+ ♔h7 41.♖1d2 ♗xb3 42.cxb6 ♕xc4

43.♔b2 ♗a4 44.♔a1 ♕c1+ 45.♔a2 ♗c2 White resigned.

□ **Slavik Sarhisov**
■ **Michael Tscharotschkin**
Neuhausen 2007

1.e4 e6 2.d4 d5 3.♘c3 ♗b4 4.♘e2 dxe4 5.a3 ♗xc3+ 6.♘xc3 ♘c6 7.♗b5 ♘e7 8.♗g5 f6 9.♗e3 0-0 10.♕d2 e5

As I mentioned in the comments to the previous game this move is Black's most popular response.

11.d5!?

Since the endgame arising after 11.dxe5 is perfectly safe for Black, White has to enter a long forced line in order to fight for an opening advantage: 11...♕xd2+ 12.♗xd2 ♘xe5 (12...f5 13.♗c4+ ♔h8 14.♘b5 ♘xe5 15.♘xc7 unclear, Gipslis-Toshkov, Jurmala 1987) 13.0-0-0 (13.♘xe4 ♗f5 14.f3 ♗xe4 15.fxe4 ♘c8! 16.0-0-0 ♘d6 17.♗d3 ♖fe8 18.♖he1 ♖e6 19.♗f4 ♖ae8∓ Gipslis-Knaak, Berlin East 1988) 13...c6 (13...f5 14.♗g5 ♘7g6 15.♘d5 c6 16.♘c7 ♖b8 17.♗a4 c5 18.h4 with compensation, Kovalev-Ulibin, Simferopol 1988) 14.♗a4 ♗e6 15.♘xe4 b5 16.♘c5 ♗c4 with equality in Hector-Müller, Hamburg 2001.

11...♘d4 12.♗xd4 12.♗c4!?. **12...exd4**

13.♕xd4 ♘f5

14.♕xe4!?

I believe this is the most challenging move, however the cunning 14.♕b4!?, once employed by Hertneck, deserves attention: 14...♘d6 15.0-0-0 ♗f5 (perhaps 15...f5!? is more in the spirit of the position, but Black looks rather safe after the text, too) 16.h4 a6 17.♗e2 ♗d7 18.h5 h6 19.♖d2 ♖fe8 20.♘d1 ♗g4 21.♗xg4 ♕xg4 22.♘e3 and White managed to get a minimal advantage in Hertneck-Uhlmann, Austria 2000/01.

14...♘d6

Black doesn't succeed in equalizing after the natural 14...c6: 15.♗e2 ♖e8 16.♕d3 cxd5 17.0-0-0 d4!? (17...♗e6?! 18.♗g4 ♕d6 19.♘xd5 ♖ad8 20.♖he1 ♕xd5 21.♕xd5 ♗xd5 22.♖xe8+ ♖xe8 23.♖xd5±, Müller-Holzke, Hamburg 1990) 18.♗g4 (18.♗f3!?) 18...♘e3! 19.fxe3 ♗xg4 20.♕c4+ ♗e6 21.♕xd4 (21.♕b4!?) 21...♕a5 22.h4 ♖ac8 23.♕b4 ♕xb4 24.axb4 ♗f5 25.♖d5 ♗e4 26.♖d2± ½-½, Spiess-Jörgens, Germany 1997/98.

15.♕a4

The only move. After 15.♕f3?! ♘xb5 16.♘xb5 ♖e8+ 17.♔f1 c6 18.dxc6 bxc6 19.♖d1 ♕e7 it was White who had to show some accuracy to keep the balance in Klinger-Lamoureux, Gausdal 1986.

15...♘xb5 16.♕xb5 ♖e8+

17.♔d2

It is necessary to coordinate the rooks. White has also tried 17.♔f1 and even succeeded to get a slight edge, but that was mostly due to Black's passive play: 17...♕e7 (17...♗f5!?) 18.♖d1 ♗d7 19.♕c4 ♔h8 20.f3 a6 21.♕d4 ♖ad8 22.♔f2, Sahm-Rosenberger, Germany 2002/03.

17...c6 18.♕b3!?

This move shouldn't be sufficient for an advantage, but at least White doesn't have to worry about his king! More ambitious is 18.♕c5!?, leading to double-edged play in which Black retains excellent compensation for the sacrificed pawn: 18...♗e6 (18...cxd5 19.♖ad1 ♗e6 20.♔c1 ♗f7 21.♖d2 b6 22.♕d4 ♕d6 23.h3 ♖ad8 24.♖hd1±, Vujadinovic-Gavric, Kladovo 1991) 19.d6 b6 20.♕d4 c5 21.♕f4 ♖b8 22.♖ad1 b5 23.b4 (or 23.♘e4 b4 24.a4 ♕a5 25.♖he1 c4 26.♖e3 ♗f5 27.♘g3 c3+, Costantini-Naumkin, Montecatini Terme 2002) 23...♕b6 24.♖he1 a5 25.♖e3 ♖bd8 26.♔e1 cxb4 27.axb4 ♗c4, Zlochevskij-Naumkin, Moscow 2002.

18...♗e6

18...cxd5?! 19.♖ad1 ♗e6 20.♔c1 d4 21.♕a4 and White is slightly better.

19.♖ae1?! The rook belongs on d1! 19.♖ad1 ♗xd5 20.♘xd5 ♕xd5+ 21.♕xd5+ cxd5 22.♖he1 ♔f7 and Black should be able to draw the ending easily.

19...♕d7

Playing on the safe side, however White wasn't really thtreatening to take on b7, so it was a bit more accurate to take on d5: 19...cxd5!? 20.♔c1 (20.♕xb7? d4) 20...♕d6 with counterplay.

20.♔c1 cxd5

There was nothing wrong with 20...♗xd5 21.♘xd5 ♕xd5 22.♕xd5+ cxd5 23.♔d2 ♔f7 and Black is just in time to protect d5 with the king.

21.♕b5!?

21...♖ad8?!

A bad strategic decision, after which White enjoys a very comfortable advantage. Better was 21...♕d6.

22.♕xd7 ♖xd7 23.♘b5 a6 24.♘d4 ♗f7 25.♖xe8+ ♗xe8 26.♖e1 ♗f7 27.♔d2 ♔f8 28.♖e3! Heading for b6.
28...g6 29.♖b3 ♖c7 30.♖b6 ♔e7 31.♘b3?!

The knight is perfectly placed on d4, so there was no reason to transfer it to a5!
31.♔d3 ♗e8 32.♖e6+ ♔f7 33.c3±.

31...♗e6 32.♘a5 ♗c8 33.c3 ♖d7 34.♔e3 ♖d6 35.♖xd6 ♔xd6

The endgame is just equal, although White could have tried a bit harder than he did in the game.

36.b4 b6 37.♘b3 ♗d7 38.♔d4 ♗a4 39.♘c1 39.♘d2. **39...♗b5 40.♘b3 ♗f1**

41.g3 ♗c4 42.♘d2 ♗e2 43.♔e3 ♗d1 44.♔d4 ♗e2 45.♔e3
Draw.

□ **Jonny Hector**
■ **Ivan Farago**
Hamburg 2004

1.e4 e6 2.d4 d5 3.♘c3 ♗b4 4.♘e2 dxe4 5.a3 ♗xc3+ 6.♘xc3 ♘c6 7.♗b5 ♘e7 8.♗g5 f6 9.♗e3 0-0 10.♕d2 f5!?
Another possible reply, leading to interesting strategic play.

11.0-0-0 a6

11...♘d5?! 12.♘xd5 exd5 13.♗xc6 bxc6 14.♗f4 ♗e6 15.h4 ♖b8 16.♕a5 ♖b7 17.♕a6±, Turner-Quillan, England 2007/08.

12.♗xc6 ♘xc6 13.♗g5 ♕d7

14.d5!?

It's hard to come up with anything better than the text-move.

14.♗f4 ♘e7 15.f3 exf3 16.gxf3 b5 17.♖hg1 ♗b7∓, V.Gurevich-Dimitrov, Werfen 1990. 14.f3 exf3 15.gxf3 e5! 16.d5 ♘d4 17.♕g2 f4∓.

14...exd5

It's a bit dangerous for Black to play 14...♘e5, but it seems that 14...♘e7 is perfectly safe.

– 14...♘e5?! 15.f3 ♘f7 16.fxe4 ♘xg5

17.♕xg5 fxe4 18.♖hf1, Kolev-Matamoros, Lanzarote 2003.

– 14...♘e7 15.dxe6 ♕xe6 16.f3 h6 17.♗xe7 ♕xe7 18.fxe4 fxe4 19.♖he1 ♗e6=, Westerinen-Thompson, Gausdal 2006.

15.♘xd5 ♕f7 16.♗f4 ♗e6?!

Black is easily equalizing after 16...♖d8! 17.♗xc7 ♖d7 18.♗f4 b5 (he might even try 18...♔h8!? if he's up for more than plain equality) 19.♕c3 ♖xd5 20.♕xc6 ♗b7 21.♕b6 ♖e8.

17.♘xc7 ♖ad8 18.♕c3 ♖c8

White obtained a slight edge after 18...♗c8 19.b3 ♕e7 20.b4 ♕h4 21.g3 ♕e7 22.h4 ♖xd1+ 23.♖xd1 ♖d8 24.♖xd8+ ♕xd8 25.♕c4+, Midoux-Roos, Gonfreville 2006.

19.♘xe6 ♕xe6 20.♖d6 ♕a2

21.♖hd1

Control over the d-file and remote prospects of getting an ♖ + ♗ versus ♖ + ♘ endgame indicate that White is firmly in control, although Black's position remains quite safe.

21...♖cd8

21...♖fe8!? 22.♖d7 ♖e7 23.♖1d5 (23.♗g5?? ♕a1+−+) 23...♕a1+ 24.♔d2 ♕f1 25.♕g3 ♖ce8 with counterplay.

22.b4 ♖xd6 23.♖xd6 ♕f7?!

Allowing White to start active operations on the queenside.

23...♖f7!? 24.♕b3 ♕xb3 25.cxb3 ♔f8=.

24.♔b2 h6 25.a4! ♖e8 26.b5 axb5 27.axb5 ♘d8 28.♗d2 ♘e6 29.♕c4 ♔h7 30.♗b4

White has definitely succeeded in making progress on the queenside, however Black should be able to hold.

30...♕g6 31.g3 ♕f6+ 31...h5? 32.♕d5±. 32.♗c3 ♕f7 33.g4!

Hector continues to pose problems on every move, and finally gets rewarded.

33.♕d5 ♖e7.

33...♖e7

33...g6 34.gxf5 gxf5 35.♕d5 ♖e7 36.h4±.

34.gxf5 ♕xf5 35.♖d5 ♕xf2 35...♖c7 36.♖xf5 ♖xc4 37.♔b3 ♖c7 38.♖e5 ♘g5 39.h4 ♘h3 40.♗d4±. 36.♕xe4+ ♔g8 37.♖d8+ ♔f7 37...♘xd8 38.♕xe7 ♕f8 39.♕d7!±. 38.♖c8 ♕f4? 38...♕f1!. 39.♕d3 39.♕xf4+ ♘xf4 40.♗b4 ♖e4 41.♖c7+ ♔e6 42.♗d2±. 39...♕f2?? 39...♘c7. 40.♗b4

Black resigned.

CHAPTER 8

Glenn Flear

Grabbing a Pawn in the Réti/Catalan

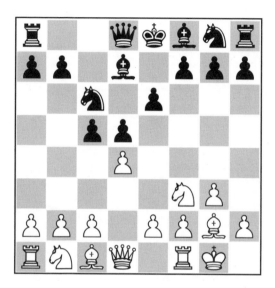

The unspectacular 5...♗d7

I once read and accepted that a reversed King's Indian Defence is OK for Black, but a reversed Grünfeld is unwise, but I no longer agree with the second of these views.

After 1.♘f3 d5 2.g3 c5 3.♗g2 ♘c6 4.d4 (a reversed Grünfeld) Black needs to find a method of deploying his pieces where White's extra tempo has little impact. So I suggest that he continues 4...e6 5.0-0 ♗d7. Now this move is definitely not the usual fare of SOS articles, where something dramatic usually happens when you least expect it. However, the thinking behind this 'modest little move' fits in nicely. By playing 5...♗d7 Black is egging White on – *Well if you don't get a move on I'm going to calmly develop my*

pieces! – and a number of white players then realise that the only way to test Black is to play 6.c4, whereupon Black grabs a pawn... 6...dxc4 7.♘a3 cxd4 8.♘xc4 ♗c5

This position becomes reminiscent of a well-known line of the Catalan, where Black has usually played ...♘f6 instead of ...♗d7. In our 'anti-Réti system' Black takes advantage of this difference by often playing his king's knight to e7 where it blocks any problems along the a3-f8 diagonal.

It turns out that in a number of lines White's compensation for the pawn is hardly convincing and even some experienced GMs playing White have found themselves with a disadvantage after the opening.

Here is how it all fits together...

1.♘f3 d5 2.g3 c5 3.♗g2 ♘c6 4.d4 e6 5.0-0 ♗d7 6.c4

Other moves suggest that White isn't particularly interested in using his extra tempo, e.g.:

– 6.b3 Black no doubt has many possible set-ups, but one reasonable one is 6...♖c8 7.♗b2 cxd4 8.♘xd4 ♘f6, when White has no pressure at all.

– 6.c3 ♖c8 7.♗e3 cxd4 8.cxd4 ♘f6 with equality or 8...♕b6!?.

– 6.a3 cxd4 7.♘xd4 ♘f6 8.♘c3 ♘xd4 9.♕xd4 ♗c6 10.b4 ♗e7 11.♗b2 b6 was equal in Janov-Wehmeier, Bundesliga 2002.

6...dxc4!

7.♘a3

The thematic and most popular move, but maybe not the best. Here are White's other options:

● 7.d5?! exd5 8.♕xd5 ♗e6 is already easy-going for Black.

● 7.♘c3 ♘f6 8.♗g5 (White soon got into a mess after 8.♗f4 ♖c8 9.♘b5 ♕b6 10.♘a3 ♕a6 11.♘e5 c3 12.♘ac4 b5 in Begun-Kapengut, Minsk 1981) and now 8...♗e7 9.♗xf6 ♗xf6 10.dxc5 ♗xc3 11.bxc3 0-0 12.♖b1 ♕c7 13.♕d6 favoured White in Haik-L.Roos, Rouen 1987, but Black should vary on move eight, e.g. 8...♕b6 9.♘a4 ♕a5 10.♘xc5 ♗xc5 11.dxc5 ♕xc5 12.♖c1 b5!? with equal chances.

● 7.dxc5 ♗xc5 8.♘bd2 (8.♘c3 ♘f6 9.♗g5 looks to be nothing special after 9...♗e7) and now:

– 8...♘a5 (risky) 9.♘e4 ♗e7 10.♘d6+ (10.♘e5 ♘f6 11.♘d6+ ♗xd6 12.♕xd6 ♗c6 13.♗xc6+ ♘xc6 14.♘xc4 ♘d4! 15.e3 ♘f5 16.♕b4 ♕e7=) 10...♗xd6 11.♕xd6 ♗c6 12.♕a3! b5 13.♗f4 ♘e7?! (13...♘b7! 14.♖fd1 ♕a5! 15.♕xa5 ♘xa5 16.♗d2 ♘b7 17.a4 bxa4 18.♘e5 ♗xg2 19.♔xg2 ♘f6 20.♖xa4 gives White a workable edge) 14.♖fd1 ♕b6, Lengyel-Skrobek, Warsaw 1979, looks bad for Black after 15.♗d6!±.

– 8...♘f6 9.♘xc4 0-0 10.♘fe5 (perhaps 10.♗g5 is better, for example 10...♖c8 11.♘d6 ♗xd6 12.♕xd6 ♘e4 13.♗xd8 ♘xd6 14.♗g5±) 10...♘xe5 11.♘xe5 ♗b5=, Rachela-Janos, Slovakia 2008.

– 8...c3!? 9.♘e4 ♗e7 10.♘xc3 (10.bxc3

♕c7 11.♘d4 a6=) 10...♘f6 (±/=) 11.♕b3
♕c7 12.♘b5 ♕b8 13.♗g5 0-0 14.♖fd1 ♖d8
15.♖ac1 e5 16.♘c3 ♗e6 17.♖xd8+ ♗xd8
18.♕b5 ♕c7=.

My feeling is that Black's route to equality is
longer and harder (than in the main line) after 7.dxc5 ♗xc5 8.♘bd2.

7...cxd4 8.♘xc4 ♗c5

9.♗f4

Here 9.e3 has been tried on a couple of occa-
sions: 9...♘f6 10.♘xd4:

– 10...♗xd4 11.exd4 0-0 12.b3 b5 (Black
was solid after 12...♘d5 13.♗a3 ♘ce7
14.♖e1 ♗c6 15.♖c1 ♖c8 16.♕d2 ♖c7 in
Pigusov-Kortchnoi, Smolensk 2000)
13.♘e3 (more active is 13.♘e5 ♘d5 14.♖e1
♖c8 15.♕g4!?) 13...♖c8 14.d5 ♘xd5
15.♘xd5 exd5 16.♕xd5 ♘b4 17.♕h5 ♖e8
18.♗d2, Jakobsen-Portisch, Raach zt 1969,
and now 18...♗g4 19.♕xg4 ♕xd2 20.♖ad1
♕c3 21.♖d7 a5 22.a3 ♘d3 is equal.

– How about 10...0-0!? 11.♘xc6 ♗xc6
12.♗xc6 bxc6, where Black may have a bro-
ken structure but the move e2-e3 rather com-
plicates White's development, so Black
should be fine, e.g. 13.b3 ♘e4 14.♕c2 ♕d5
15.♖d1 (possibly 15.f3 ♘d6 16.♖d1 ♕xf3
17.♖xd6 ♗xd6 18.♘xd6 ♖fd8 19.♗a3
♕xe3+ 20.♕f2 ♕xf2+ 21.♔xf2 a5∞; but
not 15.♗b2? ♘g5) 15...♕f5 16.♗b2
♘xg3!=.

9...♘ge7

Dubious is 9...f6?!, due to 10.♗d6! b6 11.b4!
♘xb4 12.♘xd4±, Kadar-Kiss, Hungary
2009.

10.♗d6

Less critical is 10.♘d6+ ♗xd6 11.♗xd6
♕b6 12.b4 a5 13.♗c5 ♕a6 14.bxa5 ♕xa5
15.♗xe7 ½-½, Soppe-Z.Varga, Lodi 2006.

10...♗b6

Black has a big hole on d6, but is this really a
problem? White will have to work to regain
the pawn, and this gives Black the time he
needs to get his king into safety.

11.b4

Two other moves have been tried here:

– 11.♕b3 0-0 12.♘xb6 axb6! (better than
12...♕xb6 13.♕xb6 axb6 14.♖fd1 ♖fc8
15.♘xd4±) 13.♖fd1 e5! (a neat liberating
move that relies on tactics against White's
queen) 14.♘xe5 (14.♗xe5 is well met by
14...♘xe5 15.♘xe5 ♗a4∓) 14...♗e6
15.♗xe7 ♗xb3 16.♗xd8 ♗xd1∓, Yande-
mirov-A.Sokolov, Elista 1995. That game
continued with 17.♘xc6 bxc6 18.♗xb6 ♗xe2
19.♗xd4 ♖fd8 20.♗xc6 ♖ac8 21.♗b6 ♖d6
22.♗b7 ♖c2 23.♗e3 ♖xb2, and White eventually scraped a draw in the endgame.

– 11.♗a3 0-0 12.♘xb6 ♕xb6 13.♗xe7 ♘xe7
14.♕xd4 ♕xd4 15.♘xd4 e5 16.♘b3, when a
draw was agreed in Murshed-Rahman, Dhaka
2007, as 16...♗c6 is totally balanced.

**11...♘f5 12.a4 ♗c8! 13.♗f4 ♘xb4
14.g4 ♘d5!∓ 15.♗g5**

15...♘fe7

Otherwise 15...f6!?, mentioned by Avrukh, is interesting: 16.♗c1 (16.gxf5 fxg5∓) 16...♘fe7 17.♘xb6 ♕xb6 seems to leave Black on top.
16.♘xb6 axb6

Here 16...♕xb6 17.♖b1 ♕a6 18.♘xd4 0-0 is playable, albeit slightly precarious-looking, but 19.♘b5 probably gives White enough play.
**17.♕xd4 f6 18.e4 fxg5 19.exd5 0-0
20.dxe6 ♗xe6 21.♖fe1 ♘c6 22.♕xd8
♘xd8 23.h3 h6 24.♘e5**

Khalifman-Dokuchaev, Maikop 1998, and White managed to hold.

There follow a couple of my own games where in the notes I delve a little deeper into the main line.

☐ **Arkadij Rotstein**
■ **Glenn Flear**
Port Barcarès 2005

**1.♘f3 d5 2.g3 c5 3.♗g2 ♘c6 4.d4 e6
5.0-0 ♗d7 6.c4 dxc4 7.♘a3 cxd4
8.♘xc4 ♗c5 9.♗f4 ♘ge7 10.♗d6 ♗b6
11.b4**

11...♘f5!

The best move. Instead, after 11...0-0?! 12.b5 ♘a5 13.♘xa5 ♗xa5 14.♘xd4 ♗c8 15.♘b3 ♗b6 16.♘c5 ♗c7 17.♘xc7 ♕xc7 18.♖c1, Löffler-Z.Varga, Austria 2008, Black had failed to solve his development problems.
12.b5?!

Here 12.g4! has been recommended and analysed by Akrukh:

12...♘xd6! (12...♘h4?! 13.♘xh4 ♕xh4 14.b5 ♘e7 15.♘xb6 axb6 16.♕xd4 ♘f5 17.♕xb6 ♘xd6 18.♕xd6 ♕xg4 19.a4! yields an advantage for White, as Black will have difficulty to complete his development) 13.♘xd6+ ♔e7!? (otherwise 13...♔f8 14.b5 ♘a5 15.♘e5 ♗e8 is plausible) 14.♘xb7 ♕c7 15.b5! (or 15.♘c5 ♗xc5 16.bxc5 e5 17.♕d2 ♖ad8, with double-edged play in prospect) 15...♘e5 (15...♕xb7? allows a

punishing pin with 16.♞e5) 16.♖c1 ♞xf3+ 17.♗xf3 ♕e5 isn't clear, for example 18.♕d2 ♖ac8 19.♕b4+ ♚f6! 20.h4 h6.
12...♞a5 13.♞xb6 axb6 14.♗b4 ♗xb5 15.g4 ♞e7 16.♞xd4 ♗c6 17.e4 e5

18.♗xe7?!
A slightly lesser evil is 18.♞f5, e.g. 18...♞xf5 19.gxf5 ♕xd1 20.♖fxd1 ♞c4 21.♗f1 ♖a4 22.a3 b5 23.f3 f6 24.♗d3 ♞b2∓, Sulava-Payen, Gonfreville 1999.
18...♕xd4 19.♕xd4 exd4
With the queens off the board, the position of Black's king is less worrying and the pawn deficit becomes a serious problem for White.
20.♗h4?!
Or after 20.♗b4 Black has 20...♞c4 21.♖fd1 ♖d8.
20...h5 21.g5

21...0-0
Even 21...d3 22.♖fd1 d2 is possible, e.g. 23.♖ab1 (23.♖xd2 ♞b3) 23...♞c4 24.♗f1 ♞e5!.
22.♖fd1 ♖fd8 23.g6 f6 24.e5 d3
Alternatively, 24...fxe5 25.♗xd8 ♖xd8 26.♖ac1 ♖d6 comes into consideration.
25.exf6 gxf6 26.♗xf6 ♖d6 27.♗g5 ♗xg2 28.♚xg2 ♞c4 29.♖ac1 b5 30.♖c3 d2 31.♖c2 ♖c8 32.♚g1 ♖d5!?
Or 32...♖xg6 33.h4 ♖f8 34.a4 ♖f4 35.♚h2 ♖xg5 36.hxg5 bxa4.
33.h4 ♖c6 34.♚h2 ♖e6 35.a4 ♖e1 36.♖dxd2 ♞xd2 37.♗xd2 ♖e2 38.♖c8+ ♚g7 39.♗c3+ ♚xg6 40.axb5 ♖xf2+ 41.♚g3 ♖c2 42.♖g8+ ♚f7 43.♖g7+ ♚f8 44.♗f6 ♖d3+ 45.♚f4 ♖f2+ 46.♚e4
46.♚e5 ♖xf6!.
46...♖xf6 47.♖xb7 ♖b3 48.♚d5 ♖f7 49.♖b8+ ♚g7 50.b6 ♖f4
White resigned.

□ **Carlos Nava**
■ **Glenn Flear**
San Sebastian 2004

1.♞f3 d5 2.g3 c5 3.♗g2 ♞c6 4.d4 e6 5.0-0 ♗d7 6.c4 dxc4 7.♞a3 cxd4 8.♞xc4 ♗c5 9.♗f4 ♞ge7 10.♗d6 ♗b6 11.a4 A new move!

11...0-0?!

Best is 11...♘f5! 12.♗a3 (12.b4 transposes to Khalifman-Dokuchaev, see above, when Black should opt for 12...♗c8!) 12...♗c7, with chances for both sides.

Inferior however is 11...f6?! 12.b4 (12.a5 ♘xa5 13.♘xa5 ♗xa5 14.♘xd4 is also promising) 12...e5 13.a5 ♗c7 14.b5 ♘b8 15.b6, and Black is in trouble.

12.a5?!

Here 12.♗a3 is no improvement, as both 12...♖c8 and 12...a5 seem fine.

However, 12.b4! ♗c7 13.b5 ♘a5 14.♘xa5 ♗xa5 15.♘xd4 is slightly better for White.

12...♗c7

13.♗xc7?!

This enables Black to obtain a comfortable game and retain some tension.

Instead, White should opt for 13.♘xd4 ♘xd4 14.♕xd4 ♘f5 15.♕c5 ♘xd6 16.♘xd6 ♗xd6 17.♕xd6 ♗c6, which looks rather dry.

13...♕xc7 14.♘xd4 ♘xd4 15.♕xd4 ♘f5 Otherwise 15...♗b5 16.♖fc1 ♖fd8 is about equal after 17.♕e5.

16.♕e4 Or 16.♕c3 ♖ac8=.

16...♗c6 17.♕e5 ♖ac8 18.e4?! An anti-positional move, as this pawn blocks the 'Catalan bishop'.

18...♕xe5 19.♘xe5 ♘d4 20.♘xc6 bxc6! I like this move. Voluntarily breaking one's owns pawns is counter-intuitive, but Black's superior activity is a more important factor.

21.e5?!

A more robust defence would have been possible with 21.f4 ♖b8 22.♖f2.

21...♖b8 22.♖a2 g5! 23.♖d1 ♖b4 24.a6 ♖fb8 25.♔f1 ♖8b5 26.♖c1 c5 27.♗b7

White has little to bite on, whereas Black can probe against several weaknesses.

27...♔g7

28.g4?

After 28.♔g2 c4 29.♖d1 ♘b3∓ 30.♖e1 ♘c5 something will have to be given (b2 or e5).

28...♘b3 29.♖c3 ♖xg4 30.♗c6 ♖bb4 31.h3 ♖gf4 32.♔g2 ♖b6 33.♗a4 ♘d2 34.♖c2 ♘f3 35.♖xc5 ♘e1+ 36.♔g1 ♖xa6 37.b3 ♘d3 38.♖b5 ♖c6 39.b4 ♖c1+ 40.♔g2 ♖fc4 41.♖a3 ♘f4+ 42.♔h2 ♖f1 43.♖f3 ♖cc1

White resigned.

CHAPTER 9

Dimitri Reinderman

Sicilian: Karma Chameleon

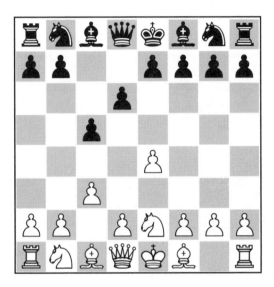

1.e4 c5 2.♘e2 d6 3.c3

When I was young, I often played the Chameleon Variation of the Sicilian, in which White, instead of ♘f3, plays ♘e2 on the second or third move.

The idea is that White can adapt to the environment: he can play the Closed Sicilian, for example if Black plays ...♘c6 and ...e6, but he can also play the Open Sicilian, which might be good if Black normally plays the Najdorf but has already put his knight on c6.

In those days I was often successful in tricking opponents in positions of my liking, but I got a bit bored with it, and so one day I wondered if I could play something different. What would happen when I moved the

knight from e2 to g3? I decided to try it out in the Dutch semi-finals and it was a big success: mate in 27 moves!

So the system I present in this article starts with 1.e4 c5 2.♘e2 d6 3.c3.

Like in the real Chameleon, there are different set-ups possible for White after this move. White can go for the centre and play d4, as in the game Nijboer-Stam.

White can also try to fianchetto his king's bishop, as in Ermenkov-Hmadi, but this does have a tactical problem.

In my game I used a setup with ♘g3, d3 and f4, putting the bishop on e2. If Black plays ...e5 though, the bishop can go to c4 (see Nijboer-Stam).

☐ **Dimitri Reinderman**
■ **Nico Kuijf**
Eindhoven 1989

1.e4 c5 2.♘e2 d6
After 2...♘c6 or 2...e6, 3.c3 would be less good because of 3...d5, but White can just play either 3.♘bc3 or 3.d4.
3.c3 ♘f6 4.♘g3 ♘c6

5.♗e2
5.d4 is possible here. Black has a lot of options, but one interesting variation is 5...h5 6.d5 h4 7.dxc6 hxg3 8.♗b5 gxf2+ 9.♔xf2 bxc6 10.♗xc6+ ♗d7 11.♗xa8 ♕xa8 when Black has enough compensation for the exchange. I avoided 5.d4 not because of this, but because I wanted to play with d3 and f4.
5...g6
The fianchetto is a logical reaction to the white system. In general in the Sicilian, when White doesn't play d4, the bishop is more active on g7 than it would be on e7.
6.d3 ♗g7 7.0-0 d5
Another idea would be to leave the situation in the centre as it is and play for ...b5-b4, just like in the Closed Sicilian.
But Black can also try to refute White's system by playing 7...h5. Since permitting ...h4-h3 is a bit unconfortable for White, 8.h4 is logical, but following this up with f4 would leave a nice square on g4 for the black knight.

White should probably leave the pawn on f2 and play ♘d2-f3 followed by d4 or ♘g5.
8.♘d2 0-0 9.f4

9...dxe4
Black was probably afraid of 10.e5 followed by ♘f3 and d4. Then Black has to play ...e6 (otherwise White will play f5), but this leaves the bishop on g7 badly placed. It isn't necessarily bad for Black, but it would be more like the French than the Sicilian.
10.dxe4
Exchanging on e4 was a small concession by Black though: after White plays e5 there will be nice squares for the knights on c4 and e4.
10...b6 11.♗f3 ♗b7 12.e5 ♘d5 13.♘c4 ♘c7 14.♕e1

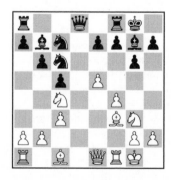

At that time I was very fond of the set-up f4, ♕e1 and ♕h4 against a kingside fianchetto,

often mating opponents quickly with it. I probably assumed I would mate my opponent now also, in at most 13 more moves or so...
14...b5 15.♘e3

15...♘a5?

White moves a knight to the centre, Black one away from it... Apart from general considerations, there is a concrete problem. White really would like to play f5, but say after 15...c4 16.♘e4 ♘e6 17.f5 gxf5 18.♘xf5 ♘xe5 the knight on e5 is a good defender. In the game the knight will be a bystander.
16.♘e4 ♘e6?

16...c4 is still stronger, though after 17.♕g3 the move f5 will be difficult to prevent.
17.f5 ♘c7

17...gxf5 18.♘xf5 ♔h8 19.♕h4 also gives White a winning attack.
18.f6?!

Pawns want to be pushed, but objectively 18.♕h4 is better, when there is no good defence for Black. For example 18...♘xe5 19.♘g5 h5 20.♗xh5 ♔g7 21.♗xg6 ♖h8 22.♗h7 and wins.
18...♗h8?

Black had some kind of defence here: 18...exf6 19.exf6 ♖e8 20.♕h4 ♗f8 after which White is better, but going for a quick mate doesn't work: 21.♘g4? ♖xe4 22.♗xe4 ♗xe4 23.♘h6+ ♗xh6 24.♕xh6 ♘e6−+.
19.♘f5

Now White gets to enjoy himself.

19...♖e8 20.♘h6+ ♔f8 21.♘xf7

Not difficult, but still nice to play!
21...♔xf7 22.♘g5+ ♔f8 23.♘xh7+ ♔f7 24.♘g5+ ♔f8 25.♕h4 ♗xf6 26.♗xb7 ♘xb7 27.♕h8

Mate.

□ **Friso Nijboer**
■ **Arno Bezemer**
Haarlem 1999

1.e4 c5 2.♘e2 d6 3.c3 ♘f6 4.♘g3 e5

Directed against 5.d4, at the cost of some white squares. Play will be a bit similar to the 1.e4 c5 2.♘f3 ♘c6 3.♘c3 e5 variation. Amongst the differences is that White can play f4 more easily.
5.♗c4

5.d4 is possible: Black probably intended something like 5...cxd4 6.cxd4 exd4 7.♕xd4 ♘c6 8.♗b5 ♗e7 9.0-0 0-0 with equality.
5...♘c6 6.d3

6...d5!?

Black as the underdog bravely goes for complications, while moves as 6.... ♗e7 or 6...g6 are perfectly reasonable.
7.exd5 ♘xd5 8.♕b3

Another idea is to play 8.♕f3 ♗e6 9.♘d2 to try to get knights on e4 and f5.
8...♘a5 9.♗b5+ ♗d7?!

Bezemer sacrifices a pawn, but does not get full compensation. Better is 9...♘c6 10.0-0 ♗e6 when White can spoil Black's pawn structure, but the weakness of d3 would compensate for that.

10.♕xd5 ♗xb5 11.♕xe5+ ♕e7 12.♕xe7+ ♗xe7 13.c4

13...♗d7

This looks a bit like 1.e4 d5 2.exd5 ♘f6 3.c4 e6 4.dxe6 ♗xe6 without queens and with better development for White.

14.♘c3 ♗e6 15.♗e3 0-0-0 16.0-0-0 ♘c6 17.♘ge2 ♖he8 18.♘f4 ♗f5 19.♘fd5 ♗f8 20.♖d2 b6

Black still has some compensation for the pawn because of the backward d-pawn and the pair of bishops, but his pieces aren't very active, so White easily consolidates.

21.h3 h6 22.♖hd1 g5 23.d4

The problem of the backward pawn is solved. Now Black only has the pair of bishops as compensation.

23...cxd4 24.♗xd4 ♘xd4 25.♖xd4 ♗c5 26.♖4d2

The normal strategy for bishops when fighting against knights is to push the knights away from good squares using pawns or pieces. In this case the knight on d5 cannot be attacked by pawns, and attacking it with pieces won't help since it's 'überdefended'.

26...♔b7 27.b4 ♗f8 28.♔b2 ♗g7 29.♔b3 ♗e6 30.♘b5

The general strategy when being a pawn up is to exchange a lot of pieces. In this case however, exchanging both rooks would be fine for Black if he can keep his bishops, but good for White if he can exchange one of his knights.

30...♗e5 31.a4 ♖d7 32.♘e3 ♖xd2 33.♖xd2 a6 34.♘d6+ ♗xd6 35.♖xd6

Mission accomplished. It's still not easy to win, but it feels like 'the rest is a matter of technique'.

35...b5 36.♘d5 bxc4+ 37.♔xc4

37.♔c3 is a good idea here, since 37...♗xd5 38.♖xd5 should be winning for White.

37...♖c8+ 38.♔d3 ♖c1

Now Black has some counterplay.

39.a5 ♖d1+ 40.♔e4 ♖e1+ 41.♔f3 ♖b1 42.♖b6+ ♔c8 43.♘e3 ♖b2 44.g4 ♔c7

45.♔g3 ♔d7 46.f4 ♖b3 47.♔f3 ♗d5+ 48.♔e2?

A mistake that could have cost White dearly – 48.♔f2!.

48...♗e4?

48...♗c6! 49.f5 ♗b5+ should draw.

49.f5 ♖b2+? 50.♔d1 h5 51.gxh5 ♗f3+ 52.♔c1 ♖b3 53.♘g4 ♗g2 54.h6 ♖xh3 55.h7

1-0.

☐ **Evgeny Ermenkov**
■ **Slaheddine Hmadi**

Tunis Interzonal 1985

1.e4 c5 2.♘e2 d6 3.c3 ♘f6 4.g3

4.♘g3 defends the pawn, but it is indirectly defended already, or is it? Well, after the text – not quite! Another way to defend the pawn is 4.f3. Putting pawns on c3 and f3 doesn't show much respects to the white knights, but in Muromtsev-Nalbandian, Alushta 2003, it turned out alright: 4.f3 g6 5.d4 cxd4 6.cxd4 ♗g7 7.♗e3 0-0 8.♘bc3 ♘c6 9.♕d2 e5 10.d5 ♘e7 11.g4!? ♘e8 12.♘g3 f5 13.gxf5 gxf5 and now 14.♘h5 would have been very nice for White.

4...♘xe4!

Black calls White's bluff!

5.♕a4+

There is an old game of two grandmasters, Tartakover-Stahlberg, Amsterdam 1950, where White tried to cut his losses and played 5.♗g2. Of course White doesn't have enough compensation for the pawn, but he did make a draw.

Playing a player with 230 rating points less, Ermenkov's move is a better practical choice and gives a very interesting position.

5...♗d7 6.♕xe4 ♗c6 7.♕e3 ♗xh1

So White is an exchange and a pawn down. However, the bishop is trapped in the corner after the next move and there's no easy way to get it out.

8.f3

♔e1-f2-g1xh1 is the threat.

8...g5

I do not think that White has enough compensation for the material deficit, but the problem for Black is that he cannot just consolidate, he has to fight for the advantage. Variations like 8...♘c6 9.d4 cxd4 10.♘xd4 h5 11.♔f2 h4 12.gxh4 e5 13.♔g1 ♕xh4 14.h3 ♗xf3 15.♘xf3 ♕g3+ or 8...♗d7 9.d4 g5 10.g4 h5 11.♘g3 hxg4 12.♘xh1 gxf3 13.♕xf3 cxd4 14.cxd4 ♗g7 look good, but aren't easy to calculate.

9.g4

The only way to prevent Black from liberating his bishop.

9...h5 10.♘g3

10...hxg4

Interesting is 10...♖h6!? threatening to win a queen. After 11.♗e2 ♗g2 12.♘xh5 White has good compensation for the exchange though.

11.♘xh1 ♕d7

11...gxf3 12.♕xf3 ♘c6 13.h3 ♕d7 is better for Black, since he's better developed. The game continuation is not bad, but more complicated.

12.fxg4 ♕xg4 13.♘f2 ♕g1 14.h3 ♖h6 15.♘e4 ♕h1 16.♘g3 ♕h2 17.♕f2 ♖e6+ 18.♘e2 ♕e5

After exchanging queens Black still would have an edge with his nice compact pawn structure.

19.d4 cxd4 20.cxd4

20...♕b5?

The wrong way: it was better to defend the

g-pawn by 20...♕g7 and then finish development.

21.♘c3 ♕d3 22.♘d5 ♘a6 23.♗xg5

White takes a pawn while developing.

23...♖c8 24.♖d1 ♕b5 25.♕f5

White is clearly better now.

25...♕xb2 26.♖d2 ♕a3 27.♖d3

27.♔f2! threatening 28.♘ef4 is very strong.

27...♕a5+ 28.♗d2 ♕xa2 29.♘f4 ♕b1+ 30.♔f2 ♗h6?

30...♘c5 31.dxc5 ♖xc5 32.♕g4 ♖ee5 is a better try.

31.♘xe6 ♗xd2 32.♘g7+

1-0.

□ **Friso Nijboer**
■ **Bart Stam**
Haarlem 1999

1.e4 c5 2.♘e2 d6 3.c3 g6

3...♘f6 is the natural move, but what happens if Black allows 4.d4?

4.d4 cxd4

I can understand that Black doesn't like 4...♗g7 5.dxc5 dxc5 6.♕xd8+ ♔xd8, but I would play 5...♘d7 here, so that White's queen's knight cannot go to c3.

5.cxd4 ♗g7 6.♘bc3 ♘f6 7.g3 0-0 8.♗g2

Now White has the centre and a smooth development, so he is a little better.

8...♘c6 9.h3 ♗d7 10.0-0 ♖c8 11.♗e3

White's next moves are easy: queen to d2, a rook to c1, king to h2. Black must move his queen to finish development, but whereto? At a5 she provokes a3 and b4, while after going to b6 or c7, ♘d5 might come. So Black keeps her at d8 and tries to win some space on the queenside.

11...a6 12.♕d2 b5 13.♔h2 ♕c7 14.♖fc1

'Which rook' is an eternal question. In this case the choice depended on which side of the board White wants to attack, and the queenside it is.

14...♕b8

At b8 the queen is safe from any attacks.

15.♘f4 b4

There is not much else Black can do (apart from waiting), but this move creates a target for White.

16.♘ce2 ♖fd8 17.♘d3 a5 18.a3

18...b3?

This loses a pawn. After 18...♕b5 White would only have a small advantage.

19.d5 ♘e5 20.♘xe5 dxe5 21.♗c5?

White probably didn't play 21.♕xa5 because of 21...♖c2, but after 22.♖xc2 bxc2 23.♖c1 ♖c8 24.♕b4 the pawn on c2 is not that dangerous.

21...a4?

Losing e7 is much worse than losing a5. Apart from that, after 21...♖e8 22.♕xa5 ♕b5 23.♕xb5 ♗xb5 24.♘g1 ♗h6 Black would have counterplay. In the game he gets none whatsoever.

22.♗xe7 ♖xc1 23.♖xc1 ♖c8 24.♖xc8+ ♕xc8 25.♕a5 ♘e8 26.♘c3

White is a pawn up and has a better position.

26...♗h6 27.♘xa4 ♕c2 28.♕a7
1-0.

As the games show, the system featured in this SOS doesn't offer much hope for a big advantage in the opening: after normal moves Black should be equal, and if Black gives White what he wants it's still only a small advantage. But it does give original positions and the possibility to 'play chess, not opening theory' without running big risks. So if you want something different against the Sicilian, why not try it out?

CHAPTER 10

Jeroen Bosch

The Centre Game in Viking Spirit

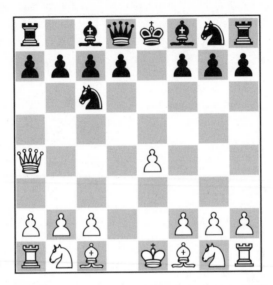

1.e4 e5 2.d4 exd4 3.♕xd4 ♘c6 4.♕a4

☐ **Dragoljub Velimirovic**
■ **Goran Todorovic**
Pula ch-YUG 1988

1.e4 e5 2.d4 exd4 3.♕xd4

3.♘f3 transposes to the Scotch, while 3.c3 would turn it into the Danish Gambit. We are concerned with the Centre Game, but we will give it a Scandinavian twist.

3...♘c6 4.♕a4

Compared to the Scandinavian (or the Centre Counter as it is sometimes called) White is a full tempo up (the pawn is on e4). As always you can argue whether it is a good thing to play a Black defence with White. The extra move has some significance, but

often Black will equalize as playing a black opening is often simply not ambitious enough when you are White.

Here I would suspect that given a certain amount of accuracy Black may obtain equal chances. However, that does not mean a sterile draw. After all White is playing rather ambitiously: having played both e4 and d4 – which enables him to develop freely, and, with the queen conveniently out of the way, queenside castling will be the rule rather than the exception. True, White has committed one sin: he has developed his queen early on in the game.

4.♕e3 is the absolute main line of the Centre Game. See our SOS weapon 4...♘b4 in SOS-12.

Instead, 4.♕d2 has been suggested by Bronstein. His idea was to continue with ♗d3, f4, ♘f3, 0-0, b3 and ♗b2. This has never gained any popular appeal. 4...♘f6 5.♗d3 d5 (Emms) is fine for Black.

4...♗b4+

Black develops with gain of time. The idea is that 5.c3 is awkward (the knight aims for this square), while 5.♘c3 is a self-pin.

5.♗d2

Worse is 5.♘d2 ♘f6 6.e5? ♕e7 7.f4 d6, and Black wins a pawn, keeping a good position, Kozel-Romanishin, Alushta 2005.

5...♕e7

Not wishing to accelerate White's development, but the queen is slightly vulnerable on e7 as we will see. Perhaps it was better to play 5...♗xd2+ 6.♘xd2 after all. When Black can either develop normally 6...♘f6 7.♗b5!? 0-0 8.♘gf3 when White is perhaps slightly better, or he can try the enterprising 6...♕f6!?.

6.♘c3 ♘f6 7.0-0-0

White has succeeded in developing his queenside first. He holds a pleasant plus in view of the threat of ♘d5.

7...0-0 7...♗xc3 8.♗xc3 0-0 9.f3 does not solve Black's problems. **8.♘d5 ♘xd5**
Here too Black could have considered taking on d2: 8...♗xd2+ 9.♖xd2 ♘xd5 10.exd5 ♘e5 (10...♕b4 11.♕xb4 ♘xb4 12.a3 ♘a6 13.d6±) 11.d6 cxd6 12.f4 ♘g6 13.♘f3±.

9.exd5

9...♕e4?

Black willingly enters huge complications, which will turn out unfavourably for him in the end. 9...♗xd2+ 10.♖xd2 ♘e5 transposes to the previous comment.

10.♗c3

White should also win with 10.c3 d6 11.cxb4 (11.♖e1!? ♕xd5 12.cxb4) 11...♗f5 12.♗c3, when Black can try to confuse the issue with 12...♘xb4! 13.♗xb4 a5, but 14.♗d3 ♕xg2 15.♗c3 ♗xd3 16.♕d4 still wins for White.

10...b5!?

Black loses after 10...♕f4+ 11.♔b1 ♕d6 12.♗e2 ♗xc3 13.dxc6 ♕b4? 14.♕xb4 ♗xb4 15.cxd7. **11.♗xb5 ♕xg2 12.♗xc6**
The desperado 12.♗xg7 is also strong. **12...dxc6** Or 12...♗xc3 13.♗xa8 ♕xh1 14.bxc3 ♕xh2 and now most accurate is 15.d6!. **13.♗xb4 ♖e8**

14.♘e2?! Velimirovic settles for a superior ending, or he may have overlooked Black's 15th move. Objectively it was stronger to play 14.♕xc6 ♗g4 15.f3. **14...♖xe2 15.♕xc6 ♕g6! 16.♕xg6 hxg6 17.♖d2** White is a pawn up, and his queenside preponderance counts for a lot. Still, the opposite-coloured bishops introduce drawing tendencies. **17...♗a6 18.♖xe2 ♗xe2 19.♖e1 ♗c4 20.♖d1 a5 21.b3!?** 21.♗c3 intending to attack the weak c7 pawn. **21...axb4?!** Better was 21...♗xb3 22.axb3 axb4 23.♖d4 ♖b8. **22.bxc4 ♖xa2 23.♖d3 ♖a1+** 23...♔f8 24.♔b1! ♖a6 25.♔b2. **24.♔b2! ♖f1 25.c5!** It's all about creating a passed pawn as soon as possible. **25...♔f8 26.d6 cxd6**

27.♖xd6! In this way the passed pawn is further away from the opponent's king, while the rook can cut off the king's approach. 27.cxd6 ♔e8 is merely equal. **27...♔e7** 27...♖xf2 28.c6 ♔e7 29.c7+−. **28.♖d2! ♖h1** 28...♖e1 29.♔b3. **29.♔b3 ♖xh2 30.♔xb4** White is winning. **30...g5** 30...♖h8 31.c6 ♖d8 is met by 32.♖d3! which is the only move that wins here. The rest is simple: **31.c6 ♖h8 32.♔c5 f5 33.c7 g4 34.♔c6 f4 35.♖d4 g5 36.♖d7+ ♔f6 37.♖d8** Black resigned.

After this inspiring game we will investigate the variation systematically.

Variation I – 4...♗c5 (4...g6, 4...d6)

1.e4 e5 2.d4 exd4 3.♕xd4 ♘c6 4.♕a4 ♗c5 Black develops the bishop without the check.

● An important alternative is a kingside fianchetto: **4...g6** The repertoire books of Nigel Davies and Mihail Marin both warmly recommend this line of play. **5.♘f3 ♗g7 6.♗g5 ♘ge7 7.♘c3** (shortening the diagonal with 7.c3 is passive but still equal: 7...0-0 8.♗b5 ♕e8 9.0-0 ♘e5, Mercier-Butler, Switzerland 1994. And now 10.♘xe5 ♗xe5 11.♘d2 or 11.♗h6 ♗g7 12.♗xg7 ♔xg7 13.♘d2 would have favoured White. However, more natural is Konikowski's 9...d6 10.♘bd2 ♗d7) **7...h6**: – **8.♗f4** Critical according to Marin in his excellent *Beating the Open Games* (Gambit 2007).

8...d6 (8...0-0?! 9.0-0-0± is Marin's verdict, who points out that White has pressure along the d-file) 9.e5!? (this is Marin's main line, but I would prefer castling queenside – the natural 9.0-0-0 ♗d7 is equal according to

Marin. This may well be true, but still the position is quite interesting after 10.♕b3 ♖b8 11.h4 b5 12.♘d5) 9...d5 (much simpler in my opinion is 9...dxe5 10.♗xe5 ♗xe5 11.♘xe5 0-0 12.♖d1 ♕e8, which 'offers reasonable chances of equalizing gradually' – Marin. Indeed, I agree there is not so much to play for here) 10.0-0-0 0-0 11.h4 (11.♗c4 ♗e6 12.♗b3 ♕d7! 13.♖he1 ♖fd8 14.h4 a6 15.♕a3 ♕e8 is equal according to Marin. White has to take care: a future ...♗f8 could be annoying; 11.♘e4 g5 12.♗g3 ♘f5 13.♘f6+ ♗xf6 14.exf6 ♘xg3 15.hxg3 ♕xf6 16.♖xd5 ♗e6 17.♖d1 ♖ad8 is also evaluated as equal by Marin) 11...♗g4 12.♗e2 a6 13.♗h2 h5 was equal in Hanghoj-Ingerslev, cr 1979. White now went wrong with 14.♘xd5?! ♘xd5 15.♕b3 ♘cb4 16.a3 c6∓. – Instead of 8.♗f4 White can also play 8.♗e3. Nikoliuk-Yanvarev, Moscow 1994, is often quoted as a problem for White, but things really aren't all that clear. It could be worth your while to investigate this move: 8...d6 9.0-0-0 ♗d7 10.♕b3 ♖b8 11.♘d5 0-0 12.h4 ♗g4

13.♗e2 (13.♘f4 or 13.h5!? ♗xh5 14.♖xh5 gxh5 15.♘f4, with compensation) 13...b5 14.♕d3 b4 15.♕d2? (only now White is more or less beyond saving; 15.♘f4!) 15...♘xd5 16.♕xd5 (16.exd5 ♕f6) 16...♕f6!. A strong sacrifice that cannot be

accepted. Nikoliuk went down after 17.♕xc6 ♕xb2+ 18.♔d2 ♗d7! 19.♕xd7 ♕c3+ 20.♔c1 ♕a3+ 21.♔d2 ♗c3+.

All in all, I think that White should either play 8.♗e3 and improve upon White's play in Nikoliuk-Yanvarev, or he should go for 8.♗f4 d6 and now 9.0-0-0 rather than 9.e5, when Black has several roads to equality. I don't want to claim an edge for White, but these positions with castling on opposite sides are interesting. You will certainly be better prepared than your opponent!

● Slightly passive is **4...d6**, but it is not illogical to place the bishop on d7 to annoy the intrepid queen. 5.♗b5 (5.♘c3 ♗d7 6.♘f3 is another idea, not fearing 6...♘e5?! 7.♕b3 ♘xf3+ 8.gxf3, when White is much better. Rather than 6...♘e5, Black should continue his development and keep the attack on the queen in reserve) 5...♗d7 6.♘c3 ♘f6 (6...a6!? 7.♗xc6 ♗xc6 8.♕d4 with about equal chances. White has space, Black has two bishops) 7.♗g5 ♗e7 8.0-0-0!? (8.♘f3) 8...0-0 9.f3 a6 10.♗xc6 ♗xc6 11.♕d4

11...♖e8 (11...♘d7 12.♗xe7 ♕xe7 13.♘ge2 ♕e5 is perhaps a tiny edge for White Lind-Wahlström, Gothenburg 2005) 12.h4?! (12.♘ge2? ♘xe4!; stronger is 12.♗e3!? and both sides have about equal chances) 12...h6 13.♗e3 ♘d7 14.h5 ♗f6 15.♕d2 ♘e5∓ 16.b3 b5 17.♘ge2 b4 18.♘d5 ♗xd5

19.♕xd5 a5 20.♔b1 a4 gave Black an attack in Resika-Lukacs, Budapest 2000.

5.♘f3

Krämer-Firmenich, cr 1965, is another game that one comes across when researching the literature on 4.♕a4. Presumably that is because Black was soon better after White allowed a queen sacrifice: 5.♘c3 ♘ge7 6.♗g5 (6.♘f3=) 6...0-0 7.♘d5 ♔h8 8.b4? (this is a blunder in view of Black's next) 8...♘xd5! 9.♗xd8 ♗xb4+ 10.c3 ♘xc3 11.♕b3 ♖xd8 and White is just lost, as ...♘xe4+ and ...♘xf2+ cannot be parried satisfactorily.

5...d6 6.♗b5

This is perhaps better than the other active bishop move: 6.♗g5 ♘f6 (also playable is 6...♘e7, when 7.♘c3 0-0 8.♘d5 – 8.♗b5 – 8...f6 9.♗e3 ♘xd5 10.♗xc5 dxc5 11.0-0-0 is about equal, Herman-Jimenez, Buenos Aires 2000) 7.♘c3 h6 8.♗h4 ♗d7 9.♗b5 a6 10.♗xc6 ♗xc6 11.♕c4

– 11...♕e7 12.0-0-0 0-0-0 13.♖he1. Now White has everything in order again. Chances are about equal: 13...♗b6?! (13...♕e6; 13...g5 14.♗g3 ♕e6) 14.♘d4 ♗xd4 15.♕xd4 ♕e5 16.♗xf6 ♕xf6 17.♕xf6 gxf6 18.♘d5 ♗xd5 19.♖xd5. The double rook ending is very pleasant, as Black has a fractured kingside structure. White won in Najer-Dervishi, Hania 1994.
– Much stronger is 11...g5! 12.♗g3 b5! 13.♕d3 b4! (13...♘xe4 14.♘xe4 ♕e7

15.♘e5! is not clear) 14.♘d5 ♘xd5 15.exd5 ♗b5 (just look at those powerful bishops!) 16.♕e4+ ♕e7 17.♕xe7+ ♔xe7 18.h4 f5 19.0-0-0 f4 20.♗h2 ♗xf2. This twice occurred in practice. Black won in Levi-West, Melbourne 2002, and in Bellon Lopez-Rivera, Santa Clara 1998. The grandmaster managed to draw by the skin of his teeth. A fair reflection of the actual chances. White has no compensation for his lost pawn here.

6...♗d7

7.0-0

It looks more accurate to develop the queen's knight first. See the next notes. In another game Lardot went for queenside castling: 7.♘c3 a6 8.♗xc6 ♗xc6 9.♕c4 ♘f6 10.♗g5 0-0 11.0-0-0 (11.0-0 is about equal and would transpose to the next note) 11...b5 12.♕d3 ♖e8 (12...h6 13.♗h4 b4 – 13...g5 14.♘xg5 hxg5 15.♗xg5 is too dangerous for Black – looks OK until you see 14.♘d5 g5 – 14...♗xd5 15.exd5± – 15.♘xg5! ♘xd5 – 15...hxg5 16.♗xg5 ♗xd5 17.exd5+– – 16.exd5 hxg5 17.♕g3!) 13.♘d4 ♗b7 14.♘f5 b4 15.♘d5 ♗xd5 16.exd5, and White is superior and won quickly after 16...♗xf2? 17.♖hf1 ♗b6 18.♘h6+ (18.♘xg7) 18...gxh6 19.♗xf6 ♗e3+ 20.♔b1 ♕d7 21.♖f3 ♗g5 22.♖g3 ♔f8 23.♖xg5 1-0, Lardot-Siljander, Kokkola 2000.

7...a6

The best move order for Black. Now the

queen cannot go to c4 after the exchange on c6. Therefore it would be natural for White to play 7.♘c3 rather than 7.0-0.

7...♘f6 8.♘c3 0-0 9.♗g5 a6 10.♗xc6 ♗xc6 11.♕c4 ♖e8 12.♖fe1 h6 13.♗h4 g5 14.♗g3 b5 15.♕d3 b4 16.♘d5 ♗b5 (16...♘xd5 17.exd5 ♗b5 18.c4 bxc3 19.♕xc3, with even chances) 17.c4 (all other moves favour Black) 17...♗d7?! (17...bxc3) 18.e5 ♘h5? (18...♘xd5 19.cxd5 ♗b5 20.♕f5) 19.exd6 cxd6 20.♖xe8+ ♗xe8 21.♖e1, with a strategically winning position, Lardot-Lehtosaari, Oulu 2002.

8.♗xc6 ♗xc6 9.♕b3

A pity but 9.♕c4? is not on in this move order, as 9...♗b5 wins an exchange.

9...♘f6 9...♘e7 10.♘c3 0-0 11.♗g5 ♔h8 12.♖ad1 f6 13.♗c1 ♘g6 14.♘d4 ♗xd4 15.♖xd4±, Nylund-Mayra, Finland 2006/07. **10.♘c3 ♕d7** 10...0-0 11.♗g5 h6 is more natural. **11.♗g5 ♕e6** 11...♘xe4 12.♘xe4 ♗xe4 13.♖fe1 f5 looks dangerous, but there is no clear refutation. Play is about equal. **12.♖fe1 ♕xb3 13.axb3 ♘g4 14.♗h4 f6 15.♖ad1 0-0 16.♘d4** with an equal game in Lardot-Mujunen, Tampere 2001.

Variation II – 4...♘f6

1.e4 e5 2.d4 exd4 3.♕xd4 ♘c6 4.♕a4 ♘f6

Perhaps the most natural response, Black does not commit his king's bishop yet. White can develop either knight now, or go for Najer's 5.♗g5 aiming for queenside castling.

5.♗g5

● An amusing miniature (known in the literature as Bronstein-NN, Sochi 1959) is: **5.♘c3 d5?! 6.♗g5! dxe4 7.♘xe4?! (7.♗b5!) 7...♕e7?! (7...♗b4+! 8.c3 ♕d4!** is a neat defence, when Black is actually slightly better!) **8.0-0-0**

8...♕xe4? (8...♗d7) 9.♖d8+! ♔xd8 10.♕xe4 and Black resigned.

Stronger is 5...♗b4, when 6.♗d2 0-0 7.0-0-0 ♖e8 8.f3 a6 9.g4 ♖b8 10.h4 b5 11.♕b3 d6 12.♗g5 was a typically exciting but unforced continuation in Nikoliuk-Mukhaev, Moscow 1994.

5...♗e7 6.♘f3 d6 7.♗f4 (7.e5 ♘g4 8.exd6 ♕xd6 9.♗f4 ♕c5=, Doncevic-Campos, Benidorm 1989) 7...0-0 8.♗e2 ♘g4 9.h3 ♗xf3 10.♗xf3 ♘d7 with approximately equal chances in Fedder-Rosenlund, Roskilde 1978.

● **5.♘f3** seems the least accurate reply. It's all about the squares e4 and d5 for the moment, and this knight move does not contribute to gaining influence on either of these central squares. **5...♗c5** (Black has other satisfactory methods as well: 5...d5 is now fully playable: 6.exd5 ♘xd5 7.♗e2 ♗e7 8.0-0 0-0 9.♖d1 ♘b6 was about equal in Zozulia-Goodger, Port Erin 2005; 5...♗b4+ 6.c3 – not 6.♗d2 as in the Velimirovic game, because of 6...♕e7! and White has problems defending e4 – 6...♗c5 7.♗d3 0-0 8.♗g5 h6 9.♗h4 d6 10.♘bd2 ♘e5 11.♘xe5 dxe5 12.♕c2 with even chances, Maciejewski-Twardon, Bydgoszcz 1979).

– 6.♗g5 and 6.♘c3 are most natural. Note that after 6.♘c3 White can ignore 6...♘g4 with 7.h3! as 7...♘xf2? leaves the knight trapped after 8.♖h2!.

– 6.♗b5?! ♕e7 7.♘c3 ♘e5 8.♘xe5 ♕xe5. This is quite pleasant for Black already. Prié now played too ambitiously with 9.f4 ♕e7 10.e5 0-0 11.♗e2 ♘g4 12.♗xg4? (12.♘d5 ♕d8) 12...♕h4+ 13.g3 ♕xg4 14.♕e4 d6 15.♘a4 ♗d7 16.♘xc5 ♗c6, and Black won in Prié-Relange, Nice 1994.

– 6.♗d3 d6 7.c3 ♗d7 8.♕c2 a5 9.♗g5 ♘e5 10.♘xe5 dxe5 11.0-0. White is effectively a tempo down on Maciejewski-Twardon. The game is still equal of course: 11...h6 12.♗h4 g5 13.♗g3 ♕e7 14.♘d2 ♘h5 15.♘c4 ♘f4 (15...♘xg3 16.hxg3 h5) 16.♘e3 ♗xe3 17.fxe3 ♘xd3 18.♕xd3 0-0-0 19.♕c4 f6 20.b4 (after a slow start the game suddenly gets exciting. Both sides need to attack, and the opposite-coloured bishops add excitement – for the moment) 20...axb4 21.cxb4

♗e6 22.♕c3 ♖d6? (22...♖hf8 was necessary – 23.b5) 23.♖xf6! ♕xf6 24.♗xe5 ♖c6 25.♗xf6 ♖xc3 26.♗xc3, and Ekström easily converted his edge in Ekström-Schaerer, Mendrisio 1988.

5...d6

● 5...h6 6.♗h4 ♕e7 7.♘c3 ♕b4!? 8.♕xb4 ♗xb4 9.0-0-0?! (stronger is 9.♗xf6 gxf6 10.♘e2, with a pleasant edge for White) 9...♗xc3 10.bxc3 d6 11.♗xf6 gxf6 12.♘e2 was equal in Ermenkov-Radev, Bulgaria 1975.

● 5...♗b4+ is a good response, as we have seen that after 4...♗b4+ White's best is 5.♗d2. 6.c3 ♗c5 7.♘f3 d6 8.♗b5 (8.♗d3=) 8...♗d7 9.♘bd2 a6 10.♗xc6 ♗xc6 11.♕c2 ♕e7, with an easy game for Black, Levi-Lane, Melbourne 2001.

● 5...d5 6.♘c3 transposes to the Bronstein miniature above.

● 5...♗e7 6.♘c3 0-0 7.♘f3 (7.0-0-0 ♘g4?! 8.♗xe7 ♘xe7 9.♕d4 d6 10.h3 ♘e5 11.f4 ♘5g6, and now it should be easy to improve upon 12.g4? ♘xf4 13.e5 ♘e6 14.♕f2 d5∓, Levi-Chapman, Melbourne 2000. White is better after 12.♕e3, 12.♕f2, 12.♕d2 or 12.g3) 7...d6 8.0-0-0 ♗d7 9.♕c4

and practice has demonstrated that the chances are equal:

– 9...♗e6 10.♕e2 ♘d7 11.h4 ♘de5 12.♘d5 ♗xd5 13.♗xe7 (13.exd5!?) 13...♘xe7

14.exd5=, Milev-Chipev, Sofia 1961.
– 9...h6 10.♗h4 ♗e6 11.♕e2 ♘d7 12.♗xe7
♕xe7 13.♘d5 ♕d8 (13...♗xd5 14.exd5
♘ce5=) 14.♕e3 ♖e8 15.♘c3 a6 16.♘d4
♘xd4 ½-½, Szabolcsi-Lukacs, Budapest
1994.

6.♘c3 ♗e7 7.0-0-0 ♗d7 8.f4!?
8.♗b5 would directly transpose to the note
to 4...d6 in the previous main game.

8...a6 9.♗xf6
More or less forced, but White certainly has
a nice space advantage in return for the
bishop pair.
9.♘f3?! b5 10.♕b3 ♗e6 11.♘d5 ♘xe4 was
the point of 8...a6.

9...♗xf6   10.♘d5   0-0   11.♘f3   b5
12.♕b3

Chances are (again) about equal. As I mentioned in the introduction, the Centre Game
with 4.♕a4 objectively promises you no advantage, but the resulting positions are certainly not a sterile draw. There is ample
room for errors (for both sides!), and a young
Najer (who was already rated 2490 at the
time) was apparently confident that he could
outplay his opponents in these tense
middlegames.

12...♗e6 13.h4 ♖e8 14.g3
Modestly cementing his space advantage for
the moment with this solid move.

14...♗g4!? 15.♕d3 ♘a5 16.♗h3!
14.g3 was not only played to fianchetto the

bishop. White is now slightly better.
16...♗xh3   17.♖xh3   ♘c4   18.c3   c6
19.♘xf6+ ♕xf6 20.♖h2
Again very patient. There is still not much
wrong with Black's game of course.
20...♕g6! 21.♘g5

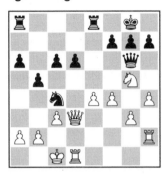

21...h5?!
Correct was 21...♖ad8!. White is better after
21...h6? 22.h5! ♘e5 (22...♕f6 23.e5+−)
23.♕e3 ♕f6 24.fxe5 ♕xg5 25.♕xg5 hxg5
26.exd6.
Still playable is 21...f6 22.h5 ♕h6 23.♘f3
f5!?, or 23...♘e5 24.♕e2±.
22.b3 f6 This is forced. 23.bxc4 Stronger was 23.f5 ♕h6 24.bxc4 fxg5
25.♕d2±. 23...fxg5 24.hxg5 ♕xe4?!
Keeping the queens with 24...♖xe4
25.cxb5 axb5 26.♕xd6 ♕e8 was a better
defence. 25.♕xe4 ♖xe4 26.cxb5 axb5
27.♖xd6

With a pawn up in the double rook ending, White has excellent chances of converting, especially because Black's king is also unsafe. **27...♖e3?** 27...♖c4. **28.♖xc6 ♖xg3**

29.g6! Pinning the king on the back rank, introducing mating motifs.
29...♖g1+ 30.♔b2 h4 31.f5 h3? 31...♖g4 32.♖b6 ♖ga4 33.a3 ♖xa3 34.♖xh4+−.
32.♖xh3 ♖g2+ 33.♔b3 ♖gxa2 34.♖c7
Now the win has become elementary.
34...♖2a3+ 35.♔b4 ♖3a4+ 36.♔c5
36.♔xb5. **36...♖c4+ 37.♔d6 ♖xc7**
37...♖a6+ 38.♔d7 ♖xc7+ 39.♔xc7 ♖a1 40.♖e3+−; 37...♖d8+ 38.♔e7 ♖xc7+

(38...♖a8 39.♖xc4 bxc4 40.♖h4+−) 39.♔xd8 ♖c5 40.♖e3 ♖d5+ 41.♔e7 and now White forces a winning pawn ending after 41...♖xf5 42.♔d7 ♖d5+ 43.♔c6 ♖d8 44.♔c7 ♖a8 45.♖d3.
38.♔xc7 ♖a3 39.♖e3 ♔f8 40.♔d7!

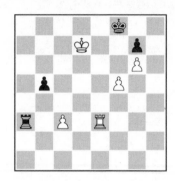

Again the threat of mate helps White to convert.
40...♖a8 41.♔c6 ♖b8 42.♔c5 ♖b7 43.♔b4 ♖b6 44.♖e5 ♖c6 45.♖xb5 ♔e7 46.♖d5 ♔f6 47.c4 ♔g5 48.c5 ♔f4 49.♔b5

Black resigned. Najer-Dorofeev, Moscow 1994.

CHAPTER 11

Efstratios Grivas

Slav: The Easy Way

The unexplored 4.♘bd2

It is well-accepted that fashion rules our lives, and chess cannot escape its fate! Nowadays a white d4-player must be ready to face the popular 'Slav Defence' and its various branches. Keeping up-to-date here can be quite time-consuming.

My proposal in this SOS survey is a line that is quite easy to handle (and at the same time fairly unexplored): 1.d4 d5 2.c4 c6 3.♘f3 ♘f6 and now 4.♘bd2. White immediately protects his c4 pawn and play may transpose into lines of the Schlechter Defence (...g6), Grünfeld Defence (...g6 and ...c5) or even Catalan (...e6) pawn-formations. These formations could easily become a nightmare for a 'Slav Defence' player as his experience

may be severely limited. Indeed, he played the Slav, didn't he?

As I was preparing for the Corus C tournament in Wijk aan Zee in 2008 I thought about this system. Further analysis convinced me that it was worth giving it a try. And it really paid-off as I was able to beat the strong German player Arik Braun in a mere 24 moves!

I have structured the material in the illustrative games that follow. First, in the game Arkell-Hamelink, Sunningdale 2007, all the rare moves are covered. Things are far from easy but it seems that White can be pleased. Second, after 4...g6 (the Schlechter Defence) White can play both 5.g3 and 5.e3. Here for reasons of space I have limited myself to the latter, see Tu Hoang Thong-Russell, Cebu City 2007. The aggressive line is 4...♗g4. This is presented in the game Grivas-Braun, Wijk aan Zee 2008 and it seems that White is doing fine. Next, there is a type of Meran Variation (4...e6). I think that White's best is to transpose to a closed Catalan with 5.g3; see section IV.

Finally, we come to the most serious answer to 4.♘bd2 and that is 4...♗f5. In my opinion White should continue with 5.♘h4, when I now think that Black should play 5...♗e4 (you will find several games with the alternative moves below).

Black's main idea is that before he withdraws his bishop to g6, to provoke the move f3, as he believes that White's weakened kingside should offer him sufficient counterplay for surrendering the bishop-pair. The future key-move for Black should be **...♕c7**, putting pressure on White's h2-pawn (after an eventual ♘xg6 and **...hxg6** the black h8-rook helps in that direction), and generally along the h2-b8 diagonal, keeping options like **...c5** or **...e5** alive.

In reply (after 6.f3 ♗g6) White should either take on g6 and forget about the option of ♕b3 (see Zambo-Drexler, 2005), or he should play 7.♕b3 ♕c7 and now my novelty 8.g4!?. See the final game in this article.

I. 4th move alternatives

☐ **Keith Arkell**
■ **Desiree Hamelink**
Sunningdale tt 2007

1.d4 d5 2.c4 c6 3.♘f3 ♘f6 4.♘bd2 a6

Instead of the text move Black has tried some other continuations too:

- 4...♕a5 5.e3 ♗g4 6.♕b3 ♕c7 (6...♗xf3? 7.♕xb7! ♗g4 8.♕xa8 ♕b6 9.♗d3+−) 7.♘e5 e6 (7...♗h5 8.cxd5 cxd5 9.♘df3 ♘c6

10.♗d2 e6 11.♖c1±) 8.h3 ♗f5 9.g4± Rogers-Stead, Canberra 2001.

− 4...h6!? preparing ...♗f5 is met by 5.♕c2! g6 6.e4 dxe4 7.♘xe4 ♘xe4 8.♕xe4 ♗g7 9.♗e2 ♗f5 10.♕f4 ♘a6 11.♗d2 c5 12.♗c3± Nikolaev-Fedoseev, St Petersburg 2008.

− 4...♕b6 5.e3 ♗f5 6.♘h4 ♗e6 7.♗d3 g6 8.0-0 ♗g7 9.b3 0-0 10.♗b2 ♘bd7 11.♕e2 ♖ac8 12.♘hf3±.

− 4...c5 5.dxc5!? ♘c6 6.♕a4 e6 7.b4±.

− 4...dxc4 5.♘xc4 ♗f5 6.g3 h6 7.♗g2 ♘bd7 8.0-0 ♘b6?! (8...e6 9.♕b3 ♘b6 10.♘fe5±) 9.♘a5! ♕c8 10.♘e5± Drabek-Schmid, Czech Republic 1995.

− 4...♘bd7 5.g3 ♕a5 6.cxd5 cxd5 7.♗g2 e6 8.0-0 ♗d6 9.♘b3±.

5.g3

5...e6

Black's alternatives mainly are:

− 5...♗f5 6.♗g2 e6 7.♘h4!? ♗g4 8.h3 ♗h5 9.g4± Houriez-Tournier, France 2009.

− 5...♗g4?! 6.♘e5 ♗h5 7.♕b3 b5 8.cxb5 cxb5 9.a4! ♕a5 10.g4! ♗xg4 11.♘xg4 ♘xg4 12.♕xd5±, Chernuschevich-Malakhov, Lvov 1999.

− 5...b5 6.cxd5 cxd5 7.♗g2 e6 8.0-0 ♗b7 9.♘b3 ♘bd7 10.♗g5± Drabek-Lednicky, Tatranske Zruby 2004.

6.♗g2 ♘bd7 7.0-0 b5

This is logical in connection with 5...a6. The other try is 7...♗d6 8.♕c2 (8.e4 dxe4 9.♘g5 0-0 10.♘gxe4±) 8...0-0 9.e4 dxe4 10.♘g5

h6 11.♘gxe4 ♗e7 12.♘f3 ♕a5 13.♗f4±
Verat-Nguyen Thanh Tong, Paris 2004.
8.b3 ♗b7 Or 8...♗e7 9.♗b2 0-0 10.♕c2
a5 11.♖fc1 bxc4 12.bxc4 ♗a6 13.e3±
Bienkowski-Walaszczyk, Lublin 1999.
9.a4
White should take into consideration the
thematic advance 9.e4!? ♘xe4 10.♘xe4
dxe4 11.♘g5 ♘f6 12.♘xe4±.
9...♗e7 10.♕c2 0-0 11.♗a3?! 11.e4!?.
11...b4 11...♗xa3 12.♖xa3 ♕e7 13.♖aa1
bxc4 14.bxc4 c5=. **12.♗b2 c5 13.cxd5
exd5!? 14.♖ac1 ♖c8 15.♕b1 ♕b6
16.♖fd1 ♖fd8 17.e3 h6?! 18.dxc5
♘xc5 19.♗d4?!** 19.♗h3! ♘e6 20.♘d4±.
**19...♕e6 20.♘e5 ♘fe4 21.♘d3 ♘xd3
22.♕xd3 ♘c5** 22...a5! 23.♘xe4 dxe4
24.♕b5 ♖xc1 25.♖xc1 ♗d5=. **23.♕b1**
23.♗xc5!? ♖xc5 24.♖xc5 ♗xc5 25.♘f3±.
**23...a5 24.♘f3 ♘e4 25.♕b2 f6 26.♘e1
♗a6 27.♖xc8 ♖xc8 28.♖c1 ♖c6
29.♘f3 ♕c8 30.♖xc6 ♕xc6 31.♗d1±
♘c3 32.♗g4 ♗d6 33.♔g2 ♗e5 34.♘f3
♗c7?! 35.♕c2 ♗b6?**

35...♗e2 36.♗xc3 ♗xf3+ 37.♗xf3 bxc3
38.♕d3±. **36.♕g6! ♗xd4** 36...♗b7
37.♘h4+−. **37.♘xd4 ♕a8 38.♗e6+**
38.♘e6+−. **38...♔h8 39.♗f5?!** 39.♘f5
♕f8 40.♘d6+−. **39...♕g8 40.♘c6 ♗c8
41.♗c2?** 41.♘d8! ♗xf5 42.♘f7+ ♔xf7
43.♕xf7+−. **41...♘e4 42.♘e7 ♕d8**

**43.♘xc8 ♕xc8 44.♗xe4 dxe4
45.♕xe4±** and White mated Black on
move 115!

II. The Schlechter line, 4...g6

☐ **Tu Hoang Thong**
■ **MKA Russell**
Cebu City 2007

**1.d4 d5 2.♘f3 ♘f6 3.c4 c6 4.♘bd2 g6
5.e3 ♗g7 6.♗e2**
The text move looks a bit passive but I regard
it to be the best. Alternatives are 6.♗d3, 6.b4
and 6.b3.
6...0-0 7.0-0 ♘bd7
Black's other options are:
− 7...♗g4 8.h3 ♗xf3 9.♗xf3 e6 10.b3 ♖e8
11.♗b2 ♘bd7 12.♖c1 ♖c8 13.♖c2±,
Hernandez-Hernandez, Mondariz 1999.
− 7...a5 8.b3 ♗f5 9.a3 ♘e4 10.♗b2 ♘d7
11.♘xe4 dxe4 12.♘d2 h5 13.♕c2±.
− 7...b6 8.b3 ♗b7 9.♗b2 ♘bd7 10.♖c1 e6
11.♖c2 ♕e7 12.♕a1 a5 13.a4 ♖fc8 14.♖fc1
♗f8 15.♗d3±, Rusev-Nikolov, Pleven 2005.
− 7...a6 8.b3 b5 9.♗b2 ♗g4 10.h3 ♗xf3
11.♗xf3±, Galego-Karim, Vila Nova de
Gaia 2010.
− 7...♗f5 8.b3 ♘bd7 9.♗b2±.
8.b4

White has also tried the more 'modest' 8.b3

c5 9.♗b2 cxd4 when I would recommend 10.♗xd4!? b6 11.cxd5 ♘xd5 12.♘c4 ♗b7 13.♖c1±.

8...a5 Here 8...dxc4 is best answered by 9.♘xc4 – this is a clear advantage of having the knight on d2. Bad is 8...e5?! 9.♘xe5 ♘xe5 10.dxe5 ♘d7 11.f4 ♕b6 12.♕b3 a5 13.cxd5 cxd5 14.♗a3±, Panchenko-Krajnak, Bratislava 1991.

9.b5 9.bxa5!? ♕xa5 10.a4 is also quite interesting.

9...c5 Or 9...cxb5 10.cxb5 a4 11.♗a3 ♘b6 12.♖c1 ♗f5 13.♘e5 ♘e4 14.♘xe4 ♗xe4 15.♗c5 ♗f5 16.♖c3±, Ratcu-Grosar, Istanbul ol 2000.

10.♗b2 ♖e8 White has a slight edge after 10...b6 11.cxd5 ♘xd5 12.♘c4 ♗b7 13.♖c1 ♖c8 14.dxc5 ♖xc5 15.♗xg7 ♔xg7 16.♘d4. The same goes for 10...cxd4 11.♗xd4 ♖e8 12.cxd5 ♘xd5 13.♗xg7 ♔xg7 14.♘c4 ♘7f6 15.♕d4 as in Simonenko-Kreisl, Turin 2006.

11.dxc5 11.cxd5 ♘xd5 12.♘c4±.

11...♘xc5 12.♖c1 ♗f5 13.♘b3 ♘a4?! 13...♘xb3 14.♕xb3 e6 15.♖fd1±.

14.♗e5!± dxc4 15.♖xc4 ♘b6 16.♖d4! ♕c8 16...♘fd7 17.♘c5 f6 18.♗g3 ♕c8 19.♘xd7 ♗xd7 20.a4±. **17.♕a1 a4 18.♘bd2 ♕e6 19.♘c4 h6 20.h3?** 20.♖fd1±. **20...g5?** 20...♘bd7 21.♖xd7 ♕xd7 22.♘b6 ♕e6 23.♘xa8 ♖xa8 24.♖c1 ♖c8 25.♖xc8+ ♕xc8=. **21.♖fd1 ♖ec8?!** 21...♘xc4 22.♗xc4 ♕b6 23.a3±.

22.♘d6!+− **exd6** 22...♖c5 23.♘xf5 ♕xf5 24.♖d8+ ♖xd8 25.♖xd8+ ♗f8 26.♗d4+−. **23.♖xd6 ♕e7 24.♗xf6 ♗xf6 25.♖xf6** Black resigned.

III. The Aggressive 4...♗g4

☐ **Efstratios Grivas**
■ **Arik Braun**
Wijk aan Zee 2008

1.d4 d5 2.c4 c6 3.♘f3 ♘f6 4.♘bd2 ♗g4 5.♘e5! ♗f5
Other options are:
– 5...♗h5?! 6.♕b3 ♕b6 (6...♕c7 7.♘df3 e6 8.♗f4 ♘e4 9.g4± Houriez-Hugaert, Puerto Madryn 2009) and now the surprising: 7.♕h3! e6 8.e3 ♗b4 9.g4 ♘e4 10.♗d3 ♘xd2 11.♗xd2 ♗xd2+ 12.♔xd2 ♕xb2+ 13.♗c2 ♗g6 14.♘xg6 ♕b4+ 15.♔e2 fxg6 16.♗xg6+ ♔d8 17.♖hb1±.
– 5...♗e6 6.♕b3 ♕c7 7.cxd5 ♗xd5 (7...cxd5 8.♘df3 ♘c6 9.♗f4 ♕b6 10.♕xb6 axb6 11.e3±) 8.♕c2 ♘bd7 9.♘xd7 ♕xd7 10.e4 ♗e6 11.♘f3 ♗g4 12.♗e3±.

6.e3 e6
6...♘bd7 7.cxd5 cxd5 8.♕b3 ♕c7 9.♘xd7 ♗xd7 10.♘f3 e6 11.♗d2 ♗d6 12.♖c1 ♗c6 13.♗d3 0-0 14.♗b4 ♖fc8 15.♗xd6 ♕xd6 16.0-0 ♖c7 17.♘e5 ♖ac8 18.♗c3 ♘d7 19.f4 f5 20.♖fc1± Grinshpun-Wapner, Israel 1996.

7.g4! ♗g6
7...♗e4 8.f3 ♗g6 9.h4 h6 10.♘xg6 fxg6 11.♗d3±.

8.h4 dxc4 8...♘bd7 9.♘xd7 ♕xd7 10.h5 ♗e4 11.f3+−; 8...h5 9.g5 ♘g8 10.♘xg6 fxg6 11.♗h3±.

9.♗xc4 ♗e4?
Not 9...♗b4?! 10.f3 ♘d5 11.♗xd5 ♕xd5 12.h5 f6 13.hxg6 fxe5 14.♖xh7 ♖g8 15.a3±. But stronger was 9...♘bd7! 10.h5 ♗e4 11.f3 (11.♘xe4 ♘xe4 12.♘xd7 ♕xd7 13.♕c2±) 11...♗d5 12.e4 ♗xc4 13.♘dxc4±.

10.♘xf7! A clear improvement over 10.♘xe4? ♘xe4 11.♕f3 (11.♘xf7? ♗b4+ 12.♔f1 ♕f6!) 11...♗b4+ 12.♔e2 ♘d6 13.a3 ♗a5 14.♗d3 ♘d7 15.b4 ♗c7 16.♗b2± ½–½ Heilinger-Schmidlechner, Vorarlberg 1998.
10...♔xf7 10...♕a5 11.♘xh8 ♗xh1 12.g5+−. **11.♘xe4 ♘xe4 12.♕f3+ ♘f6 13.g5 ♗b4+ 14.♔e2! ♘d7 15.a3 ♗e7?!** 15...♗d6 16.♗d2±. **16.♕f5! ♘f8** 16...♔e8 17.♗xe6 g6 18.♕f4! ♘f8 19.♗c4 ♘d5 20.♕e5 ♖g8 21.e4 ♘d7 22.♕e6 ♖f8 23.exd5 ♘b6 24.♗d3 ♕xd5 25.♕xd5 ♘xd5 26.h5+−. **17.gxf6 ♗xf6** 17...gxf6 18.♕h5+ ♘g6 19.♕g4 ♕d6 20.h5 ♘f8 21.♖g1+−. **18.♗d2 ♕b6 19.h5 ♖e8 20.♗b4 a6**

21.♖ag1 ♖g8 21...g6 22.♕f3 a5 23.hxg6+ ♘xg6 24.♗c3+−. **22.♖g3 ♕d8 23.♖hg1 ♕b6** 23...h6? 24.♕g6+! ♘xg6 25.hxg6 mate; 23...g6 24.hxg6+ hxg6

25.♕e4 g5 26.f4!+−. **24.h6!** Black resigned as there is no defence left: 24...♕g6 (24...g6 25.♕xf6+ ♔xf6 26.♖f3 mate; 24...g5 25.f4) 25.♖xg6.

IV. The Meran option, 4...e6

1.d4 d5 2.c4 c6 3.♘f3 ♘f6 4.♘bd2 e6 5.g3 ♘bd7
A solid continuation. Other tries for Black are:
– 5...dxc4 6.♘xc4 c5 7.♗g2 ♘c6 and now both 8.♘fe5 and 8.0-0 favour White.
– 5...♘e4 6.♗g2 f5 Black has transposed to a Stonewall Dutch. 7.0-0 ♗d6 8.♘xe4 fxe4 9.♗g5 ♗e7 10.♗xe7 ♕xe7 11.♘d2±.
– 5...♗e7 6.♗g2 0-0 7.0-0 b6 8.♕c2 ♗b7 9.♖d1 ♕c8 10.b3 ♘bd7 11.♗b2 c5 12.♖ac1± Tu Hoang Thong-Florendo, Olongapo City 2010.
6.♗g2 ♗e7
Playable is 6...♗d6 7.0-0 0-0 8.♕c2 e5 9.cxd5 cxd5 (9...♘xd5? 10.♘c4± Salov-Gayo, Oviedo 1993) 10.dxe5 ♘xe5 11.♘xe5 ♗xe5 12.♘f3 ♗d6 13.♖d1 ♖e8 (13...♗e6 14.♗e3 ♕e7 15.♖ac1± Bu Xiangzhi-Sorm, Bad Wörishofen 2007) 14.♗g5 ♗e6 15.♘d4 ♗e5 16.♘xe6 fxe6 17.e4± Rogers-Handoko, Jakarta 1993.
7.0-0 0-0 8.♕c2

This is a standard position in the Catalan.
8...b6

White seems to enjoy a pleasant advantage even with the alternatives:

– 8...c5 9.cxd5 exd5 10.b3 ♖e8 11.♗b2 ♖b8 12.dxc5 ♗xc5 13.e3 b6 14.♘d4 ♗b7 15.♘2f3 ♖c8 16.♕e2 ♘b8 17.♖fd1± Kasparov-Hartweg, simul Colmar 1998.

– 8...b5 9.c5! a5 (9...e5 10.dxe5 ♘g4 11.♘b3 ♘gxe5 12.♘xe5 ♘xe5 13.♘d4 ♗d7 14.a4± Kozul-Madina, Benidorm 2006) 10.e4 dxe4 (10...♖a6 11.♖e1 g6 12.e5 ♘h5 13.♘f1 ♖a7 14.h4± King-Rogers, Geneve 1990) 11.♘xe4 ♘xe4 12.♕xe4 ♘f6 13.♕c2 ♘d5 14.♖e1 ♗f6 15.h4 h6 (15...♗a6 16.♗g5 ♕c7 17.♕d2 b4 18.a3± Vaganian-Laznicka, Germany 2006/07) 16.♗d2 ♗d7 17.♕e4 ♗e7 18.♘e5± Ftacnik-Marangunic, Sibenik 2007.

9.e4 ♘xe4

Maybe Black should dig into the following options:

– 9...♗b7 10.e5 ♘e8 11.b3 ♖c8 12.♗b2 c5 13.dxc5 ♘xc5 14.♖fd1± Shirov-Vaganian, Germany 2006/07.

– 9...♗a6 10.♖e1 ♖c8 11.e5 ♘e8 12.b3 c5 13.♗b2 ♘c7 14.♖ad1± Shirov-Azarov, Kemer 2007.

– 9...dxc4 10.♘xc4 ♗a6 11.♖d1 c5 12.d5 exd5 13.exd5 ♗xc4 14.♕xc4± Izoria-Zhao Jun, Richardson 2007.

– 9...dxe4 10.♘xe4 ♗b7 11.♖d1 ♕c8 12.♘xf6+ ♘xf6 13.c5 with a slight plus.

10.♘xe4 dxe4 11.♕xe4 ♗b7

From the diagrammed position practice has demonstrated a slight but pleasant White advantage with the natural **12.♖d1** and now:

– 12...♖c8 13.♗f4 ♘f6 14.♕c2 ♗d6 15.♗xd6 ♕xd6 16.c5 ♕e7 17.b4 ♘d5 18.♖ab1 b5 19.h4 h6 20.♘e5± Grischuk-Bujupi, Kemer 2007.

– 12...♕c8 13.♗f4 ♖e8 (13...c5 14.d5 ♗f6 15.♕c2±) 14.♘e5 ♘xe5 15.♗xe5 ♖d8 16.♕g4 ♗f8 17.c5± Cabrilo-Radlovacki, Pancevo 2002.

– 12...♘f6 13.♕e2 ♕c7 14.♗f4 ♗d6 15.♘e5 ♘d7 16.c5! ♗xe5 (16...bxc5 17.♘xd7 ♗xf4 18.♘xf8+–) 17.♗xe5 ♘xe5 18.♕xe5± Ljubojevic-Lucena, Brasilia 1981.

V. The Main Line, 4...♗f5 5.♘h4

□ **Dragan Kosic**
■ **Petar Matovic**
Stara Pazova 2007

1.d4 ♘f6 2.♘f3 d5 3.c4 c6 4.♘bd2 ♗f5 5.♘h4 ♗g6

This is a passive move.

Black has a variety of options:

– 5...e6 6.e3 g6 7.♗d3 ♗g7 8.0-0 0-0. Now 9.h3 (Benkovic-Sokolov, Neum 2005) fails to impress. White can choose between 9.b4 dxc4 10.♘xc4 ♗xc4 11.♗xc4 ♘d5 12.♕b3 b5 13.♗e2± Miron-Kalezic, Cetinje 2009, and 9.cxd5 ♘xd5 10.a3 ♗d7 11.♘e4 ♘7f6 12.♘c5 ♗c8 13.♘f3 b6 14.♘b3 ♗b7 15.e4 ♘c7 16.♕e2± Nikolaev-Gavrilov, St Petersburg 2009.

– 5...♗c8 6.g3 dxc4 (6...e6 7.♘hf3 transposes to 4...e6) 7.♘hf3 (7.♘xc4? ♕d5) 7...b5 (7...♗e6 8.♗g2 ♕d5 9.0-0 ♘bd7 10.♕c2 unclear) 8.♗g2 ♗b7 9.0-0 e6 and now 10.e4!? c5 11.e5 leads to an interesting position which needs further analysis and test in practice.

– 5...e6 6.♘xf5 exf5 7.e3 ♘a6 (7...♗d6

8.♗d3 g6 9.h3 ♘bd7 10.♕f3 ♕e7 11.g4± Boor-Ramirez, Mesa 2009) 8.♗d3 g6 9.0-0 ♗e7 10.cxd5 ♘b4 11.♗b1 ♘bxd5 12.♘c4 0-0 13.♗d2±.

– 5...g6 6.♘xf5 gxf5 7.♕b3 ♕b6 8.e3 e6 9.♗d3±.

– 5...♗d7 6.g3 e6 7.♗g2 ♗e7 8.0-0 0-0 9.♘hf3 c5 10.cxd5 ♘xd5 and now White is somewhat better after 11.e4!? ♘f6 12.♕e2 cxd4 13.♘xd4 ♘c6 14.♘xc6 ♗xc6 15.♘c4 ♗b5 16.♗e3.

6.♘xg6

A nice alternative is 6.♕b3 and now:

– 6...♕b6? 7.♕h3! (we already saw this manoeuvre once before) 7...♘a6 8.c5 ♕c7 9.♘xg6 fxg6 10.♖b1! e5 11.dxe5 ♕xe5 12.b4±.

– 6...♕c8 7.♘xg6 hxg6 8.g3 e6 9.♗g2 ♘bd7 10.0-0 ♗e7 11.♖d1 0-0 12.e4 dxe4 13.♘xe4 ♘xe4 14.♗xe4 ♘f6 15.♗f3 a5 16.♗f4± Erdos-Figura, Germany 2008/09.

– 6...♕c7 7.♘xg6 (7.♕h3 ♕d7) 7...hxg6 8.g3 e6 9.♗g2 ♘bd7 10.0-0 ♗e7 11.e4 dxe4 12.♘xe4 ♘xe4 13.♗xe4 0-0 14.♗e3 ♘f6 (14...e5 15.♖fe1!) 15.♗f3± Harika-Sebag, Dresden ol 2008.

6...hxg6

7.e3 e6 8.a3!? ♗d6

8...♘bd7 9.♗e2 a6 10.g3 ♗e7 11.0-0 0-0 12.b3 ♕c7 13.♗b2 ♖fc8 14.♖c1±, Kosic-Mrkonjic, Subotica 2010.

9.g3 ♘bd7 10.♗g2 a5 11.b3 b5?! 11...0-0 12.♗b2±. **12.0-0 0-0 13.e4 ♗e7** 13...dxc4 14.bxc4 e5 15.♗b2±. **14.e5 ♘h7 15.♕e2?!** 15.c5!±. **15...♕b6?!** 15...bxc4!? 16.bxc4 ♖b8±. **16.c5!**

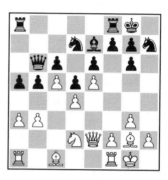

Now play is one-sided as White is winning on the kingside. His space advantage and the bishop-pair are his trumps.

16...♕a6 17.♗b2 ♖fe8 18.f4 ♘df8 19.g4 ♕c8 20.♕d3 ♗d8 21.♖ae1 ♖a7 22.♘f3 ♕d7 22...a4 23.b4±. **23.♗c1 ♕c8 24.♗h3 ♕b7 25.♖f2 ♕c7 26.♕c2 ♗e7 27.♗f1 ♕d8 28.♖g2 ♔h8 29.♗d3 ♕c7 30.h4 ♗d8** 30...♕d8 31.h5 a4 32.b4+−. **31.g5** 31.h5!? gxh5 32.gxh5 a4 33.b4+−. **31...♔g8 32.♔f2 ♖e7 33.♖h1 ♕d7** 33...♖e8 34.♖gh2 ♔h8 35.♔g3+−. **34.h5 ♕e8** 34...a4 35.b4 gxh5 36.♗xh7+ ♘xh7 37.♖xh5 g6 38.♖h1+−. **35.♖gh2 a4 36.b4** Black resigned.

□ **Efstratios Grivas**
■ **Halil Osmanoglou**
Kallithea 2008

1.d4 d5 2.c4 c6 3.♘f3 ♘f6 4.♘bd2 ♗f5 5.♘h4 ♗g4 In this way Black also cannot hope to solve his opening problems. **6.h3 ♗h5 7.g4 ♗g6 8.♘xg6 hxg6**

9.♗g2 e6

White has the bishop-pair, but in order to take advantage of this fact he must create the right environment: open centre with pawns on both flanks.

10.e4! dxe4?! Black should try to keep the centre closed: 10...♗b4!? 11.e5!? ♘e4 12.♗xe4 dxe4 13.♕b3 c5 14.a3 ♗xd2+ 15.♗xd2 ♘c6 16.♕xb7 ♖c8 17.♕xc8+ ♖xc8 18.dxc5 ♘xe5 19.♗c3 ♖xc5 20.♗xe5 ♖xe5 21.b4±. **11.♘xe4 ♗b4+** After 11...♘xe4 12.♗xe4 ♗b4+ 13.♔e2! ♘d7 14.♗e3 White's king is perfectly placed in the center, as Black has no way to embarrass him. **12.♘c3 ♘bd7 13.♕b3 ♕b6** The alternative was 13...♕a5!? 14.♗d2±. **14.♗e3 ♗a5?!** An inaccuracy. Also bad was 14...c5?! 15.0-0-0!±, but Black had to try 14...0-0-0 15.0-0-0±. **15.g5! ♘h5?!** Having a knight on the edge cannot be advisable. Black had to go for 15...♘g8 16.d5 ♕xb3 17.axb3 ♗xc3+ 18.bxc3 exd5 19.cxd5 ♘e7 20.dxc6 ♘xc6 21.b4±. **16.d5!** The correct evaluation – the position should be opened in order to create a feast for the bishop-pair! **16...♕xb3** 16...♘c5 17.♕xb6 axb6 18.dxc6±. **17.axb3 ♗xc3+ 18.bxc3 exd5 19.cxd5 ♘e5** After 19...cxd5 20.♗xd5 Black loses material with no compensation. **20.dxc6 ♘xc6**

21.b4! White could win a pawn with 21.♗xc6+? bxc6 22.♖xa7 ♖xa7 23.♗xa7, but after 23...♘f4 24.h4 ♔e7 Black should feel more than happy with the resulting position. There is no need to hunt useless pawns around. A serious player should wait for the right moment for material gain and mainly try to increase his advantage instead of hurrying to win 'suspicious' material. **21...a6 22.b5 ♘d8 23.♔d2!** Accurate. White must place his king somewhere in order to connect his rooks. On d2 the white king protects the valuable c-pawn and avoids any potential ...♘f4+ threats. Wrong would be 23.bxa6? ♖xa6 24.♖xa6 bxa6 25.♔d2 ♘e6 26.♖a1 ♘hf4 27.♗f1 ♖h5. **23...♔d7 24.♖hb1 ♔c7** Or 24...a5 25.♖a4! f6 26.h4 ♔c7 27.♖ba1+−. **25.bxa6 ♖xa6 26.♖xb7+!** White wins material while preserving his advantages. Game over! **26...♖xb7 27.♖xa6 ♖d8+ 28.♔c2 ♖d7 29.♗b6+ ♔b8 30.♗d4** Black resigned.

☐ **Zoltan Zambo**
■ **Mihaly Drexler**
Eger 2005

1.d4 d5 2.♘f3 ♘f6 3.c4 c6 4.♘bd2 ♗f5 5.♘h4 ♗d7 6.♘hf3 ♗f5 7.♘h4

♗e4 8.f3 ♗g6 9.♘xg6 hxg6 10.e3

As the white queen is not ideally placed on b3 in this set-up, maybe this logical move is better than 10.♕b3 which we will study below.

10...e6 11.♕c2 ♗d6

The key-move 11...♕c7!? 12.g3 could also be played by Black.

12.f4 ♘g4 13.♘f3 ♗b4+ 14.♔d1!

White lost his castling rights, but on the other Black also moved two of his pieces twice in an early development stage.

14...♘d7 15.a3 15.c5!? ♗a5 (15...♘df6!? 16.♗d3 ♘e4 17.♖f1) 16.h3 ♘gf6 17.♘g5 is unclear and about equal.

15...♗e7 16.♗d3 ♘df6

16...c5!? is interesting, although it leads to enormous complications after 17.cxd5 exd5 18.♗xg6 ♖c8 19.♘e5!.

17.♔e2

White has achieved piece coordination and king safety, so in general he should feel happy.

17...dxc4

17...♕c7 18.♗d2 0-0-0 19.h3 ♘h6 20.g4 looks quite nice for White.

18.♗xc4 ♕c7 19.♗d2 ♘d5 20.h3 ♘gf6 21.♘e5 ♘h5?!

Good-placed pieces should be eliminated; for that purpose 21...♘d7 was natural: 22.♖hf1 0-0 23.e4 ♘5b6 24.♗a2±.

22.♔f3! 0-0 23.g4 ♘hf6

24.h4!

White stands better due to his spatial advantage, his bishop-pair and his strong attack!

24...c5

Now 24...♘d7 is not a solution: 25.h5 ♘xe5+ 26.dxe5 gxh5 27.♖xh5 g6 28.♖h6 ♔g7 29.♖ah1 ♖h8 30.g5 ♖xh6 31.gxh6+ ♔h7 32.e4 ♘b6 33.♗b3±.

25.♗xd5?

25.h5 gxh5 26.g5± was the natural way to continue the attack.

25...♘xd5?

Black should try to defend by 25...exd5! 26.h5 gxh5 27.gxh5 ♗d6, when nothing is clear yet.

26.♖ac1? Good was 26.h5 g5 27.h6±.

26...♖ac8?

Again Black could have put-up a defence by eliminating the strong placed e5 knight: 26...♗d6 27.h5 cxd4 28.♕xc7 ♗xc7 29.exd4 gxh5 30.♖xh5 ♗xe5 31.dxe5 f6! 32.exf6 ♖xf6 33.♖e5±.

27.e4?!

27.h5! cxd4 28.♕b1 and White wins.

27...♘f6 28.♗e3 b6?!

Not pleasant but forced was 28...♘d7! 29.♘xd7 ♕xd7 30.dxc5±.

29.h5 gxh5 30.g5! ♘d7 Or 30...♘g4 31.♖xh5 f5 32.gxf6 ♘xf6 33.♖h8+! ♔xh8 34.♖h1+ ♘h7 35.♕h2 ♗h4 36.♘g6+ ♔g8 37.♕xh4.

31.♖xh5 ♘xe5+ 32.dxe5 g6

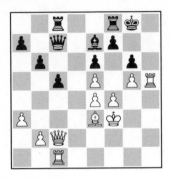

33.♖h8+! ♔g7 33...♔xh8 34.♕h2+ ♔g7 35.♕h6+ ♔g8 36.♖h1+−.

34.♖h7+!

Black resigned due to 34...♔g8 (34...♔xh7 35.♕h2+ ♔g7 36.♕h6+ ♔g8 37.♖h1+−) 35.♕h2 f5 36.♕h6 fxe4+ 37.♔g3+−.

□ **Alexey Chernuschevich**
■ **Eric Prié**
France 2003

1.d4 d5 2.c4 c6 3.♘d2 ♘f6 4.♘gf3 ♗f5 5.♘h4 ♗e4 6.♕b3

6...♕b6 7.c5?!

Nothing is offered by 7.f3 ♕xb3 8.axb3 ♗c2, but White might have tried 7.♘xe4 ♘xe4 (7...dxe4 8.g3 e6 9.♗d2±) 8.e3 e6 9.♗d3 ♘d7 10.0-0±.

7...♕c7?!

Black could safely go for 7...♕xb3 8.axb3 ♗c2 (8...♘a6 9.♘xe4 ♘xe4 10.♖a4!±) 9.e3 e5 10.b4 ♘bd7 11.b5 with unclear play.

8.f3 ♗g6 9.e4!

An active and correct response. The 'passive' 9.e3 e6 10.♕c3 transposes to Gurevich-Hauchard, Gibraltar 2009.

9...e6

White's initiative after 9...dxe4 10.fxe4 (10.♘xg6 hxg6 11.♗c4 e6 12.♘xe4 ♘bd7 13.♗e3 ♗e7 − 13...♖xh2? 14.♖xh2 ♕xh2 15.♕xb7 ♖b8 16.♕xc6 ♖xb2 17.0-0-0 ♕xg2 18.♘d2 ♖b8 19.♗f4 ♖d8 20.♗xe6+− − 14.0-0-0 0-0∞) 10...♘bd7 (10...♗xe4 11.♘xe4 ♘xe4 12.♗c4 e6 13.0-0♕) 11.e5 ♘d5 12.♘c4± looks nice.

10.e5 ♘g8 10...♘fd7!? 11.♘xg6 hxg6 12.♕c3 a5 13.a3 a4 14.b4 axb3 15.♘xb3±, Miron-Burmakin, Rochefort 2009.

11.♘xg6

11...fxg6?!

A rather optimistic capture. Black had to opt for the natural 11...hxg6 12.♕c3 ♘d7 13.♗d3±.

12.♕e3?

If White had found 12.f4! ♘h6 (12...b6 13.♕h3±) 13.♕h3 ♘f5 14.♘f3± Black would have regretted his 11th move.

12...♘h6?!

The unclear 12...b6 13.b4 a5 14.cxb6 ♕xb6

15.bxa5 ♕xa5 16.♔f2 was an 'attractive' option for Black.

13.f4?!

As 13.♗d3 ♘f5 14.♕f2 b6 15.g4 (15.b4? bxc5 16.bxc5 ♗xc5!) 15...♘h6∞ leads to nowhere, White had to admit his mistake and play 13.♕c3! b6 14.b4 a5 15.a3±.

13...a5?! Why not 13...b6!. **14.♘f3 ♗e7 15.h4** 15.♗d3 was also a possible and fair alternative: 15...0-0 16.0-0±.

15...b6?!

Now this break is not correct. Black had to opt for 15...♘f5 16.♕f2 h5 17.♘g5! ♗xg5 18.hxg5 0-0 19.♗d3 ♘a6 (19...b6? 20.♗xf5 ♖xf5 21.g4! hxg4 22.♕h4+−) 20.♗e3±.

16.♘g5! ♕d7

Or 16...♘f5 17.♕c3 ♗xg5 18.hxg5 bxc5 19.dxc5 ♘d7 20.g4 ♘e7 21.♗e3±.

17.♗d3?

White opts for a dubious tactical shot. Correct was the simple 17.cxb6 ♘f5 18.♕f2±.

17...bxc5! 18.♘xh7?

White had to admit his mistake and go for 18.dxc5 ♘a6 19.♗xa6 ♖xa6.

18...♘f5! Now Black takes over the advantage. **19.♗xf5 gxf5 20.♕g3** 20.♘g5 cxd4 21.♕xd4 c5 22.♕f2 ♘c6∓. **20...cxd4 21.♕g6+ ♔d8 22.♔f1 ♘a6 23.♕xg7 ♔c7**

Black completed his development and his king is safe. He won on move 36

☐ **Mert Erdogdu**
■ **Evgeny Agrest**
Plovdiv 2010

1.d4 d5 2.c4 c6 3.♘f3 ♘f6 4.♘bd2 ♗f5 5.♘h4 ♗e4 6.f3 ♗g6 7.♕b3 ♕c7

8.g4!?

While I was preparing for an important game around February 2010, I came across this new concept. I was not able to use this novelty but I showed it (and its merits) to my trainees (the Turkish National Men Team). One of them was 'lucky' enough to use it! White's idea is simple: he will delay the capture on g6 and he will try for an e4 advance, using the threat g5.

8...e6 More or less natural. Bad looks 8...♘bd7 9.g5 dxc4 (9...♘h5 10.cxd5) 10.♘xc4 ♘d5 11.e4±.

9.e4

The 'natural' follow-up.

9...dxe4

I do not like this move. Preferable is the passive but probably perfectly playable 9...♗e7, and now after 10.♘xg6 hxg6 White should opt between 11.cxd5 or 11.e5!?.

10.g5 e3

10...♘h5 11.♘xe4 ♘d7 12.♗d2 ♗e7 13.♘xg6 hxg6 14.0-0-0 0-0-0 15.♕e3 is nice for White (space, bishop-pair, and the edged h5-knight).

The other option is 10...♘fd7 11.♘xg6 hxg6 12.♘xe4 ♘a6 13.c5 e5 14.♗xa6 bxa6 15.♗e3 ♕a5+ (15...♖h3?! 16.0-0-0! ♖xf3 17.♖hf1±) 16.♕c3 ♕xc3+ 17.bxc3 exd4 18.cxd4±.

11.♕xe3 ♘fd7

After 11...♘h5 White can opt for 12.♘xg6 hxg6 13.♘e4 ♗b4+ 14.♔d1! ♗e7 (14...♘d7 15.c5!) 15.♔c2 ♘d7 16.♗d2 0-0-0 17.♖d1±.

12.♘xg6?!

Too early, as White mixed the variations. 12.♘e4 ♗b4+ 13.♔f2 ♗e7 14.♗d2 ♘a6 15.♘xg6 hxg6 16.♔g2± was good.

12...hxg6 13.♘e4 ♘b6?!

Why not 13...♖xh2 14.♖xh2 ♕xh2 although White has compensation after 15.♗d2.

14.♗d2

14.♕f4! was stronger: 14...♘a6 15.♕xc7 ♘xc7 16.♗f4 0-0-0 17.0-0-0±.

14...♗e7 15.0-0-0 ♘8d7

16.♗e1!

Now Black is in trouble, as the threat ♗g3 is annoying.

16...♗d6 17.♘xd6+ ♕xd6 18.♗g3?!

It would be better to preserve the queens on the board: 18.♗e2 ♕e7 19.f4 0-0-0 20.h4±.

18...♕b4! 19.♕d2 ♕xd2+ 20.♔xd2 f6! 21.f4?!

'Killing' the bishop-pair. 21.♗d3!? ♔f7 22.♔c3 still looks nice for White.

21...♔f7 22.h4 ♖ad8 23.b3 ♘c8!

Now Black can hold the position, as the bishop-pair is not strong anymore and his knight is heading for f5.

24.♗g2 ♘e7 25.♗f3 ♘b6 26.♔e2 ♘bc8 27.a4 ♘d6 28.♗f2 a6 29.♔e3 ♘df5+ 30.♔e2

Draw.

Conclusion

The 4.♘bd2 continuation is a side line of the Slav Defence, as not many top-players have adopted it. However, this means that it may well be an excellent tool for the club-player, who has a limited amount of time for the study of opening theory. Most lines are poisonous enough, and it seems that White can still achieve the advantage that the right of the first move gives him.

CHAPTER 12

Adrian Mikhalchishin

Spanish: Kortchnoi's Idea in the Central Attack

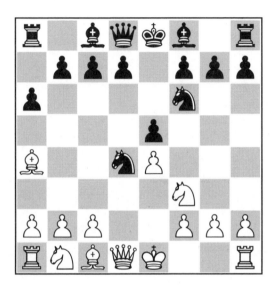

The surprising 5.d4 ♘xd4!?

The Central Attack in the Ruy Lopez arises after 1.e4 e5 2.♘f3 ♘c6 3.♗b5 a6 4.♗a4 ♘f6 5.d4. This early opening of the centre is considered to be unpleasant for strong Black players, as usually, it leads to the positions with a slight advantage for White and no real counterplay for Black.

For this reason Kortchnoi suggested the capture on d4 with the knight as the only chance to obtain some counterplay.

Before we investigate Kortchnoi's idea I first want to show you what can happen after 5...exd4.

My first ever win against a grandmaster occurred in this variation! I had carefully read the theoretical articles of the great Svetozar

Gligoric in the Yugoslav periodical *Sahovski Glasnik*, and there were several nice games won by GM Slavo Marjanovic in this line.

□ **Adrian Mikhalchishin**
■ **Yury Averbakh**
Lviv 1972

1.e4 e5 2.♘f3 ♘c6 3.♗b5 a6 4.♗a4 ♘f6 5.d4 exd4 6.0-0 ♗e7 7.♖e1 0-0
Here 7...b5 8.♗b3 d6 is a serious alternative.
8.e5 ♘e8 9.♗f4 b5 10.♗b3 d5 11.♘xd4 ♘xd4 12.♕xd4 c6 13.♕d3 ♗g4 14.♘d2 ♘c7 15.c3 ♗h5 16.♘f3 ♘e6

17.♕e3? Nowadays I would play simply with the bishop: 17.♗g3. **17...c5! 18.♗g3 c4 19.♗d1 ♗c5 20.♘d4 ♘xd4** 20...♗xd4 21.cxd4 ♗xd1 22.♖axd1 ♕d7 23.f4 was unclear. **21.cxd4 ♗xd1 22.dxc5 d4 23.♕e4 ♗h5 24.e6 fxe6 25.♗d6 ♖f6 26.♕xd4 ♗e8 27.♖ad1 ♖g6 28.♕e3 ♗c6 29.♗g3 ♗d5 30.c6 ♖c8 31.c7 ♕d7 32.♕b6 ♖xg3 33.hxg3 ♕xc7 34.♕xc7 ♖xc7 35.a3 h5 36.♖e3 g6 37.♖d4 ♖b7 38.g4 b4 39.axb4 ♖xb4 40.♖e2 hxg4 41.♖xg4**

Here the game was ajourned and my friend GM Oleg Romanishin helped me with the analysis, but our conclusion was that this position is a draw.
41...♔g7 42.f3 ♖a4 43.♔f2 ♖b4 44.♔e3 e5 45.♖d2 ♗e6 46.♖e4 ♔f6 47.f4 exf4+ 48.♔xf4 ♖b3 49.♖e3 ♖b4 50.♖d4 ♖b6

51.g4! g5+ 52.♔g3 ♔g7 53.♖de4 ♔f6 54.♖e5 ♔f7 55.♖c5 ♔g7 56.♖e2 ♔f6 57.♔f3 ♖b3+ 58.♔e4 ♗xg4 59.♖f2+ ♔e7 60.♖xg5 ♗e6 61.♖g7+ ♔d6 62.♖g6 ♖h3 63.♖d2+ ♔e7 64.♔d4 ♔f7 65.♖g1 ♖f3 66.♖e1 ♖f5 67.♖de2 ♖f4+ 68.♖e4

Black resigned.

I present you with one more beautiful and simple game, which demonstrates some of Black's problems in the theoretical lines (of those days).

☐ **Oleg Romanishin**
■ **Vladimir Tukmakov**
Tbilisi 1978

1.e4 e5 2.♘f3 ♘c6 3.♗b5 a6 4.♗a4 ♘f6 5.d4 exd4 6.0-0 ♗e7 7.♖e1 0-0 8.e5 ♘e8

9.c3!?
We already saw 9.♗f4 in the previous game.
9...dxc3 10.♘xc3 d6 11.exd6 ♘xd6
Maybe it was worth trying the paradoxical 11...cxd6. I remember that all participants were curious how powerful this pawn sac really was.
12.♗f4
Tempting, but premature, was 12.♘d5.
12...b5?! 13.♗b3 ♘c4 14.♘d5! ♗d6 15.♗g5! ♕d7 16.♖e4 f6?

**17.♗f4! ♗xf4 18.♖xf4± ♖d8 19.♕e2
♖e8** Or 19...♕xd5 20.♖xc4. **20.♕c2
♘6e5? 21.♘xe5 ♖xe5 22.♖xc4!+−
bxc4 23.♕xc4 ♔f8 24.♘xc7 ♖a7
25.♕g8+ ♔e7 26.♘d5+**
Black resigned.

□ **Oleg Romanishin**
■ **Alexander Beliavsky**
   Kiev 1978

**1.e4 e5 2.♘f3 ♘c6 3.♗b5 a6 4.♗a4
♘f6 5.d4 ♘xd4!?** In 1976 Beliavsky,
Romanishin and myself had a training ses-
sion with Kortchnoi, and this simple idea
was proposed by our teacher there!
6.♘xd4 If 6.♘xe5 then 6...♘e6.

When the lines fork:
– After 7.c3 ♘xe4 8.♗c2 d5 White has in-

sufficient compensation for the pawn.
– And 7.♘c3 b5 8.♗b3 ♗b7 9.f3 c5 promises Black comfortable play
6...exd4 7.e5
Wrong is 7.♕xd4 c5 8.♕e5+ ♕e7 9.♕xe7+
♗xe7, threatening b7-b5.
7...♘e4 8.♕xd4 ♘c5 9.♘c3 ♗e7

Now it looks tempting to eliminate the opponent's possibility to castle, but it leads to a
loss of the battle in the centre.
10.♕g4 Maybe it would be interesting to
try to castle to the queenside with 10.♗e3.
10...♔f8 Very bad is castling 10...0-0?
11.♗h6 ♘e6 12.♗b3 ♔h8 (12...♗g5
13.♗xg5 ♕xg5 14.♕xg5 ♘xg5 15.♘d5+−)
13.♗xe6 gxh6 14.♗f5. And 10...g6 weakens the dark squares too much.
11.♕f3 Better looks 11.♕f4, but Romanishin wants to prevent d7-d5.
11...♘xa4 12.♘xa4 d6

13.♗e3

It was correct to take on d6, but Romanishin in those days was convinced that he could sacrifice a pawn against everybody.

After 13.exd6 ♗xd6 14.♗e3 ♕h4 15.♘c3 ♕b4 16.0-0 ♗d7 Black can't be afraid of anything with his pair of bishops.

13...dxe5 14.♖d1 ♕e8 15.♗c5 e4

15...h5! was better, with the threat of 16...♗g4.

16.♕g3

Still harbouring ambitions. Stronger was simply 16.♕xe4 ♗f5 17.♗xe7+ ♕xe7 18.♕xe7+ ♔xe7 19.♔d2.

16...♗d7

Possible was 16...b6 17.♗xe7+ ♕xe7 18.♘c3 ♗b7 19.♘d5 ♗xd5 20.♖xd5 ♖d8 21.♖xd8+ ♕xd8 22.0-0.

17.♗d4

Not sufficient was 17.♗xe7+ ♕xe7 18.♘c3 ♗c6 19.0-0 g6 20.♖fe1 ♖e8.

17...f6 18.♘c5 ♗d6 19.♕b3

19...♗g4! 20.0-0

Or 20.♕xb7 ♗xd1 21.♖xd1 ♖d8 22.♔c1 ♗xc5 23.♗xc5+ ♔f7 24.♕xc7+ ♖d7 and Black consolidates.

20...♕h5

Possible was the sharp 20...♗xd1 21.♘e6+ ♔e7 22.♘xg7 ♕g6 23.♕e6+ ♔f8.

21.h3 ♗xd1 22.♘e6+ ♔e7 23.♘xg7 ♕g6 24.♕e6+ ♔f8 25.♘f5 ♗f3

26.♘h4 ♕f7 27.♕xf7+ ♔xf7 28.gxf3 ♖hg8+ 29.♔h1 exf3 30.♘xf3 ♖ae8

With an extra exchange Black is easily winning. Beliavsky won on move 56.

☐ **Zeljko Pavicic**
■ **Adrian Mikhalchishin**
Sibenik 2007

1.e4 e5 2.♘f3 ♘c6 3.♗b5 a6 4.♗a4 ♘f6 5.d4 ♘xd4 6.♘xd4 exd4 7.e5 ♘e4 8.♕xd4

Wrong is 8.0-0 b5 9.♕xd4? ♗b7 10.♗b3 c5 and Black arrests the b3 bishop: 11.♗xf7+ ♔xf7 12.♕e3 c4 13.♖e1 ♔g8 14.♕f4 ♘c5 15.♘c3 ♘e6 16.♕g3 ♕e8 17.f4 ♘d4 18.♕f2 ♕g6 19.♔h1 ♘xc2 0-1, Coklin-Mikhalchishin, Ljubljana 1995.

8...♘c5 9.♘c3 ♗e7 10.♕g4

Perhaps 10.♘d5!?.

10...♔f8 11.♗b3

– Even worse is 11.♗f4 d5 12.♕e2 c6 13.♗b3 h5 14.0-0-0 ♗e6 15.♗e3 b5 16.f3 a5 17.a4 ♘xb3+ 18.cxb3 b4 19.♘e4 c5 20.♔b1

20...d4 21.♕c2 ♕d5 22.♗g5 ♖c8 23.♗xe7+ ♔xe7 24.♘d2 ♕xe5 25.♕d3 ♖hd8 26.♕c2 ♗f5, with a clear advantage for Black, Acosta-Mikhalchishin, Mexico 1980.

– 11.0-0 d5 12.♕d4 (12.♕h5 d4 13.♖d1 ♘xa4 14.♘xa4 b5∓) 12...c6

13.♗b3 (13.f4!? ♗f5 14.g4!? ♘xa4!
15.♘xa4 ♗xc2) 13...h5 (13...♗f5 14.g4!
♘xb3 15.cxb3 ♗g6 16.f4) 14.♘e2 ♗f5
15.♗e3? (15.♕d1! ♕d7 16.♘d4 g6 17.c3
♔g7 18.♗e3, ± Kortchnoi) 15...♘xb3
16.cxb3 c5 and Black was clearly better in
Short-Kortchnoi, London 1980.

11...d5 12.♕f3 c6 Black does not need
to take the bishop on b3. On the contrary, it
is necessary to play as if it does not exist!
Black has to create a strong centre and to
develop his king – just that and White has
no real counterplay.

13.0-0 h5 14.h3

14...g5! First I just wanted to complete
my artificial castling with 14...g6, but
when I looked deeper into the position, I
realized, that Black actually has a powerful
initiative on the kingside

15.♗e3 It was slightly better to sacrifice a

pawn with 15.♕e2 g4 16.h4 ♗xh4 17.♗e3
♗e7 18.f3 trying to open the f-file.

15...g4 16.hxg4 ♗xg4
16...hxg4 17.♕g3 was also possible, but I
did not see the queen transfer 17...♕d7!
18.f3 ♘xb3 19.axb3 ♕f5.

17.♕g3
17.♕f4! ♘e6 18.♕h2 h4 leads to unclear
game, but I still prefer Black's position.

17...♘xb3
17...d4 18.♖ad1 ♗xd1 19.♖xd1 ♘xb3
20.axb3 c5 was clearly better for Black.

18.axb3 d4 19.f3

19...♗h4 Faster was 19...dxe3 20.fxg4 e2
21.♘xe2 ♗c5+ 22.♖f2 ♕d2.
**20.♕f4 dxe3 21.fxg4 ♗f2+ 22.♖xf2
exf2+ 23.♕xf2 hxg4** Black has won an
exchange.
24.♖f1 ♖h7 25.♘e4 g3! It is necessary to
deflect one of the white pieces. **26.♘xg3
♕h4 27.♖e1 ♖e8 28.♖e4 ♕h2+
29.♔f1 ♖g7 30.♖e3 ♖e6** More exact was
30...♖d8. **31.♕f4 ♕h6 32.♕d4 ♕g5**
32...♖g4!. **33.♔f2 ♖h7 34.♕b4+ ♕e7
35.♕f4** In the endgame Black is winning,
but it demands precise play: 35.♕xe7+
♔xe7 36.♔f3 ♖g6 37.♘f5+ ♔e6 38.♘d4+
♔d7 39.g3 c5.

**35...♕h4 36.♕f5 ♖g7 37.♕d3 ♖g4
38.♔g1 ♖eg6 39.♔f2 ♖d4 40.♕e2
♖f4+ 41.♔g1 ♖xg3**
White resigned.

CHAPTER 13

Dimitri Reinderman

Panic in the London

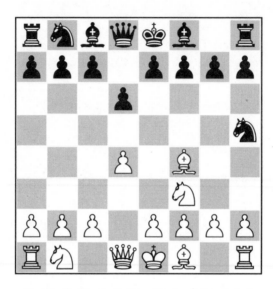

1.d4 ♘f6 2.♘f3 d6 3.♗f4 ♘h5

You probably know the type of player that doesn't want to study theory and plays the London system with white. 1.d4, 2.♘f3 and 3.♗f4, bishops to h2 and e2, knight to d2, pawns to e3 and c3 (or c4), castle short etc. It is a legal way of playing, but is it fun?

Well, that is their problem, unless you are paired against such a player. Let's say you are a King's Indian adherent, what are your options then? Well, you can study a good line against the London to get equality from the opening. However, probably your opponent will be more familiar with the position than you are. Isn't there a way to get him out of his usual pattern without playing something dubious? Yes, there is!

Start with 1.d4 ♘f6 2.♘f3 d6 (instead of 2...g6). After 3.c4 you play 3...g6 to get the King's Indian, but your opponent will probably play 3.♗f4. Now comes the surprise: 3...♘h5! Immediately your opponent has a problem: what do to with the bishop?

There are nine possible moves (that don't lose right away), of which four have been used in practice.

Many players will move their bishop to g3. Black is fine though after 4...g6, and, as our first game Bree-Kupreichik shows, Black can even get an advantage if White plays unambitiously.

If White moves the bishop to g5, Black will chase it to g3 with h6 and g5. This is slightly weakening, but Black has good chances with his pair of bishops, as you can see in the second game of this article, Mordiglia-Efimov.

4.♗c1 has been played by good players. Black can repeat moves with 4...♘f6, but 4...g6 is also good, though you have to be aware that after 5.e4 and 6.♘c3 a Pirc arises. The Pirc may not be on your repertoire, but having the free moves ...♘f6 and ...♘h5 is a nice bonus.

The fourth move that has been played in practice is 4.♗d2 and this is White's best try for an advantage. White can make use of the move ♗d2 by putting the bishop on c3. Still, in game 3, Biriukov-Golubev, Black was fine after the opening.

So far for practice, but for completeness sake I will discuss the other possibilities too. White can defend the bishop by 4.e3, 4.g3 or 4.♕c1. It's not totally stupid, but you can be happy after taking the bishop and putting yours on the long diagonal. Another move not in the database is 4.♗e3, and while it looks antipositional (blocking the e-pawn), it's actually not that bad: White can continue with g3 and ♗g2 or even ♕d2 and ♗h6, with an interesting game.

All in all, 3...♘h5 is a good way to avoid the standard London moves, and, quite importantly, it is fun for Black!

Alas, White is not obliged to play 3.♗f4 immediately, but after the annotated games I will give some options if White tries something else on the third move (like 3.h3 to transpose to the London after all).

☐ **Thomas Bree**
■ **Viktor Kupreichik**
Münster 1995

In this game White plays the usual solid moves: e3, c3 and moving the bishop back.

Since square h2 is occupied, it stands on g3 now. Black gets easy equality though and gradually outplays his opponent.

1.d4 ♘f6 2.♘f3 d6 3.♗f4 ♘h5 4.♗g3 g6 5.c3 ♗g7

6.e3

White can also play with e4 (which I think is better) but Black will castle and play ...e5 just like in the game.

6...0-0 7.♗e2 e5

Taking on g3 first is more accurate, as White can play 8.♗h4 now to keep his bishop.

8.dxe5 ♘xg3 9.hxg3 dxe5 10.♕xd8

White hopes to make a draw by exchanging a lot. Meanwhile, Black gets the d-file for free.

10...♖xd8

11.♗c4

Threatening 12.♘g5 and also making room for the king. But if the bishop is on c4, where can the knight on b1 go to? It can go to b3, but as the game shows it's not doing much there.

11...h6 12.a4 ♘d7 13.♘bd2 a5 14.♔e2 ♘c5

The knight stands well here: looking at d3 and attacking a4.

15.♘b3

Black's knight isn't allowed to stay on c5, but now the white knights will be passive.

15...♘e4 16.♘fd2 ♘d6 17.♗d3 b6 18.e4 ♗e6

The position is almost symmetrical and the pair of bishops doesn't play a role (yet), but White can't do much while Black can improve his position by activating his king's bishop and doubling his rooks on the d-file.

19.♖ac1 h5 20.c4 ♗h6 21.♖c3

21.c5 loses a pawn: 21...♗xb3 22.cxd6 ♗xd2 23.dxc7 ♗xc1 24.cxd8♕+ ♖xd8 25.♖xc1 ♗xa4.

21...♘b7!

Preventing c5 and making room for the bishop.

22.♘f3 f6

In the next four moves White does nothing, while Black improves his position to perfection.

23.♗c2 ♗f8 24.♗d3 ♖d7 25.♗b1 ♖ad8 26.♖cc1 ♗b4 27.♖hg1

White can do little but move this rook.

27...♖d6

With the idea of winning the pawn on a4 by ♗d7.

28.♘a1 ♘c5 29.b3

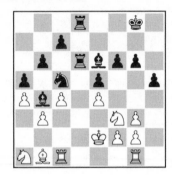

29...♗g4

Black could win a pawn with 29...♗a3 30.♖cd1 ♘xa4, but the game move is good enough.

30.♖cd1 ♖d2+ 31.♖xd2 ♖xd2+ 32.♔e3 ♖b2 33.♗c2 ♖a2 34.♖c1 ♗c3

The queen's knight was never really happy in this game, and now it dies on a sad square...

White resigned.

□ **Riccardo Mordiglia**
■ **Igor Efimov**
Arco 1999

1.d4 ♘f6 2.♘f3 d6 3.♗f4 ♘h5 4.♗g5 h6 5.♗h4 g5 6.♗g3

Black has the additional moves ...h6 and ...g5 compared to 4.♗g3, which has advantages and disadvantages, but compare this position with the one after 1.d4 ♘f6 2.♘f3 d6 3.♗g5 g6 4.♘bd2 ♗g7 5.e3 h6 6.♗h4 g5 7.♗g3 ♘h5 (a.o. Radjabov-Morozevich,

World Blitz 2008). There White has the moves e3 and ♘bd2 extra compared to the game. That variation is not known to be dangerous for White, and with the two extra tempi Black can try to get an advantage.

6...♗g7 7.e3 c5 8.c3 ♘c6

9.dxc5

Again White hopes to make a draw by exchanging queens, but in the endgame Black is a little more active, and the two bishops might play a role later.

9...♘xg3 10.hxg3 dxc5 11.♕xd8+ ♔xd8 12.♘a3 a6 13.0-0-0+ ♔c7 14.e4 b5 15.♘c2 ♗b7 16.♘e3 e6 17.♗e2 ♘e7 18.♘d2

The situation is better here for White than in the previous game: White's pieces have some activity, the knight on e7 is not doing much and the bishop on g7 doesn't bother

White (since b4 would give White square c4 for his knight). Still Black is slightly more comfortable here.

18...♖ad8 19.♗h5 ♖hf8 20.♖he1 ♖d7 21.♘b3 ♖xd1+ 22.♖xd1 c4 23.♘c5

A bit risky, since the knight cannot cannot go back anymore.

23...♗c8 24.♔c2 ♗e5 25.b4 ♗d6

And now it looks like White will lose a pawn.

26.a4 f5 27.axb5 axb5 28.exf5 ♗xc5 29.bxc5 ♘xf5 30.♘xf5 ♖xf5

And he does, but the situation is far from hopeless for White.

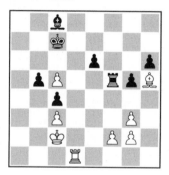

31.♗f3?

But after this move it is hopeless.

31.♖f1 ♖xc5 32.♖e1 gives good chances to draw: Black has difficulties in creating a passed pawn and h6 is weak.

31...♗b7! 32.♖e1 ♗xf3 33.gxf3 ♖xf3 34.♖xe6 ♖xf2+ 35.♔c1 ♖f3

White resigned, since after 36.♔c2 h5 37.♖e7+ ♔c6 38.♖e6+ ♔d7 39.♖h6 ♖xg3 40.♖xh5 ♔c6 he will lose another pawn.

☐ **Sergey Biriukov**
■ **Mikhail Golubev**
Alushta 2005

1.d4 ♘f6 2.♘f3 d6 3.♗f4 ♘h5 4.♗d2

The critical move. The question is whether the bishop is better on d2 than on its original square. If White plays c4 and ♘c3, the rook can go to c1, which is useful. Also there is the option of playing ♗c3. The other question is how useful the knight on h5 is. Well, on f6 it has more influence on the centre, but there it blocks the bishop on g7 (assuming Black goes for a fianchetto) and the pawn on f7. With the knight on h5, Black can play ...g6, ...♗g7, ...0-0, ...e5 and ...f5 if White plays passively. And if White plays e4, the knight might go to f4.

4...g6
The grandmasters haven't agreed so far what the best move is here.
- Kupreichik and Quinteros have played 4...f5, which you can play if you have some understanding of the Leningrad Dutch:
  – 5.e4 fxe4 6.♘g5 ♘f6 7.f3 ♘c6 8.d5 ♘xd5 9.fxe4 ♘f6 10.♘c3 h6 11.♘f3 ♗g4 was OK for Black in Prang-Kupreichik, Münster 1994.
  – 5.c4 g6 6.♘c3 ♗g7 7.e4 0-0 8.exf5 ♗xf5 9.h3 ♗d7 10.♗e3 and now 10...♘c6 would have been about equal in Glienke-Quinteros, Hannover 1983.
- Anthony Miles tried 4...♗g4 5.h3 ♗xf3 6.exf3 g6 7.♗e2 ♗g7 8.c3 ♘d7 9.f4 ♘hf6 against Sazonov in Agios Nikolaos, 1995, which is playable, but personally I like to keep my bishops.
- And then there is a very old game:

4...♘f6 5.c4 ♘bd7 6.♗c3 e6 7.e3 d5 8.c5 ♘e4 9.♗d3 f5 10.b4 g6 11.♗b2 ♗g7 and eventually Black won in 29 moves in Cohn-Nimzowitsch, Ostend 1909, but this is mainly interesting for historical reasons.
4...g6 is the move if you like to play a King's Indian.

5.c4
White can also go for the Pirc with 5.e4 ♗g7 6.♘c3 0-0 7.♗e2, and now Black has to be a bit careful. If he tries 7...e5 White can play 8.♗g5! which is annoying, e.g. 8...f6 9.♗e3 ♘f4 10.♗xf4 exf4 11.♕d2 is better for White. But Black can first play 7...c6 and on the next move play ...e5 or ...b5.

5...♗g7

6.♗c3!?
White uses the fact that Black can't play ...♘e4. After 6.♘c3 0-0 7.e4 Black has different options, but safest is 7...c6 8.♗e2 e5 followed by a quick ...♘f4.

6...0-0 7.g3
White was a bit better after 7.e3 ♘d7 8.♗e2 f5 9.d5 ♘df6 10.♘bd2 c5 11.0-0 ♕e8 12.a3 in Appel-Flores, Vlissingen 2007, but I don't think White has any advantage after the simple 8...e5.
7.g3 is more logical than 7.e3, since the bishop is more active on the long diagonal than on e2, and if White plays e4 in the future, he won't be bothered by ...♘f4.
7...♘d7

8.d5

Otherwise Black just plays 8...e5.

8...♘hf6

While it isn't necessarily terrible to exchange bishops, a King's Indian player prefers to hang on to 'his precious' if he can.

9.♗g2 ♘c5 10.♘bd2 a5 11.0-0 e5

Now 12...♘ce4 is a mini-threat.

12.dxe6

More or less obligatory, since 12.♘e1 ♗f5 13.f3 c6 isn't attractive for White.

12...♗xe6 13.♘d4 ♗d7 14.♕c2 ♖e8 15.b3

If we put the bishop on b2, the knight on c3 and the rook on d1, we get a theoretical position. This suggests that Black has won some tempi. However, if he just develops, White might consolidate and use his space advantage, so instead Black goes for an active

plan: attacking the white king.

15...h5 16.h3 ♕c8 17.♔h2 h4?!

This brings rise to interesting complications, but better would have been 17...♗f5!, since 18.♘xf5 ♕xf5 19.♕xf5 gxf5 is good for Black due to the threats 20...♘g4+ and 20...♖xe2. Instead White should play 18.♕b2 when 18...♘fe4 is equal.

18.g4 ♗h6 19.e3

Now if Black doesn't act, f4 might be on the cards one day.

19...♗xg4!? 20.hxg4 ♘xg4+ 21.♔h1

White could have played for a win with 21.♔g1!, and now either 21...♖xe3 22.♖ad1 or 21...♘xf2 22.♖xf2 ♗xe3 23.♘f1, which is not quite clear but should be better for White.

21...♗xe3 22.♗d5

And here 22.♘e4! ♘xe4 23.♗xe4 ♘xf2+ 24.♖xf2 ♖xe4 25.♕xe4 ♗xf2 26.♔g2 could have been tried.

22...♘e5 This forces the draw.

23.♗xf7+ ♔h7 24.fxe3 ♕h3+ 25.♔g1 ♕g3+ Draw.

Odds and ends

After 1.d4 ♘f6 2.♘f3 d6 White might postpone ♗f4 and play the London move(s) c3 and/or h3 first.

● 3.c3 has the idea that after 3...g6 4.♗f4 ♘h5 5.♗g5 h6 6.♗h4 g5 7.♗g3 White is a tempo up compared to Mordiglia-Efimov. It's still fine for Black, but I recommend 3...♘bd7. After 4.♗f4 there is 4...♘h5 again, and otherwise Black plays 4...e5.

● If White really wants to get a London set-up, he can play 3.h3.

Unfortunately, our pet move won't annoy White now: 3...g6 4.♗f4 ♘h5 5.♗h2 has the bishop placed on the usual comfortable square. Still it's possible to get a non-standard position.

I will give some examples:

– 3...♘bd7 4.♗f4 c5 5.e3 ♕b6 6.♕c1 cxd4 7.exd4 e5!? with complications has been tried in some games. Alas White can avoid this by playing 5.c3.

– 3...c5 is the elite choice: 4.c3 (4.dxc5 ♕a5+ 5.c3 ♕xc5 6.b4 ♕c7 7.♗b2 g6 8.e3 ♗g7 9.♘bd2 0-0 10.c4 gave Grachev an equal position against Grischuk and against Carlsen in the World Blitz 2008) 4...b6 5.♗f4 ♗a6 6.♘bd2 g6 7.e3 ♗xf1 8.♘xf1 ♗g7 9.♘1d2 0-0 10.0-0 ♘c6=, Dobbelhammer-Humer, Austria 1999 is quite a London, but at least White had to think here.

On the third move, White might also abondon the London by playing 3.♗g5 or 3.♘c3.

● 3.♗g5 ♘bd7 is OK for Black: continue either with ...g6, with ...h6/...g5/...♘h5 or ...e5 and ...♗e7.

● After 3.♘c3 you can play the Pirc (3...g6), Philidor (3...♘bd7 and 4...e5) or the Miles system (3...♗g4), but 3...♗f5 (Adams, Spassky, Tal) and 3...d5 (Morozevich, Capablanca, Euwe) aren't bad either.

Hopefully you don't have to worry about all this and can surprise your opponent with 3.♗f4 ♘h5!

CHAPTER 14

Alexander Finkel

Pirc Defence – Taking off the Gloves

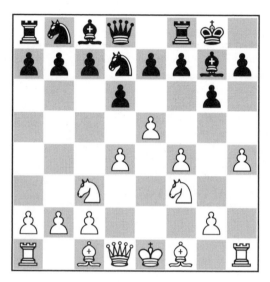

4.f4 ♗g7 5.♘f3 0-0 6.e5 ♘fd7 7.h4!?

In SOS-12 I covered the line starting with 5.e5 dxe5 6.dxe5 ♛xd1+ 7.♚xd1, indicating that one can't be absolutely sure that the queens will be swapped, due to 5...♘fd7!?, following which White doesn't really have a choice, but to opt for 6.♘f3 0-0 7.h4, transposing to our present subject. I guess I should add now that if Black meets 6.e5 with 6...dxe5 White should definitely reply 7.dxe5, entering the endgame examined in my previous Pirc article.

Since both lines are closely connected and basically combine an integral part of one whole variation (although it's hard to think of two more polar sub-lines!) it's highly recommended to carefully read both of them – it

will provide you with a complete tool box against the Pirc.

With 7.h4!? White is going for a direct assault on Black's king, intending to make good use of his rook on h1 after opening up the h-file by means of h4-h5-hxg6. The queen is transferred to h4 or h2 later on (depending on your personal taste), while the king either stays in the centre or will be evacuated to the queenside.

White's attacking set-up is quite intimidating, however, the luxury to attack from the very first moves bears a heavy price. White has to make serious strategic and sometimes material concessions (meaning major risks) to make it work.

Basically, one shouldn't be too concerned with the material concessions that have to be made; usually it's about sacrificing a pawn to keep the flame of the attack burning, a not too excessive price to pay if you ask me.

The strategic concessions have more impact though. Since Black meets White's flank aggression by breaking up the centre with 7...c5 (just as the general strategic rule prescribes), White's over-extended pawn chain (d4, e5, f4) is usually eliminated, opening up the a1-h8 diagonal for the black dark-squared bishop and freeing some squares for other black minor pieces. Moreover, White is forced to give up control over the centre, so he is highly dependent on the success of his attack.

On the positive side, when Black accepts the pawn sacrifice White's attack may become extremely dangerous, as you will see in the illustrative games.

□ **Jan Banas**
■ **Stefan Kindermann**
Trnava 1987

1.e4 d6 2.d4 ♘f6 3.♘c3 g6 4.f4 ♗g7 5.♘f3 0-0 6.e5 ♘fd7 7.h4 c5 8.h5 cxd4

9.♕xd4

In my opinion this move offers White more chances to fight for an opening advantage than the more committal piece sacrifice 9.hxg6 (as was played for example in Shirov-Smirin, Odessa 2007). I cannot really advise this course although it leads to exciting chess (with some forced draws).

9...dxe5

The best reply. After 9...♘c6? 10.♕f2 ♖e8 11.hxg6 hxg6 12.e6 fxe6 13.♗d3 ♘f8 14.♕g3 White just had a fantastic attacking position in Hector-Johansen, Gausdal 1990.

10.♕f2

It is not so easy to make a choice between the move in the game and the less popular 10.♕g1, which also offers White excellent attacking chances, but I eventually decided to concentrate on the main line and bring to your attention three highly interesting games which cover all possible developments.

10.♕g1!? e4 11.♘g5 (11.♘xe4 ♘f6 12.♘xf6+ exf6 13.hxg6 ♖e8+ 14.♔f2 hxg6 15.♗d3 ♘d7 16.♗d2 ♘c5 17.♔g3 b6 18.♖h4 ♗a6∓, Santos-Ribeiro, Lisbon 1996) 11...♘f6 12.hxg6 hxg6 13.♗e2 (13.♕h2 ♕d4 14.♘cxe4 ♖e8 – 14...♖d8 – 15.c3 ♕d5 16.♘d2 ♕c6 17.♗c4 e6 18.0-0 b5 19.♗e2±, Minic-Unger, Bad Wörishofen 1985) 13...♘c6 14.♕h2 ♕d4? 15.♗e3 ♕b4 (15...♕xe3 16.♘d5) 16.0-0-0 ♖d8 17.a3

♖xd1+ 18.♖xd1 ♕a5 19.♗c4+–, Izquierdo-Belistri, Uruguay 1982.

10...e4

This reply is considered to be Black's safest choice. The other two popular options are 10...exf4 and 10...e6, which will be examined in the next games.

11.♘xe4

This move is more popular than 11.♘g5, which leads to much sharper play.

For those of you who like to take greater risks I'd suggest to take a closer look at White's play in E.Pähtz-Schmaltz: 11.♘g5 ♘f6 12.hxg6 hxg6 13.♗e3!? (13.♕h4? ♕d4! 14.♘gxe4 ♖e8 15.♗d3 ♗f5 16.♘e2 ♕d5 17.♘xf6+ exf6∓, Matousek-Gofshtein, Prague 1989) 13...♗g4 14.♕h4 ♘bd7 (14...♕a5! is better – Vigus) 15.♘gxe4 ♖e8 16.♘f2 e5 17.f5 ♗xf5 18.0-0-0 with an initiative for White, E.Pähtz-Schmaltz, Dresden 2002.

11...♘f6 12.♘xf6+ exf6 13.hxg6

13...♖e8+!

An important intermediate move, aimed at preventing White from castling queenside.

13...hxg6?! 14.♗d2 ♘c6 15.0-0-0 ♗e6 16.♕h4 ♖e8 17.f5 ♗xf5 18.♕h7+ 1-0, Jovanovic-Martic, Bizovac 2007.

14.♗e3

Black seems to be doing fine after this, so perhaps more challenging for Black is

14.♗e2 fxg6 15.♗d2!?, with the idea to keep the rook on the h-file: 15...♕e7 16.♔f1 ♘c6 17.♗d3 with an attack.

Instead of 15.♗d2!?, practice has also seen 15.0-0 ♘c6 when play is equal after either:

– 16.♗e3 ♔h8 17.♖fe1 ♗f5 18.c3 ♕a5 19.♘d4 ♘xd4 20.♗xd4 ♗e4 21.♗f3 ♗xf3 22.♕xf3 ♕b5, Zichichi-Diaz, Havana 1966, or

– 16.♗d2 ♕c7 17.♗c4+ ♗e6 18.♗xe6+ ♖xe6 19.♖fe1 ♖ae8 20.♖xe6 ♖xe6 21.♖e1 ♕e7 22.♗c3 ♖xe1+ draw, Pulyaev-Goroschenko, Alushta 2005.

14...hxg6 15.♗d3

White got a fantastic position after 15.♗c4 ♕e7? 16.0-0-0 ♕c7 17.♗b3 ♘d7 18.♖he1 ♘f8 19.♘d4 ♗g4 20.♖d2, Fabian-Pinter, Slovakia 2002/03. However, things look far less attractive after the natural 15...♕b6! intending 16.♘e5 ♕a5+ 17.♗d2 ♕c7–+.

15...♕a5+

15...♕b6 deserves attention, after 16.♔d2 Black must choose between:

– 16...♕xb2? 17.♗c5! f5 (17...b6 18.♖hb1 ♕xa1 19.♖xa1 bxc5 20.♕xc5±) 18.♘e5 ♘d7 19.♖hb1 ♗xe5 20.♖xb2 ♗xb2 21.♖e1 ♖xe1 22.♔xe1 ♘xc5 23.♕xc5±, and

– 16...♕a5+, when White should not play 17.♔c1?!, because of 17...♘c6 18.♗d2 (18.♘d4!? ♘b4) 18...♕d5 19.♘h4 (19.♕h4 ♗f5 20.♗xf5 ♕xf5 21.♕h7+ ♔f8∓)

19...♗g4 20.♕f1 ♘d4∓, Varadi-Ianov, Nyiregyhaza 2002. Instead the white king feels quite comfortable in the centre after 17.c3!? ♘c6 18.♘d4 ♗d7 19.♘b3±.

16.c3 ♗g4 17.0-0 ♘c6 18.♘d4 f5!?

Black is trying to take over the initiative. Simply 18...♘xd4!? 19.♗xd4 f5 20.♗xg7 ♔xg7 21.a4 ♖ad8 was good enough for equality.

19.♘xc6 bxc6 20.♖fe1 ♖ad8 21.♗c2

Or 21.♗e2 ♖d7. **21...♖e7 22.♗b3 ♖de8 23.♕g3**

Preparing a trade of rooks over the e-file.

23...♗f6 24.♗f2 Of course not 24.♗d4?? ♗xd4+ 25.cxd4 ♖xe1+−+. **24...♖e2 25.♖xe2 ♖xe2 26.♖e1! ♖xb2**

26...♖xe1+ 27.♗xe1 ♕b5. **27.♕e3**

27...♕c7?

Throwing away everything that was achieved by the previous energetic play. It was much better to play 27...♔g7! 28.♕e8 ♕xc3 29.♕xf7+ ♔h6, forcing White to deal with the ...♖xf2 threat.

28.♕e8+

All of a sudden Black finds himself in a rather unpleasant situation, as all White's pieces take part in the attack.

28...♔g7?

It was necessary to play 28...♔h7 29.♗xf7 ♖b8 30.♕e6 ♔g7, although White's initiative is extremely dangerous after 31.♗e8.

29.♗c5! After this strong move Black is helpless against the many threats.

29...♗xc3

29...♗h5 30.♕f8+ ♔h7 31.♗xf7 ♕d8 32.♗e8! intending 32...♕d5 (32...♖b7 33.♔h2) 33.♗xc6! ♕xc6 34.♖e7+ ♗xe7 35.♕xe7+ ♔g8 36.♕f8+ ♔h7 37.♕f7+ ♔h6 38.♗f8 mate.

30.♕f8+ ♔h7 31.♗xf7 ♗g7 32.♕g8+ ♔h6 33.♗f8 ♕b6+ 34.♔h1

Black resigned.

☐ **Anatoli Vaisser**
■ **Mladen Palac**
Cannes 2000

1.d4 d6 2.e4 ♘f6 3.♘c3 g6 4.f4 ♗g7 5.♘f3 0-0 6.e5 ♘fd7 7.h4 c5 8.h5 cxd4 9.♕xd4 dxe5

10.♕f2

Bad is 10.fxe5?! ♘xe5 11.♕h4 ♘xf3+ 12.gxf3 ♗f5 13.hxg6 ♗xg6 14.♗d3 h5 (14...♗xc3+ 15.bxc3 ♗xd3 16.cxd3 ♕xd3 looks very dangerous for Black) 15.♗e3 ♘c6 16.0-0-0 ♕a5∓, Sax-Szpisjak, Chicago 1995.

10...exf4

Along with 10...e4 and 10...e6 one of three possible ways to deal with 7.h4, and definitely the most principled one. Black picks up a pawn, offering White to prove that his attacking prospects compensate for the material deficit.

11.hxg6 hxg6

It seems right not to spoil the pawn structure, however 11...fxg6, opening up the f-file for the rook, is perfectly playable too: 12.♖xh7!? (stronger is 12.♕h4 ♘f6 13.♗xf4) 12...♘f6 13.♖h1 ♕c7 14.♕h4 ♘h5∓, Velema-Houben, Hengelo 1997.

12.♕h4 ♘f6 13.♗xf4 ♕a5

Black loses after 13...e5? 14.♗g5 ♖e8 15.♗b5 ♘c6 16.♖d1 ♕e7 17.♘d5, Saldano-Garcia, Albacete 2004.

Perhaps Black can get away with 13...♗f5!? 14.♗d3 ♗xd3 15.0-0-0 ♕a5 16.♖xd3 ♕h5 17.♕e1 ♕f5, Kalendovsky-Babula, Brno 1969.

14.♗b5!

It's vital for White to prevent the transfer of the black queen to h5: 14.0-0-0 ♕h5! (after the exchange of queens it is much more diffi-

cult for White to prove an initiative for the sacrificed pawn) 15.♗c4 ♕xh4 16.♘xh4 e6 17.♘b5 ♘a6∓.

Also worse is 14.♘g5?! ♗g4 15.♗d3 ♘bd7 16.0-0 ♗h5 17.♖ae1 e5? (17...♕b6+ 18.♔h1 ♕xb2 19.♘ce4 ♕a3∓) 18.♗d2 ♕c5+ 19.♗e3 ♕c6 20.♗b5 ♕c7 21.♗e2 with an attack, Bronstein-Palmiotto, Munich ol 1958.

14...♕b4!

An important defensive move, halting ♗h6: 14...a6 15.♗h6 ♘h5 16.♗xg7 ♔xg7 17.g4±.

15.a3?

Based on a miscalculation, which was not exploited by Palac in the game.

It was necessary to play 15.0-0-0!? with excellent attacking chances.

15...♕xb2 16.♗e5

Gallagher has analysed 16.♘d5! as stronger, which after complications should lead to a draw by repetition. However, as I mentioned just now in my opinion White should have played 15.0-0-0!?.

16...♖d8?

Trusting the opponent or just missing the ♕c1-h6 idea, which would've put White on the ropes: 16...♕xa1+! 17.♘d1 ♕c1! 18.♗xf6 ♕h6 and Black should win.

17.♘d5?

There was a much more efficient way to trap the black queen: 17.♖a2! ♕c1+ 18.♔e2 g5 19.♕h2 ♕e3+ 20.♔xe3 ♘g4+ 21.♔e2 ♘xh2 22.♗xg7 with a technically winning position.

17...♛xe5+ 18.♘xe5 ♖xd5

The arising position is quite unclear, but it seems that Black is the one in control.

19.♘xg6! ♖xb5!
Making the right choice. After 19...fxg6? 20.♗c4 e6 21.♗xd5 exd5 22.0-0 White's initiative is highly unpleasant.

20.0-0-0 20.♘xe7+? ♔f8 21.♘xc8 ♘bd7.
20...♗d7 White is better after 20...♘c6?! 21.♘xe7+ ♔f8 22.♘xc6 bxc6 23.♖d8+ ♔e7 24.♛d4 ♖d5 25.♖xd5 cxd5 26.♛c5+.
21.♘xe7+ ♔f8 22.♘d5!? ♘xd5 23.♛d8+ ♗e8 24.♖xd5

24...♗b2+?! A serious inaccuracy, which brings up another major mistake two moves later. After the most natural 24...♖xd5 25.♛xd5 ♘c6 White would have to work very hard to keep the balance.
25.♔d2 ♘d7 26.♛g5 ♗f6?? Blunder-

ing the rook! 26...♖xd5+ 27.♛xd5 ♗f6±.
27.♛h6+ ♗g7 28.♛d6+
Black resigned.

□ **Leonid Stein**
■ **Vladimir Liberzon**
Yerevan 1965

1.e4 d6 2.d4 ♘f6 3.♘c3 g6 4.f4 ♗g7 5.♘f3 0-0 6.e5 ♘fd7 7.h4 c5 8.h5 cxd4 9.♛xd4 dxe5 10.♛f2 e6
Finally the least popular out of Black's replies, which however also leads to rather unclear positions.
11.hxg6

11...fxg6
You need guts to take with the other pawn, but it's the sort of quality you've got to have to successfully defend such positions on the Black side!
11...hxg6!? 12.♘g5:
– 12...exf4 13.♛h4 ♘f6 14.♗xf4 e5 15.♗d2 ♘bd7 16.0-0-0, Weitzer-Hoffmann, Germany Bundesliga B 1994/95, gives White the attack.
– 12...♖e8!?, and now rather than 13.♗d3?! ♛e7 14.♛h4 ♘f8 15.fxe5 ♘c6! 16.♗f4 ♘xe5 17.0-0-0 ♗d7 18.♗xe5? ♗xe5 19.♖df1 f5∓, Viksni-Fridmans, Riga 1994, White should play 13.fxe5 ♘xe5 14.♛h4 ♘bd7 15.♗e3 ♘f8 16.♖d1 ♗d7 17.♘ce4 with ongoing complications.

12.♕g3 exf4

No good is 12...♘c6? 13.♕h3 ♘f6 14.fxe5 ♘h5 15.g4 and White has a clear plus.

13.♗xf4 ♕a5

Other replies hardly promise Black an easy life:

– 13...♕f6 14.♗g5 ♕f7 15.♗c4 ♘c6 16.0-0-0 ♘de5 17.♕h4, Osterman-Nouro, Finland 1996/97.

– 13...♖xf4 14.♕xf4 ♘f8 15.♗d3 ♘c6 16.0-0-0 ♕f6 17.♕xf6 ♗xf6 18.♘e4±, Vokac-Votava, Lazne Bohdanec 1996.

– 13...♗xc3+ 14.bxc3 ♕f6 15.♗d2±.

14.♗d2 ♘f6 15.♗c4 ♘c6 16.0-0-0

We may sum up the opening stage of the game. White may be very pleased with the outcome of the opening, as his pieces are very harmonically developed and the semi-open h-file suggests that White is quite likely to get to the black king!

16...♕c5 16...♕f5!?. **17.♕h4 ♘h5**

Black's position remains highly dangerous, but defendable after 17...♕h5 or perhaps 17...b5.

– 17...♘a5 18.♘e4 ♘xe4 (18...♕xc4 19.♘xf6+ ♖xf6 20.♕xh7+ ♔f8 21.♗xa5+–) 19.♕xh7+ ♔f7 20.♗h6 ♖g8 21.♘g5+ ♘xg5 22.♖hf1+ ♔e7 23.♕xg8 ♗xb2+ 24.♔b1+–.

– 17...♕h5 18.♕e1 ♕g4 19.♕e2±.

– 17...b5!?.

18.♘e4! ♕b6 18...♕xc4? 19.♘f6++–.

19.c3 ♘a5? Just helping White to push g4! It was necessary to play 19...h6.

20.♗e2 Now Black is helpless against the forthcoming 21.g4.

20...h6 21.g4 ♘f4 22.♗xf4 ♖xf4 23.♖d8+

Black's kingside pieces don't get the chance to participate in the game, which is decided by a direct attack.

23...♖f8 23...♔h7 24.♘eg5 mate; 23...♔f7 24.♘d6++–. **24.♘f6+! ♔h8**

24...♔f7 25.♘e5+ ♔e7 26.♘d5 mate; 24...♗xf6 25.♖xf8+ ♔xf8 26.♕xf6++–.

25.♕xh6+!

Black resigned because of 25...♗xh6+ 26.♖xh6+ ♔g7 27.♖h7+ ♔xf6 28.♖xf8 mate.

A very nice finish of an inspirational attack by one of the best attacking players in the history of chess.

CHAPTER 15

Jeroen Bosch

New Recipe in Old Indian

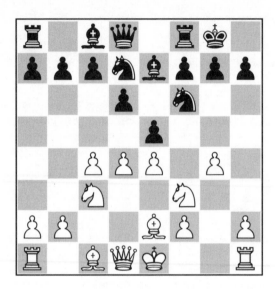

The universal antidote g4

The universal antidote to all opening problems these days is to just throw your flank pawns at your opponent. Within the SOS-series we have seen numerous lines with audacious flank pawns.

With absolutely no attempt at inclusiveness I will just mention:

– The Grünfeld with 4.h4 (SOS-3) and 4.g4 (SOS-12)
– A closed (or is it open?) Sicilian: 1.e4 c5 2.♘c3 ♘c6 3.g4 (SOS-5)
– The Shirov Philidor 1.e4 e5 2.♘f3 d6 3.d4 ♘f6 4.♘c3 ♘bd7 5.g4 (SOS-7)
– The Bogo-Indian with 6.g4 (SOS-7)
– An Anglo-Dutch 1.c4 f5 2.e4 fxe4 3.♘c3 ♘f6 4.g4 (SOS-8)

– The King's Indian with 6.g4 (SOS-9)
– The French Winawer with 4.♘ge2 and 6.g4 (SOS-12)
– The Ruy Lopez Bird with 5...h5 (SOS-12).

Many authors have noted this modern predilection for pawn moves on the flank, perhaps no one more lucidly than John Watson in his *Secrets of Modern Chess Strategy*.

Needless to say that the previous words introduce yet another flank pawn thrust in the opening. In the Old Indian experience with an early g4 (for that is what we are talking about) is as yet so limited that we present the idea here to inspire others to follow the signs of the times. Oh, by the way, this line comes with the stamp of approval of a 2700+ player...

☐ **Shakhriyar Mamedyarov**
■ **Dmitry Andreikin**
Sochi 2008

1.d4 ♘f6 2.c4 d6 3.♘c3 e5 4.♘f3 ♘bd7 5.e4 ♗e7

So Black settles for the so-called Old Indian. Not the most popular opening in the world, but one that has been played at the highest level by such grandmasters as Bent Larsen and Eugenio Torre.

6.♗e2 0-0

Black usually prefers to play **6...c6** first, but there is no need to alter our strategy in that case. White can also go **7.g4** here, when taking on g4 allows White to win back the pawn on g7 (just as in Shabalov's g4-variation in the Meran).

Let's have a closer look:

● **7...exd4** – in response to a flank attack, Black opens the centre. Now White should take with the knight on d4, as 8.♕xd4 ♕b6 (8...♘c5 9.h3 but not 9.g5 ♘e6 10.♕d1 ♘h5 and White has created a hole on f4 for a black knight to hop into) 9.g5 ♘g4 10.♗f4 (10.♕xg7 ♕xf2+ 11.♔d1 ♖f8 12.♖f1 ♘e3+

13.♗xe3 ♕xe3 is OK for Black) 10...♘de5 favours Black slightly, and after 11.0-0-0? ♕xd4 12.♖xd4 ♘xf2 13.♖f1 ♘h3 Black was winning in Wright-Xie, Canberra 2003.
8.♘xd4 and now:
– 8...d5 is well-met by 9.cxd5 cxd5 10.♘f5!.
– After 8...0-0 both the sensible 9.♗e3 and the more blunt 9.g5 ♘e8 10.h4 look attractive.
– 8...♘c5 9.♘f5 (9.f3 planning ♗e3, ♕d2 and queenside castling is entirely possible of course. This would be a similar set-up to Mamed-yarov's in our main game. However, here – with the pawn already on c6 and the king still on e8, leaving g7 undefended – the knight move makes a lot of sense) 9...♗xf5 10.exf5 ♕b6 11.♕c2 0-0-0 12.♗e3

With his bishop pair and space advantage White has an edge. Note that the 'weakening of the kingside' with g4 hardly counts – it rather gives White the possibility to gain even more space with g4-g5. 12...h5 (not wishing to continue quietly and suffer, Black seeks counterplay. 12...d5 13.cxd5 ♘xd5 14.♘xd5 ♖xd5 15.0-0 is just better for White) 13.g5 ♘g4 14.♗xg4 hxg4 15.0-0-0 ♕b4 16.♕e2 ♘a4?! (16...♘d7) 17.♘xa4 ♕xa4 18.♕xg4. White was just a pawn up and won in Anisimov-Kovalenko, St. Petersburg 2009.

● **7...♕a5 8.♗d2 ♕b6** is an -interesting manoeuvre. However, after 9.g5 ♘h5 10.c5!

– 10...♕xb2? 11.♖b1 ♕a3 12.♖b3 ♕a5, and White wins after either 13.♘b5 or 13.cxd6.

– 10...♕c7? 11.cxd6 ♗xd6 12.♘xe5 proves Tarrasch right, although he wasn't speaking of unprotected knights on the edge...

– 10...dxc5 11.dxe5 g6 Lebedev-Belmeskin, Tomsk 2007 – had White now continued with 12.♕c2 ♕c7 13.0-0-0 then he would have been guaranteed of an edge.

● Stopping the g-pawn with **7...h6** is always an important idea in g4-variations. The question usually is: which is more important, the space gained by the 'active' g4, or the squares weakened by the 'inconsiderate' pawn advance? 8.♖g1. This is played in the same spirit as 7.g4, kingside castling is now no longer on the cards for either side. (8.h3 is feasible as well, consolidating the space that has been gained on the kingside.) In Ustianovich-Pavlenko, Chervonograd 2008, Black continued with the same queen-manoeuvre as in the previous note: 8...♕a5 9.♗d2 (9.♕c2) 9...♕b6 10.♗e3 (10.c5!? ♕c7 11.cxd6 ♗xd6 12.h4 is certainly worth considering here) 10...♕xb2 11.♘a4 ♕b4+ 12.♗d2 ♕a3 13.♗c1 ♕b4+ 14.♗d2 ♕a3. Now White should perhaps have taken the draw by repetition (which means that 10.c5

is stronger than 10.♗e3), but instead he went for the unclear 15.♖b1 ♘b6 16.♘c3.

● **7...♘xg4**. Taking the pawn must always be considered. White goes 8.♖g1.

Black does not necessarily have to withdraw his knight immediately as in the old game P.Schmidt-Lange, Bad Pyrmont 1950: 8...♘gf6, now that game was quickly drawn after 9.dxe5 ♘xe5 10.♘xe5 dxe5 11.♕xd8+ ♗xd8 12.♖xg7 ♗e6, which is in itself quite surprising after 7.g4!?. However, I don't understand why White did not just play 9.♖xg7 when his chances are to be preferred.

8...♘f8 looks stronger actually, when play might continue: 9.h3!? ♘f6 (9...exd4 10.♘xd4 ♘e5, and now White should not be afraid to sac another pawn. He comes out on top after 11.♗e3 ♘fg6 12.♕d2 ♗xh3 13.0-0-0) 10.♖xg7, and now 10...♘g6? is bad because of 11.♘g5, when the inventive 11...♖g8 loses after 12.♘xf7 ♕a5 13.♖xg8+ ♘xg8 14.dxe5! (14.♘h6 ♘xh6 15.♗xh6 ♕b6) 14...♘xf7 15.exd6, and White regains the piece.

8...♘b6!? is perhaps best, when 9.dxe5 (9.h3 exd4 10.♘xd4 ♘e5 gives Black more than enough counterplay) 9...♘xe5 10.♘xe5 dxe5 11.♕xd8+ ♗xd8 12.♖xg7 does look like an equal endgame.

7.g4

Mamedyarov clearly is a child of his times.

It is very interesting to see a top grandmaster play g4 rather than go for a ± position that theory promises the first player after the more mundane 7.0-0.

One reason why Black often prefers 6...c6 over 6...0-0 is 7.d5 ♘c5 8.♕c2, when White has closed the centre (a concession of sorts) but still has the option to castle queenside. Grandmaster Andreikin does not seem to mind this too much.

Just to briefly show you that even on a high level it is not easy to make something of White's traditional slight plus in the Old Indian: 7.0-0 c6 8.♕c2 a6 9.♖d1 ♕c7. The traditional Old-Indian set-up. Black often continues ...b5, ...♗b7, ...♖fe8 or ...♖fd8, and ...♖ac8, with a solid Ruy Lopez-like middlegame. Rodshtein-Andreikin, Puerto Madryn 2009, went: 10.♗g5 h6 11.♗h4 ♖e8 12.♖ac1

12...g5!? Well, here's that g-pawn again! 13.♗g3 ♘h5 14.d5 c5 15.h3 ♘f4 16.♘h2 ♘xe2+ 17.♕xe2 ♘f6 18.♘g4 ♗xg4 19.hxg4 ♕d7 20.f3 h5!? 21.gxh5 (21.♕e3 ♔h7 22.♕xg5 ♖g8 23.♕h4 ♘xg4 24.♕xh5+ ♘h6 with obvious compensation for the pawn) 21...♘xh5 22.♔f2 ♔g7 23.♖h1 ♖h8 24.♖h3 ♘f4 25.♗xf4 exf4 26.♖ch1 ♗f6 27.♕d3 ♗e5 28.♔e2 ♖xh3 29.♖xh3 b5, with superior chances, but White managed to hold.

7...exd4

Opening the g-file in front of your king is not very logical. For example: 7...♘xg4 8.♖g1 and now:
- 8...f5 9.exf5 ♘gf6 10.♘g5 ♘b6 11.♘e6 ♗xe6 12.fxe6 exd4 13.♕xd4 favours White.
- 8...♘gf6 9.♗h6 (9.♗e3) 9...♘e8 10.♕c2.
- 8...exd4 9.♘xd4 ♘ge5 10.♗e3 and White's position plays itself.

8.♘xd4 ♘c5 9.f3 ♘e8

Black understandably wants to punish his opponent for his early g4, but White now has solid structural advantages like central control and space. It looks as if White has played the Sämisch versus the King's Indian, but Black has forgotten to fianchetto his bishop and has insufficient counterplay.

10.♗e3

The most ambitious continuation, ignoring

the threatened check, when the king will flee to the queenside anyway. Meanwhile, 10.0-0 c6 11.♗e3 was enough for a very pleasant plus.

10...♗h4+ 11.♔d2 g6 12.♔c2 ♘g7 13.♕d2

White's opening has been a total success.

13...♗d7

After 13...f5 there is either 14.gxf5 gxf5 15.♖ag1 for an all-out attack or the positional 14.exf5 gxf5 15.♖af1.

14.♖hg1

After 14.♖ad1, 14...♘a4 is an idea to relieve some of the pressure. Although White always keeps an edge.

14...♘ce6

15.♘f5!

Not difficult to find, Black cannot even contemplate to take the knight.

15...♗f6

15...gxf5? 16.gxf5 ♘c5? (16...♔h8) 17.♗h6 ♗f6 18.♗xg7 ♗xg7 19.♕h6 is a straightforward win.

16.♘h6+ ♔h8 17.g5 ♗e7 18.f4

Now in order to avoid being crushed Black has to play

18...f5 19.exf5

19.gxf6 ♗xf6 20.♘d5 is also better for White, but there is nothing wrong with the game move.

19...♘xf5 20.♘xf5 ♖xf5 21.♗g4 ♖f7 22.♖ae1 ♘g7 23.♕d5!

A double attack to win material.

23...♔g8 24.♗xd7 ♕xd7 25.♕xb7 ♖af8 26.♔b1 ♗d8 27.♕xa7 ♘h5 28.♕a4 ♕h3

Andreikin seeks counterchances with this objectively bad move, understandably he did not much like the ending after 28...♕xa4 29.♘xa4 ♘xf4.

29.♘d5 ♕xh2 30.c5! ♕h3 31.♔a1 ♕e6

32.♕c6

The beginning of a faulty manoeuvre. It was correct to keep the knight on d5 with 32.♖d1! when after 32...♖f5 33.♕b3 ♕f7 (33...c6?? 34.♘e7++−), 34.c6! fixes the beast firmly on d5 with a won game.

32...♖f5 33.♖d1

33.♘xc7.

33...♕e8!

It is hard to blame Mamedyarov for overlooking this move which paradoxically offers to trade queens. The problem is that White's light pieces suddenly hang in the air.

34.♕xe8 ♖xe8

Now it is clear that White is losing some material.

35.cxd6 35.♗c1 dxc5. **35...♖xd5 36.♖xd5 ♖xe3 37.dxc7**

37.♖e5 ♖xe5 38.fxe5 cxd6 39.exd6 ♔f7.

37...♗xc7 38.f5 gxf5 39.♖xf5 ♘f4 40.♔b1 ♗e5

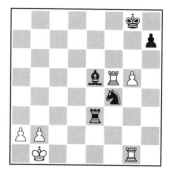

Just look at that bishop that was once stuck on d8 defending a pawn, and that knight which was formerly such a pain on the edge. Black's pieces have miraculously come alive and coordinate well. A draw is the normal result now.

41.♖f1 ♘d3 42.♖5f3 ♖xf3 43.♖xf3 ♘xb2 44.♔c2 ♔g7 45.♖e3 ♘c4 46.♖e4 ♘a3+ 47.♔b3 ♗d6 48.♖d4 ♗f8 49.♖d8 ♗c5 50.♖a8 ♘b1 51.♔c4 ♗e7 52.a4

Black also draws after 52.♖a7 ♔f7 53.a4 ♘d2+ (53...♔e6? 54.♔d3 ♗xg5 55.a5 ♘a3 56.a6 ♗h4 57.♖b7+−) 54.♔d5 ♘b3 55.♖b7 ♘a5 56.♖b5 ♗d8.

52...♘d2+ 53.♔d5 ♘b3 54.♖b8 ♘a5 55.♖b5 ♗d8 56.♔e6 ♘c4 57.♔d7

Winning the bishop, but Black drew after **57...♘b6+ 58.♔xd8 ♘xa4 59.♔e7 ♘c3 60.♖c5 ♘e4 61.♖e5 ♘f2 62.♖f5 ♘e4 63.♔e6 ♔g6 64.♖f6+ ♔xg5 65.♖f7 ♔g4 66.♖xh7 ♘g5+ 67.♔f6 ♘xh7+ 68.♔e5**

Draw.

129

CHAPTER 16

John van der Wiel

Sicilian Mission: To Boldly Go...

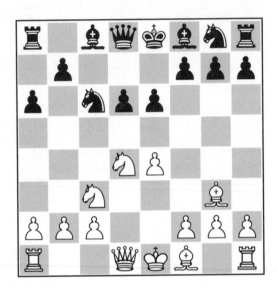

Where No Bishop Has Gone Before

Introduction

In the Sicilian after **1.e4 c5 2.♘f3 e6 3.d4 cxd4 4.♘xd4 ♘c6 5.♘c3 a6** there is nothing particularly wrong with 6.♘xc6 bxc6 7.♗d3, apart from the fact that your opponent will be prepared for it. Therefore you may want to try 6.♗f4. In the 1980s I experimented with the somewhat primitive 6.♗f4 d6 7.♘xc6 bxc6 8.♗c4, but here we shall focus on:

6.♗f4 d6 7.♗g3

A rare occurrence in a Sicilian, this bishop on g3. I don't know that many games where a bishop ends up on g3, but quite possibly a brave bishop has visited that square before. So much for the title. The questions remains:

was it inspired by recent scandals in the Catholic church or by a favourite TV-series? White's idea is to maintain pressure against d6, without deciding about the future of the knight on d4 just yet. (Another idea is 7.♘b3, when 7...b5 is a good reply). Depending on Black's reaction, White will continue positionally with ♗f1-e2 or more aggressively with ♕d1-d2 and 0-0-0. After 7.♗f4 Black's most popular reply is 7...♘f6, and next on the popularity scale comes 7...♗e7. However, 7...♗d7, 7...♕c7 and 7...e5 are quite reasonable responses too. That suggests plenty of scope for creativity. In the next four games I shall try and demonstrate the further implications.

☐ **Yaroslav Zherebukh**
■ **Anton Kovalyov**
Cappelle-la-Grande 2010

1.e4 c5 2.♘f3 e6 3.d4 cxd4 4.♘xd4 ♘c6 5.♘c3 a6 6.♗f4 d6 7.♗g3 ♘f6

This move allows White to go 8.♘xc6 bxc6 9.e5 (9...♘d5), yet it is most popular. And, indeed, White is well-advised to postpone that particular action for one more move.

8.♗e2 ♗e7

Probably it is wiser for Black to do something like 8...♕c7, as in Fernandez Garcia-Andersson, Bilbao 1987, when after 9.f4 (I would prefer 9.♕d2; or on a more peaceful day 9.0-0) 9...♗e7 10.e5?! ♘d5 White had absolutely nothing. The vast majority of mankind chooses the text, though. A case of 'database-induced herd mentality'?

9.♘xc6! bxc6 10.e5 ♘d5

The endgame cannot be to Black's liking. In Moldovan-Popa, Romania tt 1994, White didn't manage to win, but after 10...dxe5 11.♕xd8+ ♗xd8 12.♗xe5 0-0 13.0-0-0 ♗b6 14.♖hf1 ♗b7 15.♘a4! ♗a7 16.♗d6 ♖fd8 17.♗c5 he was clearly better: superior pieces and pawn structure.

11.exd6 ♗xd6 12.♘e4

12...♗xg3

A concession. White is happy to play h2xg3 and there will be weaknesses in Black's camp on the dark squares. When White

plays the same variation a tempo down, starting with 8.♘xc6 bxc6 9.e5 (so with the bishop still on f1), Black can opt for 11...♗e7! and if 12.c4 then 12....♕a5+, after which 13.♔e2!? 0-0!? has never been tested (White always played the modest 13.♘d2).

In the actual position Black doesn't have a satisfactory move: 12...♗e7 13.c4 ♕a5+ 14.♔f1 is awful for Black, and 12...♗c7 13.c4 ♘f4 14.♕xd8+ ♔xd8 15.0-0-0+ ♔e7 16.♗f3 ♖a7 (or 16...h5 17.h4 a5 18.♖d2 ♖d8 19.♖xd8 ♔xd8 20.♖d1+ ♔e7 21.♖xh5!, winning a healthy pawn in Korensky-Sideifzade, Tbilisi 1974, the oldest game with 8.♗e2 and 9.♘xc6) 17.♘c5 ♘g6 18.♗xc7 ♖xc7 19.♖he1 ♖d8 gave White a very nice advantage in W.Watson-Benjamin, New York 1987, similar to Moldovan-Popa above.

13.hxg3 f5?!

For 13...0-0 see the next game.

14.♗h5+

Unpleasant for Black's king, but even the quiet 14.♘d2 poses serious problems. We shall follow Tseitlin-Yudasin, Leningrad Championship 1987: 14...♕f6 15.♘c4 e5 16.♕d2 0-0 17.0-0-0 ♖b8 18.f4! exf4 19.gxf4 ♗e6 20.♘e5 ♘b4 21.a3 ♖fd8 22.♕e3 ♘d5 23.♕f2, highlighting White's dominance on the dark squares and winning the game soon afterwards.

14...♔f8

There was one older example: W.Watson-P.Cramling, Hastings 1985/86. That game went 14...♔e7 15.♘d2 ♕b6 16.b3 ♕d4 17.0-0 ♘c3 18.♕c1 a5?! (18...g6!?) 19.♘f3! ♕d6 20.♖e1 ♘e4 (20...g6 21.♕b2) 21.♘g5! and Black's position quickly disintegrated.

15.♕f3?

White continues in vigorous style, but he shouldn't. Stronger is 15.♘d2! ♕f6 (15...♕b6 16.c4!? – or 16.♘b3) 16.♘c4. Things are similar to Tseitlin-Yudasin, even slightly more unpleasant for Black, see 16...g6 17.♗e2 ♔g7 18.♕d2 eyeing h6, or 16...♕h6 17.♕d4.

15...♕a5+?

This prevents White from ever moving his queen to a3, but ventures too far away from the critical zone.

There were two better options:

● 15...♕e7 which threatens to win a piece by 16...♔g8 and 17...g6. Now 16.c4 ♕b4+ saves the day for Black, but White plays 16.♘d2 and still evacuates his minor pieces. Black is worse, especially since 16...g6? 17.♗xg6 ♕g7 18.♕a3+ is no good. With 16...♖b8 he can put up a good fight.

● 15...♔g8 (!) Black can't take on e4 yet, but 16...g6 will win material. White has to try 16.c4, when

– 16...g6 17.♗xg6!? hxg6 18.♖xh8+ ♔xh8 19.cxd5 fxe4 20.♕c3+ ♔g8 21.dxc6 is highly unclear.

– 16...♘e7! looks best. Then 17.♘g5 ♕a5+! (17...g6 18.♕c3!) 18.♔f1 g6 19.♗g4 h6 does not seem to help White. Perhaps something miraculous like 17.♕f4 g6 18.♘f6+ (18.♘d6 ♕a5+!) 18...♔f7 19.♕e5 could work, but I don't think so.

– 16...♘b4!? is another interesting option.

16.c3 ♖b8 17.♘d6!

Putting an end to Black's counterplay. If 17...♖xb2 then 18.♘c4!, if nothing else, is decisive.

17...♕c5?

In retrospect, both 17...♕c7 and 17...♔e7 ought to be preferred. Against the latter, White replies 18.♘c4.

18.♘xc8 ♖xc8 19.♕e2 ♘c7

A terrible move to (have to) play, but 19...♘f6 20.♕xe6, 19...♘xc3 20.♕xe6 and 19...♔e7 20.♕e5! are just not feasible.

20.0-0-0 ♔e7 21.♕d2! ♔f6 22.b4

White conducts the game with great force.

22...♕e7

For if 22...♕d5 then after 23.♕b2! ♕xg2 24.c4+ e5 25.♖he1 Black has to bleed: 25...♔g5? 26.f4+.

23.g4 g6

24.gxf5! gxh5?!

Objectively Black has to play 24...exf5 25.♖he1 ♘e6, but possibly Kovalyov (who otherwise didn't have a very bright day for his rating) judged that 26.♗e2 wouldn't leave him much hope. One example: 26...♖hd8 27.♕b2 ♖xd1+ 28.♗xd1 c5 29.c4+ and White is winning, e.g. 29...♔f7 30.♗f3, or 29...♔g5 30.f4+!.

25.♕h6+ ♔f7 26.f6 ♕f8 27.♖d7+ ♔e8 28.♖e7+ ♔d8

29.♕f4!

That seals it. Black can resign.

29...♕xe7 30.fxe7+ ♔xe7 31.♕g5+ ♔f7 32.♕xh5+ ♔f6 33.♕h6+ ♔f7 34.♖h3 ♖hf8 35.♖f3+ ♔g8 36.♖g3+ ♔f7 37.♖g7+ ♔e8 38.♕h5+

Black resigned.

□ **Sergio Mariotti**
■ **Anatoly Karpov**
Leningrad 1977 (11)

1.e4 c5 2.♘f3 e6 3.d4 cxd4 4.♘xd4 ♘c6 5.♘c3 a6 6.♗f4 d6 7.♗g3 ♘f6 8.♗e2 ♗e7 9.♘xc6 bxc6 10.e5 ♘d5 11.exd6 ♗xd6 12.♘e4 ♗xg3 13.hxg3 0-0

We already know that 13...f5 14.♗h5+ is no ride in the park for Black.

14.c4 f5!?

Most certainly the World Champion was SOS-ed in this game. The text has nothing to do with luxury or preparation, it is merely meant to avoid an inferior ending after 14...♘f6 15.♕xd8 ♖xd8. Then Sax-

Etchegaray, Benasque 1993, went 16.♗f3 ♖b8 17.b3 ♘xe4?! (17...♖b6!?) 18.♗xe4 c5 19.♗xh7+ and White was as good as winning.

15.♘d2?!

It is hard to understand why Mariotti did not opt for 15.cxd5 fxe4 16.dxc6. After 16...♕b6 (16...♕a5+ 17.♕d2 ♕xd2+ 18.♔xd2 ♖xf2 19.♔e3 surely must be winning for White) 17.0-0 ♕xc6 (17...e3 18.♗f3) all Black can do is pray and play for a draw, as White is much better.

15...♘f6 16.♘f3?!

With hindsight White should have secured some advantage with 16.♘b3. This limits the possibilities of Black's queen, and, most importantly, controls the c5-square.

16...♕b6! 17.♕d4 c5

Already Black has equalized.

18.♕c3 ♗b7 19.0-0 ♖ae8!

And now it is practically impossible to prevent e6-e5, see: 20.♘e5 ♘e4 21.♕a3?! (or 21.♕b3?! ♕c7; White should play 21.♕e3! here, however, since 21...♕xb2 22.♘d7! is highly unclear and possibly too dangerous for Black, it is hard to see Karpov going for such a line) 21...♕d6! 22.f4 ♕d4+ 23.♔h2 ♖f6.

20.♖fe1?! e5 21.♖ad1

Obviously 21.♘xe5? ♘e4 loses material.

21...a5 22.b3 ♕c7 23.♘d2 ♖d8 24.♘f3

Mariotti's meek play has earned him a passive position. Perhaps it wouldn't have been so tragic yet, had he chosen 24.♘f1 ♖d4 25.♘e3 and if 25...♘e4 then 26.♕c1.

24...♗xf3! 25.♗xf3

Probably better was 25.gxf3.

25...♖d4 26.♕e3 e4

27.♖xd4!?

A rather desperate piece sac, but an understandable one. After 27.♗e2 ♖fd8 White doesn't have a constructive defensive plan and Black may even follow up with 28...♕d6, already threatening to take thrice on d1! Or else 28.♕f4 ♕xf4 (28...♕d7 29.f3) 29.gxf4 ♖d2 and 30...♖8d4 leads to an ending that leaves White with very little hope.

27...cxd4 28.♕xd4 ♖d8 29.♕c3 exf3 30.gxf3 h5?!

This might be somewhat frivolous. True, there is no clear path to victory (yet), but 30...♖e8 was more normal, and 30...♔f7 (30...f4!?) is a good move too.

31.♖e5?!

Going after Black's loose pawns whilst leaving all the heavy pieces on the board, turns out to be too dangerous. 31.♕e5! would be the safer way to do it. I am not sure how Black would then proceed. Possibly he can choose between 31...♕xe5 32.♖xe5 f4!? and 31...♕d7 32.♕xa5 f4 (32...h4).

31...♖d1+ 32.♔g2 ♕d7 33.♖xa5 h4! 34.gxh4 ♖d4 35.♖d5

Unfortunately White cannot afford to play 35.♖xf5 ♖xh4 36.♕e5 ♕d1!, but now the ensuing endgame should be lost in the long run. A last try could be 35.♕c2!? (35...g6 36.♕b2).

35...♖xd5 36.cxd5 ♘xd5 37.♕e5 ♔f7 38.a4 ♘b4 39.♕c5 ♘d3 40.♕c4+ ♔g6 41.♔f1 ♕d6 42.♔e2 ♘f4+ 43.♔e3 ♘g2+ 44.♔e2 ♕e5+ 45.♔d3 ♘e1+ 46.♔d2 ♘xf3+ 47.♔c2 ♕h5 48.b4 ♕e1 49.♕c5 ♕d2+ 50.♔b3 ♕d3+ 51.♔b2 ♘d2 52.♕c3 ♕b1+ 53.♔a3 ♕e1 54.♔b2 ♕xf2 55.♕xg7 ♘e4+ 56.♔b3 ♕e3+ 57.♔b2 ♕d2+ 58.♔b3 ♕d5+ 59.♔b2 f4 60.♕h8+ ♔g4 61.h5 ♕d2+ 62.♔b3 ♕d3+ 63.♔b2 f3 64.h6 ♘g5 65.♕c8+ ♔h5 66.♕e8+ ♔xh6 67.♕f8+ ♔h5 68.♕e8+ ♔g4 69.♕c8+ ♔g3 70.♕c7+ ♔g2 71.♕c6 ♕e4 72.♕c5 ♘e6

White resigned.

Intermezzo

After these games we know that 7...♘f6 and 8...♗e7, though played relatively often, is actually quite bad for Black. He had better follow up with 8...♕c7, once he has selected 7...♘f6. Now it is time to look at other 7th moves by Black. Before we move on to the next two games, a few words about 7...e5, which is a good attempt to break the pressure of ♗g3. The positions often resemble the Najdorf. In practice this may be to White's advantage: when Black starts out with ...e6, ...♘c6 and ...a6 he is usually not a Najdorf expert. White can choose a treatment with ♕d1-d2 and f2-f4, the tempi being the same as in the 6.♗e3-system, or something slower with ♗g3-h4 as a useful tool in the struggle for control over the d5-square.

7...e5 8.♘b3 ♘f6

and now:

● **9.♗c4 ♗e7 10.0-0 0-0** 10...b5!?. **11.a4 b6 12.♕e2 ♗b7 13.♖fd1** with some advantage to White, as ♗g3-h4 is coming up (Janosevic-Hartoch, Amsterdam IBM 1970).

● **9.f4 exf4 10.♗xf4 ♗e7 11.♕d2 0-0 12.0-0-0 ♗g4?!** 12...♘e5; 12...♗e6!?. **13.♗e2 ♗xe2 14.♕xe2 ♕c7?!** 14...♖e8. **15.g4! ♘e5 16.g5 ♘fd7 17.♘d5 ♕d8 18.h4** And White had a great position in Fernandez Garcia-Mendoza Contreras, Spain 1990.

Black can consider postponing e6-e5 to a better moment, as we shall see in the next game.

□ **Andrey Lukin**
■ **Alexey Suetin**
Moscow tt 1972

1.e4 c5 2.♘f3 e6 3.d4 cxd4 4.♘xd4 ♘c6 5.♘c3 a6 6.♗f4 d6 7.♗g3 ♗e7

For 7...♗d7 and 7...♕c7 see Game 4.

8.♕d2

An original (but not so strong) approach was to be seen in Tseitlin-Vyzhmanavin, Soviet Army Championship 1983: 8.♘xc6 bxc6 9.e5 d5 10.♕g4 g6 11.♗d3 ♘h6 12.♕f3 ♘f5 13.♗f4 h5 14.♗d2 (14.g4!?) 14...♕c7 15.0-0-0 ♕xe5 16.♖he1 ♕c7 (16...♕g7! looks safer) 17.♗xf5 gxf5 18.♘e2 c5?! (and here 18...♗d7 ought to be preferred) 19.♘f4 and now White had dangerous compensation, but mainly due to Black's careless play.

8...♘xd4 9.♕xd4 ♘f6

10.♗e2

In a game Zolnierowicz-Svenn, Gothenburg 1989, White opted for the more powerful 10.♗c4 0-0 11.0-0-0 e5 12.♕d3 ♗e6 13.♗b3 ♗xb3 14.axb3 ♖c8 15.♔b1 ♖c6 16.♕e2 ♕a5 17.♗h4 ♖fc8 18.♗xf6 ♗xf6 19.♕g4 and held a clear advantage. I think there is something to be said for 10...b5

11.♗b3 ♘h5!? (12.a4!) or rather 10...♘h5!?, letting White know his bishop should have gone to e2. After eliminating ♗g3 there is less central pressure and no need to give up the d5-square, but White still has chances on the kingside.

10...e5 11.♕e3 ♗e6 12.0-0-0 ♕a5 13.a3 ♖c8 14.f3 If 14.♗h4 then 14...♖xc3!.

14...0-0 15.♗h4 The alternative is 15.♗e1, paving the way for the g-pawn.

15...d5?!

A radical solution, but maybe not the best one. My money would be on 15...♘g4!? 16.fxg4 ♗xh4. After 17.♖xd6 (17.g5 ♕c5!) 17...♗e7 18.♖d3 ♗c5 Black surely has good compensation. White does not have to eat the pawn, of course. 17.♔b1 is about equal. 15...♘xe4 16.♗xe7 ♘xc3 17.♗xf8 is not quite enough.

16.exd5 ♖xc3

The problem with 16...♘xd5 is not so much 17.♘xd5 (17...♗xh4 18.♕xe5 ♖c5 then looks acceptable for Black), but 17.♖xd5!, see: 17...♖xc3 18.♖xa5! ♖xe3 19.♗xe7 ♖xe2 (19...♖e8 fails to 20.♔d2!) 20.♗xf8 ♔xf8 21.♖d1 ♖xg2 22.♖xe5 and Black does not have enough. Therefore another endgame is reached by force.

17.♕xc3 ♕xc3 18.bxc3 ♗xa3+ 19.♔d2 ♘xd5 20.♖b1 b5 21.c4

21.♖a1 b4 is fine for Black.

21...♘f4

White was hoping for 21...♗b4+? 22.♖xb4 ♘xb4 23.♗e7. Black could have chosen 21...bxc4 22.♗xc4 ♗b4+ though. As the white king has no squares, there follows 23.♖xb4 ♘xb4 24.♗xe6 fxe6 25.♗e7 or 25.♖b1 which looks like a draw.

22.cxb5 axb5?!

Strange. After 22...♘xe2! 23.♔xe2 axb5 Black's advantage looks minimal. So, did Suetin fear 23.bxa6 ? I don't believe White can win after 23...♘d4 24.a7 ♗c5.

23.♗xb5 ♘xg2 24.♗g3

From here onwards it's a game of two results: 1-0 or ½-½.

24...f6 25.♗d3 ♗d5 26.♖b5 ♖d8

White had set a little trap: 26...♗xf3? 27.♖b3 attacks two bishops, because of ♗d3-c4+. **27.♔e2 ♗c6 28.♖b6 ♖c8 29.♖hb1 ♔f7 30.♖b8**

30...♖xb8

Another weird decision. With the last Black rook gone, White's dominance is doubled. 30...♖c7 would have made Lukin's task much harder.

31.♖xb8 h5 32.♖c8 ♗d7 33.♖c7 ♔e6 34.♔f2 ♘f4 35.♗xf4 exf4 36.♗f5+ ♔xf5 37.♖xd7 g5 38.♖h7 ♗c5+ 39.♔e2 ♔g6 40.♖c7 ♗d4 41.c4 ♗e5 42.♖d7 g4 43.c5 g3 44.♔f1 h4 45.♔g2

Black resigned.

□ **Mark Tseitlin**
■ **Valery Loginov**
Rostov on Don 1976

Finally we shall turn our attention to 7...♗d7 and 7...♕c7. These moves can often inter-transpose.

1.e4 c5 2.♘f3 e6 3.d4 cxd4 4.♘xd4 ♘c6 5.♘c3 a6 6.♗f4 d6 7.♗g3 ♗d7

8.♕d2 ♕c7

The usual approach. Black wants to protect d6 first and then develop his kingside. One exception is Khalifman-Gdanski, Leningrad 1989: 8...♘f6 9.0-0-0 ♖c8 10.♘xc6 ♗xc6 11.f3 (11.♗xd6?! ♕xd6 12.♕xd6 ♗xd6 13.♖xd6 ♗xe4) 11...d5 12.e5 ♘d7 13.♘e2 ♗e7 14.♘d4 0-0 15.♔b1 ♘c5 16.h4 ♕b6

17.h5 ♖fe8 18.♗h4 ♗f8 19.♖h3 ♔h8 20.♖g3 and White developed a dangerous initiative.

9.0-0-0 ♖d8

Black could defend d6 by means of 9...0-0-0, but no one has ever played that. The reason: after 10.f3 (10.f4) and 11.♗f2 the b6-square is vulnerable and, having castled, Black does not want to weaken himself by b7-b5 (in order to stop ♘c3-a4).

10.♗e2

A good universal move. Other, more extreme, examples are:

– 10.♘b3 ♗c8 11.f4 ♘f6 12.♗h4 ♗e7 13.g4?! (13.♕e1!?) 13...♘xe4 14.♘xe4 ♗xh4 15.♘xd6+ ♔f8 16.g5 h6 17.♖g1 e5 with a big advantage for Black in Pietrusiak-Wl.Schmidt, Gdynia 1973.

– 10.h4 ♘f6 11.h5 ♗e7 12.♔b1 h6 13.f4 ♗c8 14.♕e1 0-0 15.♗h4 b5 16.♘xc6 ♕xc6 17.♗d3 and White was slightly better and after 17...b4 18.♘e2 e5 19.♕xb4 exf4 20.♘xf4 ♖fe8 21.♘d5 more than slightly, Pavlov-Ogaard, Bucharest 1976.

Probably in this game Black should try 13...♘xd4 (13...b5 14.♗xb5!?) 14.♕xd4 ♗c6, intending to follow up with b7-b5.

– 10.f4, a good way to play for the initiative, retaining the option of ♗f1-c4. This has never been tried.

10...♗e7

It is very difficult to develop with ♘g8-f6 here, as White has tactics in the centre on his side, viz.: 10...♘f6 11.f4 ♗e7 12.e5! dxe5?! 13.fxe5 ♘xe5 14.♕g5! and Black has no reply.

11.f4 ♗c8 12.♗f2

12...b5?!

Loginov underestimates the power of White's mobilization. He wants to prevent ♘c3-a4 once and for all, but here it was necessary to go 12...♘f6. When needed the knight can go to d7, in Scheveningen style. After 13.g4 we have a full-blooded fight that might be called slightly better for White. Now White can sacrifice:

13.♘cxb5! axb5 14.♕c3 ♗d7

14...♗b7! looks better (15.♗xb5 ♖c8 or 15.♘xb5 ♕b8) because d6 is not as weak. Maybe the players discarded it on account of 15.♘xe6 fxe6 16.♕xg7, but after 16...♘f6! White probably cannot justify his action.

15.♘xb5 ♕b8 16.♕xg7 ♗f6 17.♕g3 ♗c8

Or 17...♗e7 18.♕c3 ♘f6 19.♗h4!.

18.♕a3! d5 19.e5 ♗e7 20.♗c5

With three pawns up and so many positional and dynamical trumps for the piece, White must be close to winning.

20...♖d7 21.c4! dxc4 22.♗xc4 ♗xc5 23.♕xc5 ♖xd1+ 24.♖xd1 ♘ge7 25.♘d6+ ♔f8

26.f5!

Not too difficult, but nevertheless quite effective! White wants to crack open the black king's position and have his queen join the fun.

26...exf5

Even 26...♕b4 27.♕xb4 ♘xb4 28.♘xc8 ♘xc8? (28...♘xf5) 29.♖d8+ ♔g7 30.f6+ cannot save Black.

27.♕e3 ♖g8

Or 27...h6 28.♘xf7.

28.♕h6+ ♖g7 29.♘xf7 ♘g6

29...♕b4 30.♘d6 threatens a big check on f6.

30.♕g5?

My first impression was that this was a very nice game by Mark Tseitlin, who employed this SOS-system several times. However, this decisive-looking manoeuvre does not win! I am convinced that time-trouble played a significant part in the remainder of the game. Anyhow, the position is far from easy. For instance, 30.♘g5 ♕xe5 31.♘xh7+ ♚e8 doesn't quite do the trick. Possibly, 30.♖d6 ♕b4! 31.b3 wins eventually, but even that is not guaranteed.

30...♕c7 31.♕f6

Leaving Black no choice...

31...♖xf7 32.♗xf7

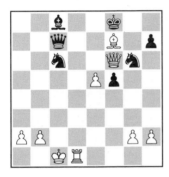

32...♕xf7?

...but here there was another option! Instead of this blunder Black could and should select 32...♘cxe5+ 33.♗c4+ ♚e8, when White can play on with 34.b3 ♘xc4 35.bxc4 ♕xc4+ 36.♚b1, but there is no win in sight.

33.♕xc6 ♗e6 34.♖d6 ♘xe5

This hastens the end, but Black's position was beyond salvation anyway.

35.♕c5!

Setting up a murderous discovered check or winning the knight. Black resigned.

Conclusion

My database produced 56 games stemming from the position after 7.♗g3. White scored 63%. Not bad, but this is not a large sample of course.

Strangely enough, Black's percentages after 7...♘f6 are relatively best (around 45%), although we have seen that White obtains a big advantage after 8.♗e2 ♗e7?! 9.♘xc6 bxc6 10.e5.

Black does better to avoid this white thrust by 8...♕c7 or 8...♗d7, which might transpose to a 7...♕c7/7...♗d7 line, which I slightly distrust: see Tseitlin-Loginov.

For Black, I would mainly put my trust in 7...♗e7. One reason being that Portisch once played it, and did anyone ever study any line more in-depth than he did? Nevertheless, White has some options here too: especially 10.♗c4 and 15.♗e1, as mentioned in Lukin-Suetin. And if, in the only recent game, a 2600-player can be lured into the 'headache variation' and defeated, then we can safely say: this is a typical SOS-system!

CHAPTER 17

Ian Rogers

Surprising Sacrifice in the Giuoco Piano

The cunning 8.♕xd2

1.e4 e5 2.♘f3 ♘c6 3.♗c4 ♗c5 4.c3 ♘f6 5.d4 exd4 6.cxd4 ♗b4+ 7.♗d2 ♗xd2+

This position has been reached thousands of times, with the reply being automatic. Yes, we all know that White would prefer to put his b1 knight on c3 rather than d2, but surely any other move than 8.♘bxd2 loses a pawn?

8.♕xd2!

An idea discovered about 35 years ago and first played (as a deliberate sacrifice rather than a pawn blunder!) by this writer in an unnoticed Zonal Tournament game in Japan in 1978. White is sacrificing the e-pawn, but in many variations wins it back immediately, with a better position than in the usual

8.♘bxd2 lines. When Black decides to keep the pawn, he will be subject to considerable pressure, which can lead to trouble in surprisingly quick time.

8...♘xe4

'The only way to refute a gambit is to accept it!' said Steinitz. Though other moves are undoubtedly playable, they tend to lead to inferior versions of other Giuoco Piano variations.

● **8...d6 9.♘c3**

This is the same as the position which would usually arise via 1.e4 e5 2.♘f3 ♘c6 3.♗c4 ♗c5 4.c3 d6 5.d4 exd4 6.cxd4 ♗b4+ 7.♗d2 ♗xd2+ 8.♕xd2 ♘f6 9.♘c3. Black's position is not disastrous, but it is clear that not many players would enjoy sitting with the black pieces here either – otherwise 4...d6 would have emerged from oblivion at some point.

Play has continued 9...0-0 10.0-0 ♗g4 (10...♖e8 11.♖fe1 ♗d7?! 12.♖ad1 ♘e7?! 13.e5!± was Sleczka-Kopera, Polanica Zdroj 2008; 10...♘xe4!? is a serious try – only slightly better for White after 11.♘xe4 d5 12.♗d3 dxe4 13.♗xe4) 11.♘e1! h6?! (11...♖e8 is more sensible, but still better for White after 12.f3!) 12.f3 ♗h5 13.♘c2 ♗g6 14.♘e3 and Black was living in a counter-play-free zone in Sarsam-Djikerian, Beirut 2007.

● In the original game with 8.♕xd2, Black tried to follow the main line by playing 8...d5, but after 9.exd5 ♘xd5

(Note that White has reached a position which could arise via 1.e4 e5 2.♘f3 ♘c6 3.♗c4 ♗c5 4.c3 ♘f6 5.d4 exd4 6.cxd4 ♗b4+ 7.♗d2 d5!? 8.exd5 ♗xd2+ and now 9.♕xd2 'exclam' – say the books – 9...♘xd5 and, as with the ...d6 lines, noone has been rushing out to recommend 7...d5.)

White has a pleasant choice:

– 10.♘c3 ♘xc3 (10...♗e6 11.♘xd5! ♗xd5 12.♕e2+ is awkward for Black, while after 10...♘ce7?!

hoping for something like the main 8.♘bxd2 line, 11.♕g5! shows one of the tactical points behind 9.♕xd2) 11.bxc3 (11.♕xc3!? 0-0 12.0-0± Kaplan-Giblon, Kemer 2007) 11...♕e7+ 12.♕e3 0-0 (12...♕xe3+ 13.fxe3±) 13.♕xe7 ♘xe7 14.0-0±.

– 10.♗xd5!? ♕xd5 11.0-0 0-0 12.♘c3 ♕d8 13.d5 ♘e7 14.♖ac1 ♗d7 15.♖fe1 ♘g6 16.♕d4 and Black was rather passively placed but hung on to draw in Rogers-Shaw, Itoh zonal 1978.

– 10.0-0 is perhaps a little too slow – after 10...0-0 11.♘c3 (11.♖e1!? Jirousek-Cizek, Frymburk 2000) Black has time for 11...♘ce7.

● 8...0-0!? has rarely been played but might be one of Black's best replies. After 9.e5 (9.♘c3?! ♘xe4!) 9...d5 (9...♘e4 10.♕e3 d5 gives White more options for a bishop retreat) 10.♗b3 ♘e4 11.♕e3 we have a messy,

Open Spanish-style position. Quite possibly Black is fine, but White's plan – starting with ♘c3 and 0-0 and later looking for a kingside attack – is probably easier to carry out than Black's.

● 8...♕e7 most likely leads to an inferior version of the 8...0-0 lines after 9.e5 d5 (9...d6?! looks too risky after 10.0-0 dxe5 11.dxe5 ♘g4 12.♘c3!, while on 9...♘e4?! 10.♕f4! ♕b4+?! 11.♘bd2 Black is already lost) 10.♗b3 ♘e4 11.♕e3, ± since the d5 pawn is needing help.

9.♕e3 ♕e7

If Black wishes to hang onto the pawn then this is necessary.

The alternative is 9...d5

10.♗xd5! ♕xd5 11.♘c3 ♕d8 (11...♘b4? loses to 12.♘xd5 ♘c2+ 13.♔e2! ♘xe3 14.♔xe3, but Black has many alternative queen moves, of which 11...♕f5, never played, is the most serious alternative. After 12.♘xe4 0-0 13.0-0 ♗e6 14.♖fe1 ♗d5 15.♘g3 ♕f6 16.♘e5 the black bishop on d5 is a great piece but ♘h5-f4 should neutralize it. If Black is looking for an equalizer, this may be the way to play – though 7...♘xe4!? – beyond the scope of this article – is probably a better way to play for a draw) 12.♕xe4+ ♕e7 looks as if it should be a safe equalizer, but 13.♕xe7+ ♘xe7 14.0-0 0-0 15.♖fe1 gave White a nagging

edge in Guo-Mareckova, Chotowa World Girls U20 2010, and in fact White won rather easily.

10.0-0 0-0

● 10...♘f6 11.♖e1 ♕xe3 12.♖xe3+ leads to the sort of endgame White must not be scared of if he or she wishes to play 8.♕xd2. Play can continue 12...♔f8 13.♘c3 ♘a5 14.♗d3 d5 15.♖ae1 ♗d7 16.♘e5 ♗e6, and now 17.♘b5 ♘e8 18.f4 g6 19.g4, Song-Mendes da Costa, Ryde-Eastwood 2005, could have been well met by 19...♘c4!, so White should prefer 17.f4, e.g. 17...g6 18.f5 ♗xf5 19.♗xf5 gxf5 20.♖f3, with more than enough for the pawn.

● On 10...♘d6

White does not even need to exchange queens:

– 11.♕b3!? 0-0 (11...♘a5 12.♕c3!; 11...♘xc4 12.♖e1 ♘4e5 13.dxe5) 12.♗d3 and Black's development will remain difficult, while White has ♘c3-d5 coming.

– 11.♕xe7+ is not bad either, e.g. 11...♘xe7 12.♗b3 (12.♗d3!?) 12...0-0 13.♖e1 ♘g6 14.♘c3 c6 15.♖ac1 ♘f5 and now 16.d5! is a typical idea for White, since after 16...d6 17.dxc6 bxc6 18.♘e4 ♗b7 19.g4! ♘fh4 20.♘xh4 ♘xh4 21.♘xd6! ♘f3+ 22.♔g2 ♘xe1+ 23.♖xe1 ♗a6 24.♖e7 White has much the easier position to play.

11.♖e1

11...♖e8?!

The most natural move in the world, but it also loses by force! Black's other options also have their downsides, e.g.:

– 11...♘b4?! 12.♘c3! ♘c2 (12...c6 13.d5!

♘c2 14.♕xe4 ♕xe4 15.♘xe4) 13.♕d3! ♘xe1 14.♖xe1, when the two pieces are worth far more than rook and pawn.

– 11...♕b4!? 12.♕xe4 ♕xc4 13.♘c3 d6 14.d5, when White will win back the pawn with a slightly better endgame.

– 11...♘d6 12.♕d3 ♕f6 13.♘c3 ♘xc4 14.♕xc4 ♕d8 (otherwise 15.d5 wins back the pawn) 15.d5 ♘e7 16.d6 looks horrible.

12.♕f4!

Far stronger than the 12.♘c3 of Song-Mendes da Costa, Sydney 2005. Now, incredibly, Black must lose a piece due to the pin on the e-file and the threats against f7.

This opening trap has never yet happened in a game – using this SOS you might be the first!

The SOS Competition

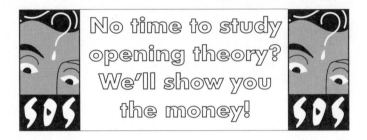